MURDER BY
POISON

Poison bottles from the turn of the century. (© Martin Latham)

MURDER BY POISON

A CASEBOOK OF HISTORIC
BRITISH MURDERS

NICOLA SLY

The
History
Press

First published 2009

The History Press
The Mill, Brimscombe Port
Stroud, Gloucestershire, GL5 2QG
www.thehistorypress.co.uk

British Library Cataloguing in Publication Data.
A catalogue record for this book is available from the British Library.

ISBN 978 0 7524 5065 0

Typesetting and origination by The History Press
Printed in Great Britain

Contents

About the Author

Nicola Sly's lifelong fascination with crime and criminal behaviour led her to complete a degree in Psychology, followed by a Masters Degree in Forensic and Legal Psychology. As well as writing, she currently teaches Psychology and Criminology to adult learners. She and her husband live in Cornwall.

Also by Nicola Sly

A Ghostly Almanac of Devon and Cornwall
Bristol Murders
Cornish Murders (with John Van der Kiste)
Dorset Murders
Hampshire Murders
Herefordshire Murders
Oxfordshire Murders
Somerset Murders (with John Van der Kiste)
Shropshire Murders
West Country Murders (with John Van der Kiste)
Wiltshire Murders
Worcestershire Murders

Introduction
and Acknowledgements

The modern crime dramas of film and television have largely sanitised our view of the poisoner and his or her victim, who is often depicted lying in a clean bed, with crisp, white sheets, looking pale and wan and occasionally groaning weakly. In order to truly appreciate the horror of this method of murder, we must go back in time to a period when poisons were freely available

Poison bottles from the turn of the century. (© Nicola Sly)

at every corner shop for the purposes of killing mice, flies and bedbugs; for treating illnesses such as venereal diseases; for quietening crying children; for agricultural, veterinary and garden use; and even for beauty treatments, sexual stimulants and aphrodisiacs. The symptoms of the majority of poisonings involved copious sickness and diarrhoea, all of which had to be disposed of and, in the days before modern sanitation, must have been extremely unpleasant to deal with to say the least. There were no flushing toilets, no hot water on tap and no automatic washing machines for dealing with fouled bedding and clothing and homes were frequently overcrowded, often with several people sharing a small cottage, half a house, or even a single room.

By the 1840s, concerns were growing about the number of deaths from poisoning – either by accident, suicide or murder – almost a third of which were caused by arsenic, a poison which is virtually tasteless. The Arsenic Act of 1851 was an attempt to control sales of the poison and, hopefully, reduce deaths resulting from its ingestion. Following the introduction of this Act, all arsenic sold had to be coloured with soot or indigo in order to distinguish it from common household substances such as flour and sugar. Sellers were obliged to keep records of every sale and could only sell the poison if they personally knew the prospective purchaser. However, accidental and deliberate poisonings continued almost unabated.

In 1856, *The Times* reported indignantly on two apprentices, aged eighteen and thirteen years, who were left in charge of a pharmacy while the owner was out. A customer produced an order, in writing, for a bottle of 'black draught' – a mild laxative preparation. The older apprentice, Mr Lundie, asked the younger, Master Barrett, to fill a bottle with 'black draught', which Lundie then labelled 'aperient draught' and sold to the customer. However, the young apprentice either misheard the instructions or mistook the bottle of 'black draught' for one of 'black drop' – a powerful opium preparation. The medicine was given to an eleven-year-old boy by his mother and 'in less than an hour, he was a corpse'.

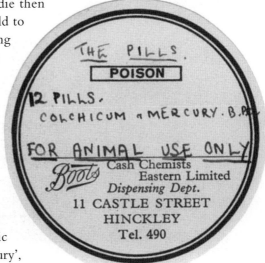

The newspaper bemoaned the fact that deadly poisons were often known by familiar names. Arsenic was frequently referred to as 'mercury', for example, while tartarised antimony was commonly called 'quietness'. Deadly poisons were routinely kept on shelves next to harmless chemicals, rather than under lock and key, and few apprentices were properly trained to understand the dangers of the compounds they were freely dispensing. 'Why, at Ashton only the other day, we had a lad scarcely older than Barrett selling arsenic by the pound as if it had been so much meal!' stated *The Times*.

Poisons were still used as ingredients in many patent medicines, such as Godfrey's Cordial, Dr J. Collis Browne's Chlorodyne and Fowler's Solution, which could be bought over the counter and usually cost less than a visit to the doctor. Across Britain people rushed to embrace the practices of those foreigners who regularly took small doses of arsenic to promote '...a blooming complexion, a brilliant eye, and an appearance of embonpoint.' *Chambers Journal* of July 1856 contained an article written by a Dr Inman on arsenic eating, which recommended anyone wishing to adopt the practice:

> To use only a preparation whose real strength they know; Fowler's solution contains 1-120th of a grain in every drop. Very few indeed can bear to take five drops three times in a day. It is best borne on a full stomach. It soon produces griping, sickness, and purging. It is well to remember the Styrian rule, and invariably suspend its use every alternate fortnight. The dose cannot be increased indefinitely or with impunity. When once the full dose which can be borne is ascertained, it is better to begin with that, and go on diminishing it to the end of the fortnight, than to begin with a small dose, and go on increasing it daily.

The article ended with a dire warning: 'Lastly, let me urge upon all who adopt the Styrian system, to make some written memorandum that they have done so, lest, in case of accident, some of their friends may be hanged in mistake' [*sic*].

More stringent regulations were obviously needed and The Pharmacy and Poisons Act of 1868 covered not only arsenic but also the twenty most commonly used poisons, such as strychnine and Prussic acid, restricting the selling of poisons to authorised retailers, as determined by the Pharmaceutical Society. Yet drugs like opium and cocaine were still freely available without prescription. On 12 October 1895, *The Nursing Record and Hospital World* called for more stringent legislation on the sale of laudanum (a tincture of opium), saying, 'In many country places...laudanum is sold wholesale by local grocers and agricultural folk not only take it in somewhat large quantities themselves, but they dose their children – especially the babies in the teething stage – to a very deleterious effect.' As little as two drops of laudanum could prove fatal for a baby and many mothers (and sometimes fathers or nursemaids) were charged with either murder or manslaughter as a result. Yet, by and large, the final verdict in such cases tended to be one of acquittal for the defendant, since it was recognised that accidental overdoses were all too easy to administer and it was difficult to prove any malice aforethought.

It wasn't until the Pharmacy Act of 1908 that it became a requisite for purchasers of opiates to be known to the seller and for the Poisons Register to be signed. Even so, drugs like heroin, morphine and cocaine were still freely available, with 'gift sets' sold at shops such as Harrods, for sending to soldiers fighting on the front in the First World War. It took the Dangerous Drugs Act of 1920 to restrict the sale of drugs to medical and legitimate users only.

Poisons were also heavily used in household and industrial capacities, the prime example of this being arsenic, which was used to provide green colouring in wallpapers, clothing dyes, food wrappers, and even in actual foodstuffs. In Greenock, Scotland, a nineteenth-century cake decoration was found to contain seven times the fatal dose of arsenic and, even as recently as 1954, the associations of green colouring with arsenic was reputed to make Scottish people the lowest consumers of green sweets in the Western World.

So, historically, poisons were freely available and had the added advantage of being very difficult to detect, particularly since the symptoms of their misuse mimicked the symptoms of diseases like cholera and dysentery, which were endemic at the time. Busy doctors, treating a succession of cases of genuine illness, were unlikely to spot the rare cases of deliberate poisoning among them and, even if they did, testing for poisoning was unreliable, making it difficult to prove in a court of law. Advances in medical science saw the development of the Marsh Test in October 1836, the first diagnostic test for arsenic. In 1832, chemist James Marsh was called by the prosecution in the trial of John Bodie, who was accused of poisoning his grandfather with arsenic in coffee. The jury was not convinced by the scientific evidence and acquitted Bodie, who subsequently confessed his guilt. Marsh was so incensed by this that he developed his own test, first used in 1836 and still occasionally used today. Tests for other poisons quickly followed, with inventive and intrepid scientists often administering samples suspected of containing poison to animals and frequently resorting to tasting samples such as urine and stomach contents themselves.

Having examined *how* people poisoned, the next question to be addressed is *why* they did. Every murder has its own individual motive but, in the case of poisonings, a number of common threads are observed.

The near impossibility of obtaining a divorce meant that poisoning an unloved partner was often believed preferable to spending the rest of one's life trapped in an unhappy marriage, particularly if there was a prospective alternative partner in the equation. Until 1949, when Legal Aid was granted for those seeking a divorce, the legal dissolution of a marriage was for the very

Prudential Assurance Company, 1904. (Author's collection)

rich only and was heavily biased towards the interests of men. The nineteenth century also saw the growth of Life Assurance in the United Kingdom, with companies like Prudential deliberately targeting the working classes from 1854 onwards and providing penny policies for infants from 1856. The lack of reliable contraception meant that many families produced more children than they had the money to feed and the bonus of a cash sum from a life assurance policy or a payout from a friendly society or a work-based scheme ensured that many children and partners received 'a helping hand' to hasten their death.

Some people poisoned for love – or lack of it – and some poisoned for financial gain. Others resorted to poison in the course of robbery, some to rid themselves of a person or persons who had become a nuisance to them. And some people poisoned just to see what it would be like.

In compiling this collection of nineteenth- and twentieth-century poisonings from the United Kingdom, I have tried as far as possible to include a wide variety of methods, motives and geographical locations. Some cases, such as that of Hawley Harvey Crippen, who poisoned his wife in 1910 and William Palmer, who poisoned a number of people in the Rugeley area, were notorious throughout the country while others, such as the case of Christiana Edmunds who randomly poisoned people in Brighton in the early 1870s, are less well known but hopefully just as intriguing.

It may help readers to understand two common terms of measurement used throughout the book. A 'grain' of poison is a measurement of weight roughly

'The man from the Pru'. A Prudential Insurance Agent in the 1920s. (Author's collection)

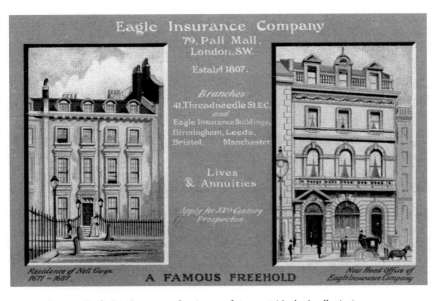

Eagle Star Insurance advertisement from 1907. (Author's collection)

equivalent to the weight of a grain of barley. There are 437.5 grains to the ounce and 15 grains equal one gram. Another measurement of weight is the drachm, which equals approximately 28.8 grams.

As usual, there are numerous people to be thanked for their assistance in writing this book. I drew heavily on contemporary newspaper reports in compiling this collection. These, and any books consulted, are listed in detail in the bibliography at the rear of the book. I was particularly privileged to be able to study the original notes made during his apprenticeship by my father, John Higginson, who spent his entire working life as a pharmacist and dispensing chemist. Author Linda Stratmann very kindly supplied a picture of Dr Palmer and Scotsman Publications and the *Daily Echo*, Bournemouth generously gave permission for me to use their pictures of Dr Cream and Charlotte Bryant.

My husband, Richard, acted as a general sounding board for which cases to include and which to leave out. As usual, he read every chapter and, surprisingly, having read them all, he still continues to eat my cooking, although perhaps a little more warily than before.

Finally, I must thank my editor at The History Press, Matilda Richards, for her continued help and support.

Every effort has been made to clear copyright, however my apologies to anyone I may have inadvertently missed; I can assure you it was not deliberate but an oversight on my part.

Nicola Sly, 2009

I

'You hussy!
You have murdered your baby!'

BUCKFASTLEIGH, DEVON, 1817

In 1817, Frances Clarke, also known as Frances Puttavin, went before the parish at Buckfastleigh in Devon, homeless and about to give birth to an illegitimate baby. She was placed in lodgings with labourer William Vesey and his wife Susannah and, at the beginning of October, gave birth to a healthy baby boy, whom she named after his father, a gentleman farmer called George Lakeman.

On 24 October, Frances spent most of the morning sitting by the fire, her child asleep in her lap. At about two o'clock in the afternoon, Susannah Vesey suggested that she should put the baby upstairs. This Frances did, laying the

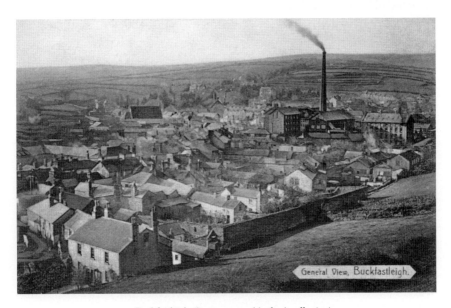

Buckfastleigh, Devon, 1909. (Author's collection)

child on the bed and going downstairs, returning to the baby a minute or so later with an apron over her arm.

Seconds later, William Vesey heard choking sounds coming from the room in which the baby had been put down. He called out to ask Frances what the matter was and was horrified when Frances calmly replied that the baby was dying.

Frances then snatched up her baby and ran downstairs with him, where she met Susannah. The boy was now 'strangling' – coughing and choking and struggling to breathe. Frances told Susannah that the infant was dying too.

Susannah asked how the baby could possibly be dying when he had been so well just minutes earlier. 'Let me have it,' she asked Frances, but Frances refused, clutching her baby tightly to her breast and rushing upstairs again with him. Susannah followed, and Frances promptly went back downstairs to avoid her, still clinging desperately to baby George.

Eventually, Susannah Vesey managed to catch up with her and took the screaming baby from her grasp, carrying him over to the window for more light. The baby's mouth was open and Susannah was later to describe '…stuff boiling in its mouth'. There was what looked like a bloodstain on the baby's garments but when Susannah touched it with her finger and then placed the finger in her mouth, her tongue burned unbearably. 'You hussy! You have murdered your baby!' she screamed at Frances, who showed no reaction and made no denial of the accusation.

Susannah sent for surgeon Mr Nicholas Churchill, who, having heard that a child had been poisoned, rushed straight to the Vesey's home. There he found the baby being held by Susannah, blue in the face and struggling to breathe, its lips, tongue and mouth burned as if by some kind of acid. Unable to help the child, Churchill called in another local surgeon, Thomas Rowe, and between them the two men battled to save the baby's life. However their efforts were in vain and baby George died at midday the following day.

Both doctors were of the opinion that the child had died as a result of being given oil of vitriol (sulphuric acid). There was a small mark on the side of the baby's nose, which was bluish in colour and, according to Churchill, this was characteristic of the application of sulphuric acid to skin. To support his theory, Churchill applied a little oil of vitriol to his own finger and compared the resulting injury with that on the child's nose. While other acids caused white or yellowish burn marks on the skin, Churchill maintained that only oil of vitriol cast a bluish stain, which corresponded exactly to the burns both on his own finger and the baby's nose.

An inquest was held before coroner Mr Joseph Gribble and the cause of death given as poisoning by oil of vitriol. Frances Clarke was indicted for the wilful murder of her baby and brought for trial before Mr Justice Holroyd at the next Assizes in Exeter.

The court heard first from William and Susannah Vesey, followed by their maid, eleven-year-old Sarah Maddock. Having established that young Sarah could fully understand the importance of speaking the truth, the court heard her testimony that about six weeks before the baby's death, Frances had sent her on an errand to Richard Butcher's shop in the village. Frances had asked Sarah to buy a penny's worth of oil of vitriol, instructing her to say that it was for the Veseys if she was asked. Sarah was sold the oil of vitriol by Butcher and given a strict warning that, if she drank the liquid, it would kill her. Sarah swore that she had relayed this warning to Frances Clarke when she handed over her purchase. Shopkeeper Richard Butcher corroborated her account of the purchase of oil of vitriol from his shop, although he stated that the girl had told him at the time that the acid was for Fan Clarke.

The court next heard from Mr Churchill and Mr Rowe, the surgeons involved in trying to save the baby. An apron and a spoon were produced in court and Churchill agreed that burns on the apron had been produced by some kind of acid. However, he was not prepared to state that the spoon had last held oil of vitriol, saying that this was outside his experience as a medical man. Two empty bottles had been found at the Vesey's house after Frances Clarke's arrest, one in a box belonging to her and the other on the fire. It was thought that either might once have contained the dose of oil of vitriol administered to baby George and both Sarah Maddock and Richard Butcher testified that they were similar to the one bought by Sarah on Frances Clarke's behalf, although neither could be sure that they were that particular bottle.

By chance, William Hallett was in court. A wholesale druggist and chemist for more than thirty years, he was called to give his opinion. He too told the court that it was impossible to be certain just what the bottles had contained. Had they contained oil of vitriol and if they had not been washed then they would retain the pungent smell of the acid, which would corrode anything it came into contact with. The bottle being burned in a fire would not have affected any residue of its contents.

Turning his attention to the spoon, Hallett pointed out that vitriolic acid applied to iron produced a black discolouration. The spoon in question was iron, which had been plated with lead and it showed a white rather than a black discolouration. Hallett stated that it was impossible for him to swear that oil of vitriol was the last thing put into the spoon, saying that all acids would produce whiteness. Finally Hallett examined the baby's clothes and Frances Clarke's apron, saying that both appeared to have been burned by acid, although he was unable to state precisely what type.

Mr Justice Holroyd then summed up the evidence for the jury who did not even find it necessary to retire for deliberation, finding Frances Clarke 'Guilty' as charged. It was then that the judge dropped a bombshell.

Assize Court and County Council offices, Exeter, 1909. (Author's collection)

The judge told the court that Miss Clarke had been indicted for the wilful murder of her son, George Lakeman Clarke. However, the boy had officially been christened just George Lakeman and he was therefore doubtful of the legitimacy of the entire trial. He had thought fit to proceed in order to establish the defendant's guilt or innocence but now found himself unable to pass sentence and would be forwarding the case to the appropriate authorities for their consideration

This resulted in a retrial for Frances Clarke, who was eventually acquitted on the grounds that the new indictment against her specified that baby George Lakeman had died as a result of oil of vitriol passing into his stomach. However, the medical witnesses disagreed, stating that the oil of vitriol had not reached the child's stomach and that his death had occurred as a result of damage to his throat, which had caused him to suffocate. This left the court no alternative but to acquit Frances Clarke of the wilful murder of her son.

Yet, even after two appearances in court, the officials had not finished with Frances, who in August 1819 found herself back at the Assizes in Exeter before Mr Justice Best. This time the indictment against her was most specific – she was charged with the wilful murder of George Lakeman '…by compelling the infant to take a large quantity of oil of vitriol, by means whereof he became disordered in his mouth and throat and by the disorder choking, suffocating and strangling occasioned thereby, died on the following day.' A second count stated that the baby had '…died of a certain acid called oil of vitriol administered by the prisoner and taken into his mouth and throat whereby he became incapable of swallowing his food and that his death was the consequence of the inflammation, injury and disorder occasioned thereby.'

Asked to plead, Frances Clarke evoked her former acquittal. Mr Justice Best could not accept this plea, telling the court that the defendant must plead either 'Guilty' or 'Not Guilty'. If she pleaded not guilty, then '…she may have a writ of error to the Court of the King's Bench', the supreme court in England. Otherwise, he would submit the case for the opinion of twelve judges. In other words, Best stressed that, regardless of the result of the court case, Frances Clarke would be allowed to appeal.

Frances immediately pleaded 'Not Guilty' and the prosecution, led by Mr Selwyn, opened the case by calling William Vesey as a witness. This time, Mr Tonkin and Mr Merewether were in court to act as defence counsels.

As in the original trial, the court heard from the Veseys and Sarah Maddock. This time however, the Vesey's married daughter, Sarah Tupper, was called to testify. At the time of the death of baby George, Sarah Tupper had had a young baby of her own and, on the morning of the alleged murder, the two mothers had sat together breastfeeding their respective infants.

Sarah Tupper's child had been a sickly baby, unlike George who was thriving. Understandably, Sarah had been somewhat upset about the health of her own child but Frances had assured her that she didn't believe that her own baby would be a 'long-lived child'. The two women had talked about the fact that Frances had a 'nice bosom of milk to go wet nursing' but Frances said that if her baby should die she would allow her milk to dry up and move away from the area, somewhere in the countryside.

At that, Sarah Tupper had to leave to go to work but when she returned to her parents' house at about half-past twelve in the afternoon, she found Frances sitting in the same place, her child still not dressed. Frances told her that the baby had been asleep all morning and that she had not wanted to disturb him.

Sarah had witnessed the drama of Frances Clarke running around the house with her choking son in her arms and had observed the damage to the child's mouth and throat, watching in horror as 'liquor' ran from the baby's mouth and burned his clothes. She told the court that both she and Frances had later tried to breastfeed George but that he had been unable to suckle. She added that Frances had not seemed at all upset at her son's distress.

Cross-examined by the counsel for the defence, Sarah was asked about the medicine bottle subsequently found in Frances Clarke's box. Sarah admitted that the box concerned did not specifically belong to Frances but was an open box, into which any member of the family might put things.

Shopkeeper Richard Butcher took the stand to tell the court that he had sold oil of vitriol to Sarah Maddock and that the amount she had purchased was sufficient to cause death.

Next the two doctors were called and both Churchill and Rowe told the court that the child had been given acid and that his symptoms were consistent with drinking oil of vitriol, which had caused inflammation and swelling of the his throat and prevented him from breathing. They had not conducted a post-mortem examination.

Finally, Frances Clarke submitted a written statement in which she denied her guilt. She insisted that she had, in the past, raised other children 'tenderly' and spoke of three former masters who had given her a good character reference at her previous trial. Throughout the proceedings, Frances Clarke frequently fainted and had to be revived by prison warders so that the trial could continue.

It was left to Mr Justice Best to summarise the case. He told the jury that it was for them to decide if the child had died as a result of an act by the prisoner, and then carefully dealt with all the evidence that had been presented in court, pointing out that even things that might appear insignificant acquired weight when considered cumulatively.

The jury retired for a few minutes before returning with a verdict of 'Guilty'. Frances Clarke was promptly sentenced to death for the wilful murder of her son but, as soon as the verdict was returned, the counsel for the defence objected to the indictment. As promised, Mr Justice Best agreed to forward the case for appeal.

In the event, Frances Clarke did not hang for the murder of her son. King George III, who was the reigning monarch at the time of the murder of baby George Lakeman, died on 29 January 1820 and was succeeded by his son, who became George IV. One of his first acts as King was to issue a statement marked for the attention of 'Our Trusty and Wellbeloved Justices of Gaol Delivery for the Western Circuit' [*sic*]. The King made it known that, having considered a report on the case, he was 'graciously pleased to Extend Our Grace and Mercy unto her and to Grant her Our Free Pardon for her said Crime' [*sic*].

Note: Cotemporary accounts of the case show some variation in spelling of the names of those concerned. Frances Clarke is also referred to as Frances Clark and, on one occasion, Elizabeth Clark. Sarah Maddock is alternatively named Sarah Moddick; the surgeon is named as both Mr Rowe and Mr Row and the chemist William Hallett and Hallet. I have used the most common variations for this account.

2

'Why should Emery be hanged?'

In 1821, Sarah King lived in a cottage in White Notley near Chelmsford in Essex with her father and her younger siblings. Like many a teenager before and since, she allowed herself to be seduced by an older man, a twenty-five-year-old servant from the neighbouring parish. James Emery was described in the contemporary newspapers as 'a well-looking man' and before long, Sarah almost inevitably found herself pregnant.

She steeled herself to break the news of her condition to Emery and eventually told him when he came to visit her at home. Her younger sister, to whom Sarah had confided her predicament, shamelessly eavesdropped on the conversation between the lovers and heard her sister say, 'Emery, I am with child by you.'

White Notley, Essex, 1904. (Author's collection)

White Notley, Essex, 1905. (Author's collection)

'If you like anybody better than me, you may swear the child to him,' Emery replied but Sarah assured him, 'I have not been with any other person but yourself and therefore I shall swear it to you.'

When James Emery left that evening, he and Sarah were apparently on good terms and indeed Emery returned to the cottage to visit Sarah again on 29 May at about six o'clock in the evening. Once again, as the couple sat together in the parlour, Sarah's sister listened intently to their conversation.

'How do you do?' he asked her, to which Sarah replied, 'I am worse.'

At that, James Emery apparently produced a small box from the pocket of his coat. 'Oh, you are worse, are you? I have brought you a box of pills and I will give you a £1 note if you will take them.'

James then went home, leaving Sarah and her family to eat a hearty dinner of boiled cabbage, after which Sarah went to her bed, first taking seven of the pills that her lover had left for her. Soon afterwards, she awoke 'in great torture' and was violently sick.

Her agonising stomach pains gradually increased in intensity until, in desperation, she sent her sister to the nearby public house to purchase a measure of gin with which she hoped to ease her suffering. However the gin just made things worse and merely increased the frequency of her vomiting and diarrhoea and the intensity of the pain.

In spite of her illness, Sarah remained conscious and lucid. She expressed concern for her boyfriend and begged her younger sister to hide the remaining pills in the field behind the house, along with two small phials that had contained medicine previously brought for her by Emery, which she had been taking for the past week. 'Why should Emery be hanged?' she asked.

The girl did as she was asked, returning minutes later to find that her sister's agony appeared to have worsened. Now Sarah thought that she might try some beer to alleviate her symptoms and her sister was once again dispatched to the pub. By the time she got back, Sarah was dead.

A surgeon, Mr Tonkin, was called and he performed a post-mortem examination on the body of Sarah King at which he determined that she had died as a result of arsenical poisoning. The remaining pills were sent for analysis by chemist Mr Baker, who found that each tablet contained about six grains of arsenic and gave his opinion that taking just half of a single tablet would have been sufficient to cause Sarah's death.

As soon as he heard about Sarah's fate, James Emery remarked to a colleague, 'Then I shall be had up before the magistrates.' Telling the man that he had taken some 'stuff' to Sarah, he went on to sell him some of his clothes and personal possessions, using the money he obtained to hurriedly leave the area. Yet even though he was fleeing the law, he was hardly discreet. In conversation with a man in a public house in Boxwell, he told him, 'I dare say you have heard what I have come away for. I dare say you heard that I have come away on account of that cursed wench who was poisoned at Notley.' He admitted to another acquaintance that he had got some 'stuff' but insisted that he had never intended for it to cause Sarah any harm.

Emery was soon apprehended by the police and charged with the wilful murder of Sarah King by poisoning. He was brought to trial at the Essex Assizes in Chelmsford before Mr Justice Burrough on 10 August 1821. Mr Knox and Mr Brodrick prosecuted the case and Emery, who pleaded 'Not Guilty', was not defended.

The court heard from Sarah King's sister about the conversations between the couple that she had overheard and surgeon Mr Tonkin and analyst Mr Baker testified to the cause of Sarah King's death. Witnesses were then called to testify to the fact that Emery had approached a local blacksmith about a fortnight before Sarah died, asking if he could recommend anything that might bring about a miscarriage. The blacksmith had refused to give him any information, so Emery had gone into Chelmsford, where he visited a horse doctor.

He persuaded the horse doctor that his bedroom was infested with mice, which gnawed his clothes hutch and ate his clothes. He was eventually able to purchase half an ounce of *nux vomica* and half an ounce of arsenic for the purpose of killing them. A fellow servant, who shared his bedroom, told the court that there was no evidence of mice in their room and neither had Emery's clothes been damaged.

Shire Hall, Chelmsford, site of the Assizes. (Author's collection)

Invited to speak in his own defence, Emery categorically denied any wrongdoing, saying, 'I have nothing to say. I am quite innocent of what the girl says. I did not do it.'

In his summing up of the case for the jury, Mr Justice Burrough explained the legal position with regard to the administration of poison in order to bring about a miscarriage. He told them that, even if this had been the defendant's intention rather than murder, the fact that Sarah had died meant that if Emery had administered the poison, he was guilty of murder and must take the consequences.

The jury didn't even feel the need to retire, immediately finding James Emery 'Guilty' and leaving the judge to pronounce the death sentence. Emery, who by now seemed resigned to his fate, showed very little reaction.

He was hanged at Moulsham Gaol on 13 August 1831, just three days after the conclusion of his trial.

3
'There you go, you varmints!'

Burnham Market, Norfolk, 1835

On the evening of 4 March 1835, Mrs Talbot received a message to say that her sister, Mrs Mary Taylor, had been taken ill and she immediately set out to visit her at her home in Burnham Market, Norfolk. She found Mary sitting in a chair, with her concerned husband, Peter, by her side. Mary was screaming in agony, begging for water and shouting over and over again that her stomach was on fire. Yet as soon as she was given the water she craved, she vomited it straight back up again.

Mrs Talbot went to her sister's next-door neighbour, Mrs Lake, where she met the lodger, Catherine Frarey, and asked her if she might have some gruel. There was a pot standing on the stove and Mrs Talbot was told to help herself.

Market place, Burnham Market, 1914. (Author's collection)

Burnham Market. (Author's collection)

When she took the bowl in to her sister, Catherine followed her, protesting that it was too thick. She took the dish back to her house, returning minutes later with the watered-down gruel.

'I hope, my dear, you'll take some of it now from me and that it will do you all the good I wish,' Catherine told Mary Taylor.

At that moment, Peter Taylor called Mrs Talbot out of the room and when she returned, she noticed that Mary had eaten some of the gruel. However, it didn't appear to have helped her at all and indeed, she seemed much weaker than she had before eating it. Mrs Talbot asked Catherine Frarey to go for the doctor but Catherine didn't seem willing. 'She's a dead woman,' she protested, although she did reluctantly agree to fetch medical assistance when Peter Taylor asked her to. Sadly, Catherine's prediction proved to be correct and Mary Taylor died before the doctor's arrival.

Several neighbours gathered at Mrs Taylor's house to help lay out her body and, according to the local newspaper accounts, they '...regaled themselves with copious streams of tea after the ceremony, in the very room in which the dead body lay.'

As soon as the unfortunate Mary Taylor breathed her last, tongues in the village of Burnham Market began wagging. Mary's husband, Peter, had for some time been engaged in an illicit affair with a neighbour, Frances 'Fanny' Billing, a mother of fourteen children, nine of whom were still living. It was widely known that Mary Taylor had found out about her husband's affair and was angry and very jealous. In addition, Mary Taylor's was not the only suspicious sudden death that had recently occurred in the village – just a couple of weeks earlier, Catherine Frarey's husband, Robert, had died in very similar circumstances. In view of the fact that Catherine Frarey had been closely connected with both deaths, it was decided to hold a post-mortem examination on the body of Mary Taylor and, when her remains were tested, they were found to contain large quantities of arsenic. Arsenic was also found in foodstuff taken from the Taylor's home, including a bin of flour.

The police began investigating the recent activities of Catherine Frarey and their interviews with the villagers of Burnham Market soon proved fruitful. Peter Taylor acted as the village barber and, on the evening of Mary Taylor's death, the blacksmith had called at his house for a haircut. He had seen Catherine Frarey raking out the ashes in the Taylor's fireplace, after which she briefly left the house, returning with a small pan of gruel, which she placed on the embers. As the blacksmith watched, she unfolded a paper packet and removed nearly a teaspoonful of white powder, which she added to the gruel. The blacksmith had thought nothing of her actions at the time, assuming the powder to be either sugar or salt. However, soon afterwards, Fanny Billing came in and asked how Mrs Taylor was.

'She's very ill but the man will do,' replied Catherine.

'That's just right,' said Mrs Billing.

'I'm boiling her a little gruel and I shall sit with her husband and keep him company in his lonesomeness for an hour or two. I hope it will settle her, poor thing.'

A second witness, Mrs Southgate, told the police that she had been drinking tea with Catherine and Robert Frarey when Fanny Billing had come to the house carrying a jug of porter. Fanny had asked Catherine for a teacup and, when Catherine gave her one, she poured some of the porter into it. Fanny then turned her back on the room and, when she turned around again, she was stirring the cup of porter with her finger. She passed it to Robert Frarey who drained its contents. Mrs Southgate noticed a powdery, white residue in the bottom of the cup and commented to Robert that she could never drink porter with sugar in it.

Fanny Billing left with the remains of the porter and, later that night, Robert Frarey was taken ill. He later died, after two days of agonising stomach pain and vomiting.

Catherine had buried her husband as soon as she possibly could and Mrs Southgate told the police that she had advised Catherine, 'If I were you, I'd have my husband taken up again and examined for I'm sure the world will talk and I'd shut the world's mouth.'

Catherine said she would not like to do that, asking Mrs Southgate, 'Would you?'

'Yes, I would like it, for if you don't it will be a check upon you and your children after you.'

Once the police learned the story of the porter, they applied for the exhumation of Robert Frarey's body and found that, like Mary Taylor's remains, it too contained a large quantity of arsenic. Enquiries at the village chemist's shop revealed that, prior to the deaths of Robert Frarey and Mary Taylor, Catherine Frarey and Fanny Billing had together purchased three pennyworth of white arsenic, telling the chemist that they had been sent by a Mrs Webster, the wife of a local tradesman, to purchase the arsenic on her behalf. The chemist had put the arsenic into two small paper packets, which he had clearly labelled 'Poison' but, when the police contacted Mrs Webster, she denied ever having requested any such purchase.

The police also discovered that Catherine Frarey had recently hired a horse and buggy and driven several miles to see a notorious 'cunning woman'. She had asked the woman to 'tie' the tongue of Mr Curtis, the village policeman, and to 'witch' her mother (as she called her landlady, Mrs Lake) so that she would not be able to answer any questions about her. Having first extracted a fee from Catherine, the 'cunning woman' had promised to carry out her wishes straight away.

An inquest was opened into the death of Mary Taylor, which was attended by Fanny Billing, Catherine Frarey and Peter Taylor. At one point, Catherine was heard to say to Peter, 'There you are, Peter dear; we should all have been done if it had not been for mother [Mrs Lake], God bless her. The gruel was made in her house.' Catherine seemed to be under the impression that because the gruel had been made in Mrs Lake's house, it could not be traced back to her.

The coroner's jury determined that Mary Taylor had died from arsenic poisoning and at the end of the inquest, Fanny Billing, Catherine Frarey and Peter Taylor were arrested on suspicion of her murder. As they were transported to prison, Fanny was heard to whisper, 'Hold your tongue, Peter, and then they can't do nothing with you, I feel sure.'

All three were committed for trial at the next Norfolk Assizes, although the Grand Jury eventually decided that there was no case to answer against Peter Taylor and he was subsequently released. Hence only Catherine Frarey and Fanny Billing stood trial at Norwich on 7 August 1835, before Mr Baron Bolland. Mr Prendergast and Mr Cooper prosecuted the case while Mr Palmer appeared in defence of the two women, who both pleaded 'Not Guilty'.

They were charged only with the murder by poison of Mary Taylor, although the prosecution counsel freely discussed the alleged murder of Robert Frarey from the outset of the trial. Mr Prendergast told the court that the two women had conspired together to murder Mary Taylor. Fanny Billing, who was having an affair with Peter Taylor, had an obvious motive, so, to divert any suspicion from herself, had recruited Catherine Frarey to actually commit the murder. In return for Catherine's assistance, Fanny Billing had agreed to murder Robert Frarey, knowing that his wife would be the most likely suspect.

Although both defendants protested their innocence, their defence counsel had little to offer in response to the prosecution witnesses and, after a short consultation, the jury found them both guilty as charged.

Catherine Frarey and Fanny Billing were then immediately tried for the wilful murder by poison of Robert Frarey. The prosecution told the court about the cup of porter given to Robert before his death by Mrs Billing and produced Mrs Southgate as a witness to testify to the fact that Fanny appeared to have added some white powder to the porter and stirred it with her finger. The exhumation of Frarey's body and the discovery of arsenic in his remains supported Mrs Southgate's observation that he had apparently been given a white powder shortly before his death. The prosecution stressed that there was no apparent quarrel between Fanny Billing and Robert Frarey and neither had there been any ill feeling between Catherine Frarey and Mary Taylor. However, Catherine and Robert did not live happily together and she wanted him dead, while Fanny wanted Mary Taylor out of the way so that she could pursue her affair with Peter Taylor.

Once again, the jury needed little time for deliberation, pronouncing both defendants 'Guilty' of the wilful murder of Robert Frarey. The judge then donned his black cap and Catherine Frarey went into hysterics as he pronounced sentence of death on her and Fanny Billing, ordering that their bodies should be buried within the confines of the prison walls after their execution.

'Thus ended an inquiry into one of the most atrocious deeds of violence ever perpetrated in this country,' stated *The Times* at the conclusion of the trial. However, nothing could have been further from the truth.

Both Catherine Frarey and Fanny Billing were to make a full confession to the murders shortly before their executions, saying that they believed it was the best way to atone for the injuries they had done to society and that they hoped it would act as a warning to others. Fanny Billing, once a religious woman who regularly attended church, was driven from the path of righteousness when she '…admitted into her bosom a guilty passion for the profligate husband of a neighbour'. Peter Taylor was described as the 'wicked paramour', who had enticed her with promises of marriage, if his wife and her husband were not standing in the way. To this end, Fanny had recruited the assistance of Catherine Frarey and together the two women had placed arsenic in the gravy, flour and sugar at the Taylor's house. Catherine had compounded the deed by mixing still more poison into some gruel and feeding it to Mary Taylor.

Norwich Castle, c. 1911. (Author's collection)

Catherine Frarey admitted to trying to poison her husband once before, saying that she had become frightened by reports in the newspapers of the arrest of a woman, Mary Wright, for a similar offence. Mary Wright and Catherine Frarey had both consulted Hannah Shorten, the 'cunning woman', for help in their respective quests to rid themselves of their spouses. On 19 February 1835, Fanny Billing had mixed arsenic with some pills that Robert Frarey had to take and, after taking two of them, he became very ill. Yet he didn't die as expected, forcing the two women to give him a further four doses of arsenic, administered in either tea or porter.

The two women had planned to despatch Fanny's husband by the same means had they not been apprehended. Catherine Frarey named some other people as accomplices to the murder, including a Mr Gridley, with whom she had been having a dalliance. She swore that she had never had a sexual relationship with Mr Gridley, although it emerged that she had previously boasted to Fanny Billing that the affair was a physical one.

Frances Billing, aged forty-six, and Catherine Frarey, aged forty, were executed on 10 August 1835 at Norwich Castle. Among the 10,000 spectators was Peter Taylor, who was heard to say, 'There you go, you varmints!' as the trapdoor fell.

Peter Taylor went back to Burnham Market after the execution and was taken in by one of his brothers. As soon as his whereabouts became generally known, an unruly crowd descended on the property, baying for his blood. Peter managed to escape unnoticed out of a back entrance and, once the lynch mob realised that he had evaded them, they stoned the cottage windows.

Such was the public feeling against him that the police reopened their investigations into the murder, now finding a witness who had heard Peter Taylor conspiring with Fanny Billing to murder his wife. A warrant was issued for Taylor's arrest and he was eventually captured at his father's house in Whissonsett and charged with being an accessory before the fact to the murder of Mary Taylor. He stood trial on 2 April 1836 before Mr Justice Gaselee. Mr Prendergast again prosecuted, assisted by Mr Cooper and Mr Palmer, and Mr O'Malley defended Taylor in a trial that lasted eleven hours.

The prosecution called a witness who had seen Peter Taylor at Robert Frarey's house on the day of his death. Fanny Billing had also been present and had said to Peter, 'Peter, the doctor has been but it is no use. It is all over for him in this world.'

Peter's reply had been telling: 'Well, go about her as soon as you like.'

On the day of his wife's death Peter was at Fanny Billing's house. At about noon, he visited the outside privy, where Fanny Billing soon joined him. She was seen to give him a small paper packet, saying, 'Here's enough for her.' Later that day, Peter was also seen in earnest discussion with Catherine Frarey in the washhouse of her home.

Peter Taylor's defence was that he and his wife had both been taken ill as a result of eating a lunchtime meal containing too many onions. Catherine Frarey had offered to make some gruel for them and he had accepted, not knowing what the gruel contained. However, the fact that Peter had not been too ill to visit Catherine Frarey's home at five o'clock in the afternoon, coupled with his damning words at her husband's deathbed, proved persuasive to the jury, who consulted for only a short time before finding Peter Taylor 'Guilty' as charged. He was executed on 23 April 1836 at Norwich Castle.

Note: There are some discrepancies in reports of the case in contemporary newspapers. Fanny Billing is frequently named as Fanny Billings and Robert Frarey is sometimes referred to as William Frarey. There are also anecdotal reports that a child was murdered, its body exhumed and found to contain traces of arsenic. The child is not mentioned in newspaper accounts of either of the two trials of the female defendants for the murders of first Mary Taylor and second Robert Frarey, neither is it mentioned at Peter Taylor's trial.

4

'What have I done that I must be suffering this way?'

Fifteen-year-old William Eccles had worked for more than three years as a bleacher at Messrs Eden and Thwaites Mill, where he was known as a good, reliable worker who had never before been ill or needed to take any time off work. On 26 September 1842, William went to work as normal in the morning and worked until lunchtime, when he went home for his midday meal of potato hash. When he returned to work in the afternoon, he appeared to have been crying and complained of feeling terribly sick.

William vomited several times that afternoon and was so ill that it was decided to send him home. He left work at about three o'clock to walk the mile to his house. An hour later, Thomas Davenport, another bleacher from the works, was walking the same route when he came across William lying in the bottom of a ditch.

'What made thee lie down there?' Davenport asked Eccles, who replied that he couldn't walk any further.

Davenport helped the young man to his feet. Eccles was complaining of a pain in his stomach and was constantly retching, throwing up a watery substance. Davenport supported William Eccles and began to walk him towards his home but they had not gone far when they met William's stepmother, Elizabeth 'Betty' Eccles.

Davenport handed the sick boy over to his stepmother, who took him home. William's stomach pains and sickness continued unabated throughout that night and into the next day. At one stage, William tearfully laid his head on his stepmother's lap and asked her, 'What have I done that I must be suffering this way?' Betty reassured him that he would soon feel better but no doctor was summoned to attend him and he died in agony the following afternoon.

On the very afternoon of William's death, Betty went to Eden and Thwaites to ask for the allowance of fifty shillings, normally made by the company towards the burial costs of anyone in their employ. She was no stranger to the bookkeeper there, having made another application for burial money just ten days earlier, after the sudden and unexpected death of ten-year-old Alice Haslam, her daughter from a previous marriage. It had been explained to Betty then that the money was only paid out in the event of the death of a child actually employed at the mill, or of the child of a current mill employee.

On William's death, Betty's neighbours had been keen for her to arrange a post-mortem examination in case the boy had died from an infectious disease. Betty had angrily refused, telling the neighbours that she had enough on her mind at the moment without adding more. Now the concerned bookkeeper at Eden and Thwaites communicated his suspicions to the police and Betty was left with no choice in the matter.

On 28 September, surgeon Mr Joseph Denham made an examination of William's remains. Having noted nothing untoward about the external appearance of the boy's body, Mr Denham found that William's stomach and intestines appeared very inflamed. He removed the stomach and duodenum and delivered them to analyst Mr Henry Hough Watson for further testing.

The chemist found that William's stomach contained a mixture of blood and mucus, along with a quantity of undissolved whitish powder. Watson tested the powder to find that it was white arsenic, amounting to a total weight of 28 grains, from which the chemist estimated that William had ingested a more than fatal dose of between 35 and 40 grains of arsenic.

In the course of their investigations, the police discovered that William Eccles and Alice Haslam had not been the only recent bereavements suffered by Betty Eccles. Alice's sisters, Nancy and Hannah, had died in the previous two years, as had Betty's first husband and William Hatton Haywood, a ten-month-old baby she had been caring for.

The police decided to exhume the bodies of the other dead children. Hannah's body was almost completely skeletonised but the contents of the stomachs of the other three children were retrieved by Joseph Denham and sent to Henry Hough Watson for analysis. He was able to determine that arsenic was present in the stomachs of all three.

Betty Eccles was arrested on 29 September and charged with the wilful murders of William Eccles and Alice and Nancy Haslam. Inspector James Harris interviewed her about William's illness and Betty told him that she had called on the doctor to ask him to visit but that Dr Mallett had been out. She had therefore given William some senna but he had died about six hours later, before she had a chance to contact the doctor again. Asked about Alice's death, Betty told the Inspector that her daughter had been ill for about three days. Again, Betty said that she had asked Dr Mallett to call and, finding him out, had left a message with his apprentice. The doctor had finally arrived minutes after Alice's death. Betty denied ever having had a child called Nancy.

The police made enquiries in the neighbourhood and questioned local chemists and druggists. One of these, Mr Mosscrop, told them that Betty Eccles was a regular customer of his and that, six weeks before William's death, she had come into his shop and asked for a pennyworth of arsenic to kill mice.

He had refused to sell it to her since she was alone and it was a legal requirement for arsenic to be sold in front of a witness. Betty had left the shop, returning half an hour later with another woman. Only then had she been allowed to purchase the arsenic, which the chemist had wrapped in a paper packet and clearly labelled 'Poison'.

Betty Eccles was committed for trial at the Spring Assizes in Liverpool before Mr Baron Parke, with Mr Armstrong and Mr Brandt prosecuting and Dr Brown defending. Although Betty was charged with the murders of William Eccles and Nancy and Alice Haslam, the only case tried was William's murder, with the other two charges being held in reserve should she be acquitted.

The court heard that Betty had been married to her present husband since 1841. Henry Eccles, who was described as 'a man of irreproachable character', worked as a carter and, until shortly after his marriage, had been employed by Messrs Hardcastle & Co. of Bolton and Manchester. However, about nine weeks before William's death, Betty had done something to upset her husband's employer, described in the newspapers of the time as 'a faux pas', and Henry had been dismissed. He had been forced to move to Manchester to find work and now lived there during the week, returning to Bolton and his wife and family only at weekends.

On his last trip, he had said to Betty as he was leaving, 'Now, Betty, look to the children while I am away and in a week or two we will remove to Manchester.' Betty assured him that she always looked after the children and Henry Eccles could not dispute that, since she always appeared kind and caring towards them. However, it seemed that things were not as they appeared to Henry, since the prosecution produced witnesses in court who had seen Betty cruelly beating the children and, when the witnesses remonstrated with her, she told them that they were her children and she could do as she liked with them.

The prosecution called Richard Mangnall, the sexton of the parish church at Bolton-le-Moor and Benjamin Brown, the relieving officer of Great Bolton, both of whom recalled the death of Nancy Haslam, the daughter Betty had denied. James Haywood, a rag dealer from Bolton, was also called and told the court of the sudden death of his baby son, for whose care Betty Eccles had been paid a weekly sum of 3s 6d.

Mr Denham and Mr Watson gave their medical evidence and Mr Barlow, the assistant to Mr Mosscrop the druggist, testified to the defendant's purchase of arsenic at his employer's shop.

The prosecution then rested, leaving Dr Brown to argue for the defence. He pointed out that no trace of arsenic had ever been found at Betty Eccles's home and that all the evidence therefore pointed to William Eccles having been poisoned elsewhere, possibly by accident. Brown therefore insisted that there was sufficient doubt for the jury to return a verdict of 'Not Guilty' on his client.

The jury obviously gave the matter of Betty Eccles's guilt or innocence their full consideration, since they deliberated for almost an hour before returning with a verdict of 'Guilty'.

Betty Eccles was executed on 5 May 1843 at Kirkdale Gaol. Although she was only tried for the murder of her stepson, she had actually given birth to ten children in her lifetime, eight of whom had died suddenly, as well as her stepson and the baby she was caring for. Her first husband had been ill for some time before his death and, although he too had died suddenly, there was initially no suspicion of foul play in respect of his death. Yet after Betty's execution, the contemporary newspapers hinted that perhaps she had been responsible for his demise after all. 'All her family,' it was written, 'excepting those alive, have received a helping hand.' If this was indeed the case, then Betty Eccles poisoned at least ten, possibly eleven people, in her thirty-eight years.

5

'My station in society places me above or beyond suspicion'

SLOUGH, BERKSHIRE, 1845

On 1 January 1845, Mary Ann Ashley was disturbed by strange noises coming from her neighbour's cottage in Salt Hill, Slough. The sound resembled a woman's stifled screams and when they continued unabated for more than a minute Mary Ann picked up a candle and went to investigate. As she went outside, she heard the front door of the neighbouring cottage closing and saw a man walking up the garden path to the front gate.

Although Mary Ann did not know the man by name, she recognised him as a frequent visitor to her neighbour, Sarah Hart. As the man walked into the street, Mary Ann noticed that he appeared agitated and was trembling violently.

Town Hall, Slough. (Author's collection)

Slough Station, c. 1910. (Author's collection)

She asked him what was the matter with her neighbour but the man didn't reply, brushing past her and continuing briskly on his way towards Slough.

As the stifled moans continued from within Sarah Hart's cottage, Mary Ann walked inside and followed the sounds to her neighbour's bedroom. There she found Sarah Hart lying on her back on the floor breathing hard, her skirts above her knees and one stocking torn and pulled down. Her cap had fallen off and her hair had escaped its pins and hung around her face. It looked to Mary Ann as though Sarah had been engaged in a violent struggle.

Mary Ann ran to alert her other neighbours and Mrs Margaret Burrett accompanied her back to Sarah's cottage, attempting to give the stricken woman a drink of water. As soon as the liquid touched her lips Sarah began to foam at the mouth, so Mrs Burrett stayed with her while Mary Ann went to fetch surgeon Mr Champneys. By the time the surgeon arrived, Sarah Hart had stopped moaning. Mr Champneys felt for her pulse and thought that he could still detect a faint beat so he attempted to bleed her, but when he put his hand beneath her bodice to check her heart he realised that she was dead.

Immediately suspecting that Sarah Hart had been poisoned, Mr Champneys called for the police who, on hearing from Mary Ann Ashley that a man had been seen leaving the cottage shortly before Sarah's death, surmised that their prime suspect could be heading for the local station and set off in hot pursuit. Mary Ann was adamant that the man was dressed as a Quaker.

Another person had the same thought as the police. When the Revd E.T. Champnee heard of the suspicious death, he too guessed that the murderer might try to leave town as quickly as possible. Champnee went directly to the station, where he saw a man answering to the description that Mary Ann had provided entering a first-class carriage on the 7.42 p.m. train bound for Paddington Station, London. He sought out Henry Howell, the superintendent of Slough Station but, by the time he had spoken to him, the train bearing the stranger had departed. Knowing that Slough had recently installed an electric telegraph system, Champnee suggested sending a message to London so that the man could be intercepted and detained on his arrival at Paddington.

A wire was sent to Paddington with the message:

> A murder has just been committed in Salt Hill and the suspected murderer was seen to take a first class ticket to London by the train that left Slough at 7.42 p.m. He is in the garb of a Kwaker [*sic*] with a brown greatcoat on which reaches his feet. He is in the last compartment of the second first class carriage.

The machine did not have the letter Q, hence the improvisation of the spelling of the word Quaker.

The message was received by William Williams, a police sergeant at Paddington Station. Unsure about the legalities of arresting someone on instructions received by telegraph, he decided instead to just tail the suspect, following him to The Jerusalem Coffee House in Cornhill, near London Bridge and from there to a private lodging house, then back to The Jerusalem the following morning. A watch was kept on the premises and, as soon as orders were received by a more conventional means, Inspector William Wiggins arrested the man, by now identified as Mr John Tawell.

Wiggins approached Tawell in the coffee house and asked him to confirm his identity. He then told Tawell that he was arresting him for having been the last person to be seen with a woman in Slough, who was now deceased. Tawell immediately denied knowing anybody in Slough, telling Wiggins that he had not been there and had not left London at all on the previous day. 'You must be wrong in the identity,' he told Wiggins. 'My station in society places me above or beyond suspicion.'

John Tawell was not a true Quaker, although he had adopted the Quaker ways after entering the service of a member of the Society of Friends as a young man. However he found himself unable to adhere to the Quaker's strict moral codes, especially those relating to relationships. At the age of twenty-two, he seduced a servant girl who became pregnant and, much to the disapproval of the Quaker community, he was forced to marry her. Then, having worked for some years in a druggist's shop, Tawell got his hands on an engraved copper plate, with which he attempted to forge a £10 note. He was caught and tried for the offence and given a sentence of fourteen years transportation to Australia.

There he worked on the coal boats before progressing to a job at a convict hospital then to a job as a clerk at the Sydney Academy. He so impressed his employer there that Mr Isaac Wood petitioned the governor for a pardon for him and, after only three years, Tawell was granted his freedom.

He immediately opened a shop selling drugs and chemicals and was given permission to dispense by the local medical board, soon having a small chain of highly successful drugstores. News of his success reached his wife and son in England and they eventually sailed out to Australia to join him. A second son was born and Tawell, who continued to pass himself off as a Quaker, became wealthy.

Eventually the Tawells returned to London and settled in Southwark. Not long after their arrival, the family suffered the deaths of their two sons. Mrs Tawell also fell ill and her husband engaged a nurse, Sarah Lawrence, to care for her. The temptation of a pretty young woman living in his home, along with a wife who was too ill to share his bed, was too much for Tawell and Sarah soon became pregnant, giving birth to a son. A year later, she gave birth to a daughter, by which time the long-suffering Mrs Tawell had died.

Sarah fully expected to become the next Mrs Tawell after a decent interval. But in 1841 Tawell met and married Mrs Sarah Cutforth, a Quaker widow with one child, who had previously run a school in Clerkenwell. Her choice of husband led to her being excommunicated by the Society of Friends.

Having tired of Sarah Lawrence and ever fearful of his new wife finding out about their past relationship, Tawell installed her in a cottage in Slough, where she became known as Sarah Hart. She told people that she was married but that her husband was abroad, explaining Tawell's visits to her cottage by passing him off as her father-in-law. Tawell's fortune had declined after his second marriage. His bank accounts were overdrawn and the payment of almost £1 a week in maintenance for Sarah and their two children was draining him financially. He apparently began to default on his payments to Sarah as, at the time of her death, the quarterly rent on her cottage, due the previous month, remained unpaid and several pawn tickets were found in her home. This, coupled with the constant worry that the new Mrs Tawell would find out about Sarah, necessitated dramatic action on the part of John Tawell.

Drawing on his experience as a druggist, Tawell visited a chemist's shop on 1 January 1845 and asked assistant Henry Thomas for two drachms of Scheele's Prussic Acid, saying that he wanted to use it to treat a varicose vein he had developed. He had brought his own bottle, but Thomas found himself unable to remove the stopper, so supplied the acid in a new bottle, which, at Tawell's request, he did not label.

By now, Mr Champneys had conducted a post-mortem examination on Sarah's body, finding no injury or natural illness that might have accounted for her death. However, on opening the body, Mr Champneys believed that he could smell Prussic acid. He removed the stomach and its contents and took them to Mr J. Thomas Cooper, a chemist and lecturer in chemical jurisprudence. In the presence of his son, Joseph, who was also his assistant, Cooper ran a series of tests on the stomach contents. Mr Champneys observed the tests along with two other surgeons, Mr Nordblad and Mr Pickering. Cooper found no trace of poisons such as arsenic, oxalic acid, opium, all of which he tested for, but was able to isolate Prussic acid. In all, almost 50 grains of the poison were extracted from the contents of Sarah's stomach. Sarah Hart was obviously expecting a visitor on 1 January, since she went to the Windmill Inn and purchased a bottle of Guinness. It was believed that Tawell added Prussic acid to Sarah's glass of beer and so poisoned her.

Prussic or hydrocyanic acid, so called because of its Prussian Blue colour, is one of the deadliest poisons known to man and a single drop in its pure form placed on the end of a rod and inserted into the mouth of a cat or dog would be sufficient to cause instant death. Found naturally in some fruit stones and in the leaves of trees such as beech and laurel, about two thirds of a grain dissolved in water would be capable of killing seven people. For obvious reasons, Prussic acid was not readily available in its pure form, although it was the active component of Scheele's Prussic Acid, which comprised five grains of pure acid to ninety-five grains of water and was used for external application.

Arrested for the murder of Sarah Hart, sixty-year-old Tawell was tried at Aylesbury in March 1845 before Mr Baron Parke. Mr Sergeant Byles and Mr Prendergast prosecuted the case, while Tawell was defended by Mr Fitzroy Kelly, Mr O'Malley and Mr Gunning. Tawell appeared in his customary Quaker garb and looked pale and somewhat anxious, although he made his 'Not Guilty' plea in a firm and decisive voice.

The prosecution outlined the circumstances of Sarah Hart's death, calling on her neighbours to give their accounts of the events of 1 January. Most of them positively identified Tawell in court as the man they had seen either leaving Sarah's cottage or making his way to the station on the night of her murder. They were followed into the witness box by the medical experts, who testified first about trying to save Sarah's life then on the post-mortem examination and the results of the tests that had been carried out on her remains. The staff from Slough Station testified, as did the police officers involved in Tawell's arrest and druggist's assistant Henry Thomas, who had sold Prussic acid to Tawell. Another witness, Charlotte Howard, told the court that Sarah Hart had unaccountably been violently ill once before after sharing a drink with John Tawell.

It was then left to the defence to present their case. Mr Fitzroy Kelly began by reminding the jury that John Tawell had paid for his previous misdeeds and had now re-established himself in society as an honest, Christian, charitable man. Kelly went on to point out to the jury that the medical witnesses, Mr Champneys, Mr Pickering and Mr Nordblad, were all relatively young and inexperienced and had never seen an actual case of poisoning by Prussic acid, instead gaining all their knowledge on the subject from books and records of a science that was as yet still in its infancy.

Poisoning by Prussic acid was comparatively rare, said Kelly. There were, at that time, only about thirty-eight or thirty-nine known incidences and, of those, all but two had been shown to be suicide rather than murder. Tawell's initial statements to the police had accused Sarah Hart of blackmailing him for money and threatening to kill herself if she didn't get it.

Now the defence told the jury that they did not believe that Sarah had taken any poison of her own volition and set out to place reasonable doubt in the minds of the jury, suggesting that the Prussic acid found in Sarah's remains had occurred naturally after she had eaten an unusually large quantity of apples. Sarah was known to have received a big basket of apples as a Christmas gift just days before her death, and chemist's assistant Mr Thomas had conducted an experiment in which he had managed to obtain two-thirds of a grain of pure Prussic acid from the pips of just fifteen apples. Kelly also suggested that Mrs Burrett might have suffocated Sarah Hart in attempting to give her a drink of water, a suggestion that provoked first startled gasps then nervous laughter from the body of the court.

Mr Kelly addressed the purchase of Prussic acid on 1 January, pointing out that it was a perfectly legitimate transaction since Tawell had a varicose vein and the Scheele's Prussic Acid had been prescribed for him. He also told the court that Henry Thomas had stated that Tawell had bought a similar quantity of Prussic acid on the following day, telling the chemist's assistant that he had accidentally broken the first bottle. If the Prussic acid had been bought for the express purpose of killing Sarah Hart, why buy yet more on the day after her death?

It only remained for the judge to summarise the case for the jury. Mr Baron Parke championed the scientific evidence, telling the jury that as far as he could see from the evidence presented in court, there was absolutely no doubt that Sarah Hart had died from poisoning by Prussic acid and stating that death from eating apple pips could only have occurred had the pips first been crushed and distilled. He reminded them that Sarah had become violently ill on another occasion after drinking with the defendant and suggested that the motive for murder was both financial, in that Tawell could no longer afford to pay her allowance of £13 a quarter, and personal, in that Tawell did not want his present wife to know about his past 'connexion' [*sic*] with Sarah and was also very keen to be accepted as a member of the Society of Friends. Finally the judge ridiculed the idea that Mrs Burrett may have unwittingly asphyxiated Sarah Hart in trying to help her.

The judge stressed that if the jury had any doubts whatsoever then they should give the prisoner the benefit of those doubts, saying that they were not bound to convict anyone. With that, he left the matter entirely in the hands of the jury to do their duty as they saw fit.

Before the jury could retire to consider their verdict, counsel for the defence, Mr Gunning, interjected to ask the judge to mention the fact that the defendant had received numerous good character witnesses. The judge concurred and resumed his summary to read aloud all the testimonies on Tawell's character.

With that the jury retired. In their absence, the judge began the trial of three men charged with burglary, while Tawell remained anxiously in court, his face alternately flushed and pale. However, the new case had barely begun when, after thirty minutes, notice was received that the jury had reached a verdict. When they returned to court and pronounced Tawell 'Guilty' a spontaneous burst of applause broke out in the court, which the judge quelled with some difficulty in order to pronounce the death sentence on the prisoner.

Tawell faced his sentence in silence and it was only after he left the court and went to the cells below that he fell to the ground in a fit. He was later heard pacing the floor saying repeatedly, 'Oh dear, oh dear.' It emerged that he had been so confident of his acquittal that he had arranged for a carriage to be waiting at the conclusion of the trial to convey him home.

Sarah Hart's two young children had been in rooms close to the court throughout the trial and would have been called to give evidence had there been any doubt about Tawell's identity. The boy in particular was said to bear a strong physical relationship to John Tawell, his alleged father. Immediately after the death of their mother, Mary Ann Ashley had generously taken in the children. Now in the care of their grandmother, the children were called to the courtroom and Sarah's son was presented with the watch that his mother had always worn.

Tawell was taken to the condemned cell at Aylesbury Prison to await his execution, which went ahead in spite of appeals to the Home Secretary and even the Queen on his behalf. Before his death, John Tawell made a full confession to the murder of Sarah Hart to prison chaplain Mr Cox, although it was conditional on the contents not being made public. In spite of everything, Tawell's wife was still convinced of her husband's innocence and Tawell expressed a wish that she should be allowed to get over the shock of his execution before learning the details of his admission of guilt.

A gallows was specially constructed on an iron balcony on an upper floor of the Town Hall at Aylesbury A modest crowd of between 2,000 and 3,000 people watched Tawell's execution by William Calcraft – it was suggested that most people assumed that he would be reprieved and so didn't bother attending. One person who did make a special effort to be there was a Mr Thompson from St Austell in Cornwall who, having seen an engraved picture of Tawell in the *Pictorial Times*, believed that Tawell was a 'Mr Lawrence', a Quaker who had absconded owing a considerable amount of money after the purchase of some land.

Thompson had hoped to have an interview with Tawell in person but, after a comparison of a sample of Tawell's handwriting with that of 'Mr Lawrence', he instantly realised that Tawell was not the man he was seeking after all. When Mr Thompson's presence was communicated to Tawell, he asked on what date

Aylesbury County Town Hall, 1905. (Author's collection)

the fraudulent transaction in Cornwall had taken place. When he was told that it was in October 1836, Tawell immediately wrote a short note to Mr Thompson, telling him that he had been in Australia at the time.

Calcraft apparently miscalculated the necessary drop required for John Tawell and instead of dying instantly, Tawell convulsed for almost ten minutes on the end of the rope, wringing his hands and pulling up his legs. It was pointed out in the newspapers of the time that his prolonged and agonising death mirrored that of his unfortunate victim.

It also emerged that Sarah had experienced a strange premonition about her own death. On the afternoon of her murder she had spoken to baker Mr Hawker, promising to pay his bill when she next saw him. She explained that 'the old gentleman' would be visiting her soon to bring money, adding, 'I am very uncomfortable, very uncomfortable indeed. I don't know how it is, Mr Hawker, but I assure you I quite dread his coming.' Less than three hours later, Sarah was dead.

Note: There are some variations in the accounts of the murder in the contemporary newspapers. John Tawell's second wife is named as both Sarah Cutford and Sarah Cutforth and Mary Ann Ashley is alternatively called Ashlee. There also appears to be some confusion as to who it was who initiated the sending of the telegraph from Slough to Paddington, probably because of the similarity in names between Mr Champneys the surgeon and the Revd Champnee. Some accounts state that the surgeon was responsible, others name the clergyman. There are variations in the spellings of both names.

6
'It's dumpling night'

Having known each other for several years, Catherine Morley and John Foster married in October 1846 at All Saints' Church, Acton, near Sudbury in Suffolk. The newlyweds set up home in the village with Catherine's mother, Maria, although within days of her marriage, Catherine asked her husband's permission to visit her aunt at Pakenham for a short holiday. John willingly gave his consent, telling her to take a month if she liked, but she was gone for just ten days.

On the day after her return – a Sunday – John complained to his sister of a headache but was well enough to go to his work as a farm labourer the next day, when he appeared to be in perfect health and good spirits. On the Tuesday, Catherine went to visit her mother-in-law. She was given her midday meal and spent most of the day with Mrs Foster until five o'clock in the afternoon, when she suddenly seemed in a hurry to go home. 'It's dumpling night,' she told her mother-in-law.

When Catherine got home, the only person in the house was her eight-year-old brother, Thomas, who watched as his sister made two dumplings, wrapped them separately in cloth and put them to boil in the copper.

John Foster returned home from work and, having washed his hands at the pump in the yard, sat down to his evening meal of dumpling and potatoes, washed down by tea with sugar. He had eaten barely half of his meal when he began to feel ill and was forced to rush out of the cottage to vomit. Catherine followed him, returning moments later to pick up the remains of the dumpling from her husband's plate and take it outside.

When Maria Morley got home from her work as a washerwoman at seven o'clock in the evening, her son-in-law had taken to his bed and was vomiting a coffee-coloured liquid into a basin. Throughout the night, the basin was repeatedly emptied into a ditch behind the cottage.

At eight o'clock the next morning, John was still very ill and Catherine set out to walk the two miles to consult Robert Jones, a surgeon from Melford. The short walk took her almost two hours. Catherine told Mr Jones that her husband had a bowel complaint. She mentioned nothing about sickness or vomiting and Jones assumed that John had a case of English cholera, which had been very prevalent in the area over the summer months. Jones gave Catherine some mercury, chalk and rhubarb powders for her husband and when she mentioned that John had wanted the doctor to call, he promised to do so later that day.

By the time Catherine got back to Acton, her mother had already gone to work, leaving John alone at home, still very ill. When Maria Morley returned home at three o'clock that afternoon, John's condition had worsened considerably and at four o'clock, he died. Mr Jones arrived an hour later and was most surprised to learn of Foster's death, since Catherine had communicated no urgency or undue concern to him when she visited his surgery that morning. Jones happened to be passing the cottage on the following day and called in to ask if he might see John's bed linen, so that he could '…ascertain what passed through his bowels'. Having inspected the sheets, he formed an opinion that John had died from bilious diarrhoea or English cholera.

As John had been a strapping, healthy man, in the prime of his life, Jones carried out a post-mortem examination on the instructions of the coroner. He found what he described as ulceration of the vena cava – a blood vessel to the heart – which, had it burst, would certainly have caused Foster's death. Knowing that Foster had been taken ill shortly after beginning his evening meal, as a precaution, Mr Jones removed Foster's stomach contents and sent them to another surgeon, William Image, who was well known for his skill and experience in chemical analysis.

Yet even before the results of Mr Image's tests were received, there was convincing evidence that Foster had been poisoned. Maria Morley's house was the middle one of a terrace of three and both neighbours on either side had found that their chickens had unexpectedly died almost immediately after the death of John Foster. The birds' crops contained suet, which, when analysed, was found to contain arsenic. Not only that, but neighbour Mrs Simpson had found a piece of dumpling in her garden, which she had fed to a hen. The hen died soon afterwards and, once again, its crop was found to contain arsenic. The police had also removed two pudding cloths from Maria Morley's home, one of which was contaminated with arsenic.

Once Mr Image had confirmed that John Foster's stomach contents contained a large quantity of the poison, the coroner ordered his body to be exhumed so that further samples could be taken. These too showed the presence of arsenic. An inquest was held at the Crown Inn, Sudbury, before coroner Harry Wayman, at which the jury determined that John Foster had been wilfully poisoned by his wife, Catherine. One of the key witnesses was young Thomas Morley, who originally testified that Catherine had made only one dumpling on the night John died, which all three of them had eaten. However, when later questioned again by the police, he admitted that she had made two; one that she shared had with him and another that John alone ate. Thomas told the police that he had lied to please his sister, who had previously told him exactly what he should say if asked.

Catherine was committed for trial at the Suffolk Lent Assizes before Chief Justice Baron Pollock. Mr Gurdon prosecuted the case and Mr Power acted for Catherine Foster, who pleaded 'Not Guilty'.

It was the contention of the prosecution that Catherine Foster had been unwilling to marry John but that he had been so persistent in his courtship of her that she had acquiesced, realising her mistake as soon as the wedding ring was on her finger. Thus the prosecution called several witnesses to whom Catherine had supposedly expressed her discontent, while the defence countered with witnesses who believed that she was perfectly happy to be married to John.

John's mother, Elizabeth, told the court that she had not been told that her son was ill, only finding out after his death that he had been 'purging upwards and downwards' and asking for her.

Catherine's mother stated that John had been very keen to marry Catherine and that she had asked him to wait a year, since Catherine was only seventeen. Catherine had seemed happy and comfortable with his courtship and had seemed quite keen to marry. However, other witnesses told a different tale.

Mary Ann Chinery lived with her grandfather, William Pawsey, in the cottage adjoining Maria Morley's home. She recalled the day of John's post-mortem, when Catherine had asked to sit at her house while the examination of her husband's body was going on next door. Catherine had told Pawsey that, had she gone to Bury before her marriage, she wouldn't have married at all. Catherine had also told people that she much preferred a young man named Spraggons to

her husband and, when asked by a friend how she liked being married, had replied, 'Not at all.'

Perhaps the most important person to testify was Thomas Morley, who had actually watched the drama unfold from start to finish. Thomas appeared frightened in court and was allowed to stand next to the judge himself to give his evidence.

Thomas told the court about his return from school on the day on which John was taken ill. He watched his sister making the dumplings, using flour from her flour bin and adding salt to the mixture, and had then seen her add the contents of a small paper packet, which she took from her pocket, burning the paper afterwards. He and Catherine had been eating their dumpling when John returned home from work and was given his own dumpling, rushing outside to vomit within minutes. Thomas told the court that there had been no dumpling left over and none thrown away. He swore before God that his sister had not told him what to say in court.

Maria Morley's neighbours told the court the fate of all thirteen of their chickens and PC George Green testified to searching the house and taking away samples of flour and pudding cloths. It was then left to Mr Image the analyst to tell the court of his findings.

The defence made much of the fact that John had allowed Catherine to visit her aunt for a holiday and that, even though he had told her to 'take a month', she had returned in ten days. Would she have come back so quickly if she had been unhappily married? As far as defence counsel Mr Power could elicit, Catherine returned John's affections and had written him letters that clearly demonstrated this.

Mr Power also suggested that John Foster had been ill, following a fall from a hay wagon two weeks before his death. However, the prosecution had anticipated this line of defence and had already called a fellow farm labourer of John's, William Steed, to testify that he had suffered no ill effects from the fall.

In the end, the prosecution won the day as, after retiring for fifteen minutes, the jury returned a verdict of 'Guilty'. Catherine Foster remained almost unmoved as the judge pronounced the death sentence upon her, merely dabbing at her eyes with a handkerchief.

Five days before her execution, she made a full confession to the prison governor, in which she admitted, 'I am guilty, very guilty of this awful crime and well deserve the death I am condemned to die.' She stated that she had bought poison from Mr Ely, a chemist in Sudbury, and mixed it with her husband's dumpling. Her husband was always good and kind but she had no affection for him and wished to go back into service. Her confession also included the words, 'I do not wish to live, for I could never be happy in this world.'

Some years previously, Catherine's father, William Morley, had been strongly suspected of murder and robbery and there is also anecdotal evidence that her grandfather was hanged for murder. Regardless of her family history, on 17 April 1847 seventeen-year-old Catherine Foster walked unsupported to the drop with a firm step and a crowd of more than 10,000 people witnessed her last moments in what was to be the last public execution at Bury St Edmunds Gaol.

7

'Take that devil away from me!'

William Palmer was born on 6 August 1824, one of eight children of a sawyer, Joseph Palmer, and his wife, Sarah. Accounts of William's early life in the contemporary newspapers are contradictory but it appears that Joseph made a fortune from his timber business, not all of it honestly. Described as a 'coarse, unscrupulous, insolent, pushing fellow, who had no friends', Joseph died when William was only twelve years old, leaving £7,000 to William on the condition that he didn't marry before his twenty-first birthday, and a staggering £75,000 to Sarah, providing she didn't marry again after his death.

William left school at seventeen and was apprenticed to Messrs Evans and Evans, a wholesale chemist in Liverpool. Unfortunately, as soon as William started to work there, money began to disappear. In due course, William was caught red-handed in the act of opening a letter containing money addressed to his employers and was immediately dismissed from his job. He was saved from prosecution only because his doting mother repaid all the money he had stolen.

The missing money had been used to impress William's older girlfriend, Jane Widnall, who, it seems, was courting William with the sole intention of getting her hands on his inheritance. Her ardour cooled rapidly when she discovered that he wouldn't inherit anything if he married before he reached twenty-one and the couple parted.

William's mother found him another position as an apprentice to Dr Edward Tylecote, a surgeon at Great Haywood. Soon, Jane Widnall turned up again, more determined than ever to forge a future with Palmer, whom she still believed to be very wealthy. In order to make William jealous, she turned her attentions briefly to another man. Her plan worked and William became so inflamed with passion that he poured acid over his rival's clothes and cut up his boots.

Once again, money went missing from William's place of employment and once again William was dismissed. He and Jane then ran away together but were forced to return when their money ran out. Palmer's mother pleaded with Dr Tylecote to give William his old job back, but the doctor refused. Hence she paid the sum of five guineas for him to become a 'walking pupil' at Stafford Infirmary. Meanwhile, Jane Widnall married the man she had been flirting with to make William jealous and the newlyweds emigrated to Australia.

Great Haywood. (Author's collection)

Stafford Infirmary, 1912. (Author's collection)

It was while Palmer was working at Stafford Infirmary that he began to take an interest in poisons and his time there also marked the start of a long association with a series of sudden, suspicious deaths. He was first implicated in the death of a man named George Abley. Abley, a weak and sickly man, was challenged by Palmer to drink a large quantity of brandy for a bet. Unused to drinking, Abley died after the contest and, although his death was certified as being due to natural causes, rumours abounded that Palmer was attracted to Abley's wife and had deliberately set out to kill him so that she would be free to marry him.

Palmer did not stay long at Stafford Infirmary, leaving for St Bartholomew's Hospital in London to train to become a doctor. However, rather than studying, he wasted his time pursuing women, drinking and gambling. The hospital eventually contacted his mother to advise her of her son's extra-curricular activities and Mrs Palmer engaged the services of a personal tutor, Dr Stegall, to help William cram for his exams. Stegall was promised £100 if Palmer qualified as a doctor and, although Stegall fulfilled his duties and William graduated, the promised payment was not forthcoming. Stegall sued Mrs Palmer for his money, the case eventually being settled out of court.

William, now Dr Palmer, returned to Rugeley and rented a house in Market Street, fixing a brass plate to the wall by the door, declaring himself a surgeon (MRCS). His medical practice thrived and he was soon able to employ Benjamin Thirlby as his assistant. Soon Thirlby all but ran the practice, since Palmer was too preoccupied with gambling, having developed a consuming passion for horse racing. Not content with just being a spectator, Palmer was to purchase numerous horses, which he put into training. He obviously managed to find some spare time for other activities besides horse racing as it was rumoured that he fathered at least fifteen illegitimate children.

Palmer soon ran up large gambling debts, which led to him being banned from Tattersall's, the main auctioneers of thoroughbred horses in England. He was also not above trying to fix the outcome of horse races by doping horses before they ran if he thought they were likely to beat his own horse. His failures on the racecourse and his large gambling debts soon took care of his inheritance from his father, at which Palmer began to look for another source of income.

He settled on Anne Thornton. Anne was the illegitimate daughter of Colonel Edward Brookes, a wealthy but eccentric Rugeley resident, and his housekeeper, Mary Thornton. Anne's father committed suicide and, since her mother had a serious drink problem, under the terms of his will, his daughter was assigned guardians. One of these was Palmer's old employer, Dr Tylecote, who, suspecting that Palmer's true motives for courting Anne were purely financial, vigorously opposed any relationship between the doctor and his ward.

Upper Brook Street, Rugeley, c. 1910. (Author's collection)

However Anne, who had first met Palmer while he was working for Tylecote, declared herself deeply in love with William and the couple eventually obtained a court order to allow them to marry. The wedding took place on 7 October 1847, when Anne was twenty years old.

Anne came to the marriage with an inheritance of £8,000, which soon went the way of Palmer's own inheritance. Now, Palmer turned to his mother-in-law, Mary Thornton, and although she had initially been against her daughter's marriage, Mary obliged by lending William small sums of money. After the death of Colonel Brookes, Mary Thornton's alcohol consumption grew even more excessive and she existed almost solely on a diet of gin, eating very little food. In January 1849, she moved in with her daughter and son-in-law as a paying guest but within days she was suffering from attacks of biliousness.

Palmer was unable to relieve her symptoms and called in another doctor to attend to her, deliberately choosing Dr Bamford who, at eighty years of age, was semi retired. Aware of his own shortcomings as a doctor due to his advanced age, Bamford repeatedly suggested that Mary's own doctor, Dr Knight, was consulted, but Palmer refused. Mary Thornton grew more ill by the day and eventually died on 18 January 1849, aged fifty. Almost her last act before her death was to point to her son-in-law and scream, 'Take that devil away from me!'

It is not clear whether Mary died as a consequence of her alcoholism or as a result of any direct intervention by her son-in-law. What does seem certain is that Palmer had expected that the considerable sum of money and numerous

The residence of William Palmer at Rugeley, as illustrated in the Illustrated London News. *(Author's collection)*

properties that Mary had inherited on the death of Colonel Brookes would go to Anne. However, this was not the case and the courts ruled instead that Mary's fortune should go to Brookes' nearest relative, a man named Mr Shallcross. Newspaper reports of the time are contradictory, with some saying that Anne inherited nothing at all, some saying that she inherited money but was unable to gain access to it since it was left in trust, and some saying that Anne inherited £12,000. Whatever the truth of the matter, there is no dispute that William Palmer's finances were still in a perilous state since he owed numerous gambling debts and was now unable to find bookmakers who were prepared to take his bets. By now, the Palmer's had one child, a boy named William after his father who was known as 'Little Willy' to avoid confusion. William and Anne were to have five children, all but Little Willy dying in infancy. Although it was never proven, many people believed that Palmer had poisoned his four children.

In 1850, William was at Chester racecourse with a friend, Leonard Bladon, to whom he owed £600. Bladon enjoyed a successful day at the races, winning £500, which was presented to him in cash. Palmer told him that he was now in a position to repay his gambling debt and suggested that Bladon return with him to Rugeley. Bladon wrote to his wife, telling her where he was going and also mentioning his good fortune, informing her that he would be home in a couple of days with around £1,000. However, almost as soon as he reached Rugeley, he was taken ill with severe indigestion.

Palmer treated him but Bladon's illness worsened and again Palmer called in the ageing Dr Bamford. Quite by chance, a mutual friend of Palmer and

Rugeley, as illustrated in the Illustrated London News. *(Author's collection)*

The High Street and Town Hall, Rugeley, as illustrated in the Illustrated London News.
(Author's collection)

Bladon visited Palmer's house and was shocked by Bladon's condition, asking Palmer if Bladon's wife had been notified. Palmer told him that it wasn't necessary to trouble her, since he fully expected Bladon to recover soon. Some time earlier, Bladon had been injured in an accident and had been advised by his doctors to rest. Instead, he had gone to the races, against the wishes of his wife. The friend ignored Palmer and notified Mrs Bladon, who immediately travelled to her husband's bedside. By the time she reached Rugeley, Leonard Bladon was so ill that he no longer recognised her and he died shortly after her arrival. There was no trace of the money he had won and when Mrs Bladon enquired about it, Palmer denied any knowledge of it. He also denied his debt to Leonard Bladon, telling Mrs Bladon that, on the contrary, Bladon actually owed him £60.

Palmer certified Bladon's death himself, citing the cause as an injury of the hip joint and an abscess in the pelvis. He dissuaded Mrs Bladon from arranging for her husband's body to be taken home, instead organising a quick burial in Rugeley. Mrs Bladon consulted with her family about the missing money and it was suggested that she contacted the police. Fearful of incurring costs, Mrs Bladon eventually decided to let the matter drop, although she refused to pay Palmer the £60 he continued to insist that her husband owed him.

Some newspapers later carried an account of another friend of Palmer's, a Mr Bly or Blyth, who suffered a similar fate to Leonard Bladon, dying in suspicious circumstances at Palmer's home at a time when Palmer owed him £800. However, this story has never been reliably confirmed.

Still in dire straits financially, Palmer then took to using the services of moneylenders, forging the signature of his wealthy mother in order to guarantee repayment of his loans. To aid him in his deception, Palmer enlisted the services of the Rugeley postmaster, Samuel Cheshire, who ensured that all of Mrs Palmer's mail was delivered first to her son's house. Cheshire was later tried for his part in Palmer's devious scheme and was sentenced to twelve months hard labour at Newgate Prison.

In October 1852, Palmer's uncle, Joseph 'Beau' Bentley, came to stay with his nephew. Widely known as a womanising rogue and an alcoholic, Beau was challenged to a drinking contest by William and died hours later from what was recorded as a 'malignant disease of the stomach'. As with Mary Thornton, the actual cause of his death was uncertain – it could have been due to his alcoholism or to the administration of poison by his nephew. Then, an aunt who visited the Palmers home for a short holiday was taken ill during her stay and was given some pills by William. Rather than take them, she threw them out of her bedroom window, where they landed in a chicken run. When several of the birds were found dead the next morning, William was most insistent that their bodies were destroyed rather than being prepared for the table.

The Accurst Surgeon

Dr William Palmer. (By kind permission of Linda Stratmann)

Palmer then devised another scheme to obtain money. In collusion with crooked solicitor, Jeremiah Smith, he insured his wife's life for £13,000, agreeing to pay a premium of £760 a year. Without Smith's assistance, the Prince of Wales Insurance Company might well have questioned why a young, apparently healthy woman merited such a large sum assured. However, Smith acted as an agent for the company and the insurance proposal went through without a hitch, with Palmer borrowing the money to pay the premium.

In September 1854, Anne Palmer went to stay with some friends at Liverpool. She caught a chill and, feeling poorly, cut short her stay and returned to Rugeley after just three days, where she went straight to bed. William nursed her but instead of getting better, Anne gradually became worse, complaining of severe sickness and diarrhoea with agonising stomach cramps. Palmer called in Dr Bamford but the ageing doctor was far from happy to treat Anne and insisted that another doctor was called. Dr Knight was summoned and, having examined Anne, diagnosed the early stages of cholera and put her on a starvation diet. Anne's condition gradually improved but then suddenly worsened and, although Dr Knight was called back to the house, he arrived just after Anne had died. After consulting with Dr Bamford, Dr Knight certified her death as being due to English cholera.

At the end of June 1855, within nine months of Anne's death, Palmer's housemaid, Eliza Tharme, gave birth to a baby boy, Alfred, apparently sired by Palmer. Palmer arranged for the child to be fostered by a nurse but in November 1855, he expressed a desire to see the baby, who was brought to his home. Having spent a few minutes alone with his father in his dispensary, Alfred experienced convulsions on the way back to his nurse and died soon afterwards. The cause of his death was recorded as erysipelas – a skin infection.

With the payout of £13,000 from the insurance company on Anne's death, Palmer was able to settle some of his debts. Yet he still owed a considerable amount of money to moneylenders who were beginning to pressure him for repayment. Palmer's insurance scheme had been so successful that he next insured the life of his brother, Walter, for £14,000. This was accomplished with some difficulty, as Walter was an alcoholic in poor health, who lived apart from his wife. Several insurance companies turned down Palmer's request but somehow Palmer managed to find a doctor willing to pronounce his brother 'healthy, robust and temperate'.

Unfortunately, should Walter die, the insurance money would automatically go to his next of kin – his wife, Agnes. William managed to talk Walter into signing the insurance policy over to him, for which he offered his brother a cash sum of £400. When that was done, William went to visit his brother in Stafford, staying at the Grand Junction Hotel there.

At a chemist's shop in Wolverhampton, Palmer purchased Prussic acid, which he was later seen mixing into a medicine bottle in his hotel room. Palmer then went to see his brother and, by the following morning, Walter had died.

William did not bother to inform his brother's estranged wife of his death and by the time Agnes found out, Walter had already been buried. Agnes was furious, especially when William told her about the life insurance policy and added that Walter owed him a considerable sum of money.

An independent doctor certified Walter's death as being due to 'general visceral disease and apoplexy'. However, the insurance company was suspicious, as Walter had died only four months after the policy had been activated. They refused to pay out, telling Palmer to take them to court.

Palmer did not initiate court proceedings against the insurance company, instead hatching a scheme to insure a man named George Bates. Bates is variously described in the contemporary newspapers as a mentally retarded youth, employed by Palmer as his groom and as a friend of Palmer's, a gentleman farmer who was down on his luck. Whatever the facts of the matter, Palmer represented Bates to the insurance companies as 'a gentleman of leisure' and tried to insure his life for £25,000.

In view of the large sum assured requested, the insurance companies sent inspectors to investigate the proposal before accepting it and discovered that Bates was far from a gentleman of leisure. Not only that but he evidently did not understand the concept of insurance and was under the impression that he was going to receive a large sum of money, not realising that the money was only paid out after his death.

Palmer's proposal to insure Bates was turned down, leaving Palmer still poverty stricken and under ever increasing pressure from the moneylenders to whom he owed a substantial amount. He was also now being blackmailed by a woman named Jane Burgess, who was in possession of some damning letters in which Palmer discussed arranging to carry out an illegal abortion on her.

On 13 November 1855, Palmer went to Shrewsbury races with a friend, twenty-eight-year-old John Parsons Cook. Cook was also an occasional patient of Palmer's and, it was rumoured, was being treated by the doctor for syphilis. He had once been articled to a solicitor but had inherited a large sum of money and had turned instead to drinking and gambling.

Cook had a mare, 'Polestar', running at the race meeting at Shrewsbury, which romped in first in one of the races, securing a prize purse of £3,000. That evening, Cook threw a celebration dinner at the Raven Hotel in Shrewsbury and, following a night of overindulgence and the consumption of copious amounts of alcohol, he was taken ill. A doctor was called and Cook was given an emetic to encourage him to vomit, which seemed to cure him. Cook accused Palmer of poisoning his drink but Palmer dismissed

THE HONYWOOD HOTELS

Raven Hotel, Shrewsbury.   *Telephone : Shrewsbury 476 & 477.*
Telegrams : Raven Hotel, Shrewsbury.

The Raven Hotel, Shrewsbury in the 1930s. (Author's collection)

Cook's allegations of poisoning to the doctor, saying that Cook was just drunk.

On the following day, Cook was well enough to go back to the races, where Palmer lost money. That evening, Cook dined with friends, including Palmer, at the Raven Hotel where Palmer was observed apparently adding the contents of a small bottle to some brandy. When Cook drank the brandy, he immediately complained that his throat was burning. 'There's nothing in it,' insisted Palmer, snatching the tumbler from him and drinking from it, before passing it to another dinner guest and demanding that he too tasted the contents. However, there had only been about a teaspoonful of brandy left in the glass for Palmer to drink and he had completely drained it.

Once again, Cook felt unwell and a doctor was sent for. Cook told Dr Gibson that he had been poisoned and the doctor gave him a large quantity of warm water and recommended that he tickled the back of his throat with a feather in order to make himself vomit. Cook maintained that he could make himself sick with the handle of a toothbrush and, having watched Cook vomit up all the water, Dr Gibson sent some medicine to the hotel. By the following morning, Cook was well enough to get up and eat a little breakfast. He then agreed to return to Rugeley with William Palmer and the two left that evening, with Cook booking into the Talbot Arms Inn, which was situated directly opposite Palmer's house. Having first attended a dinner party at Palmer's house, Cook went back to his hotel after midnight when, according to the hotel porter, he was perfectly sober.

Nevertheless, Palmer appeared at the hotel very early the following morning asking the staff to prepare a cup of black coffee for him to take up to Cook's room since Cook had drunk to excess the previous evening and would no doubt be suffering from a severe hangover. Within minutes of drinking the coffee, Cook vomited and began writhing around with severe stomach pains.

Throughout that day, Palmer was extremely solicitous towards Cook, ferrying several cups of coffee upstairs to his sick friend. On one occasion, he took a bowl of soup and, when Cook didn't finish it, chambermaid Elizabeth Mills took a few spoonfuls from the half-empty bowl. The broth tasted of turnips and celery but Elizabeth immediately experienced terrible stomach pains and vomiting and was ill for the rest of the day.

Palmer called in the trusty eighty-two-year-old Dr Bamford, who agreed with him that Cook's illness was a result of overindulgence in alcohol. Leaving Cook ill in bed, Palmer travelled to London with Cook's betting receipts and managed to get his hands on most of Cook's winnings. He also purchased three grains of strychnine.

On 18 November 1855, Palmer eventually called in Cook's own doctor, Dr Jones, but continued to treat Cook himself and, on 20 November, purchased six grains of strychnine as well as a solution of opium and some Prussic acid and morphia. Dr Jones arrived on the train from Lutterworth on 20 November and, in the early hours of the next morning, was sleeping in Cook's room when Cook began to convulse. Jones called for Palmer to assist him and Palmer arrived almost immediately, giving Cook what he said were two ammonia pills that he had brought with him. Cook continued to suffer from convulsions, his muscles stiffening and his spine arching, bending his whole body upwards like a bow. He finally died at 1 a.m. on the morning of 21 November.

Dr Jones left Rugeley and went straight to London to notify Cook's stepfather, William Stevens, of the death of his stepson. Stevens immediately travelled to Rugeley, where he met Palmer and apparently took an instant dislike to him. Palmer told Stevens that his stepson had died with debts of £4,000. Stevens asked to see Cook's betting books and, after making a pretence of searching for them for a few minutes, Palmer told him that he couldn't find them, casually telling Stevens that he expected they would turn up sooner or later. This wasn't good enough for Stevens, who ordered Cook's room to be locked and hastened back to London to consult his solicitor. Returning to

The Talbot Arms Inn, Rugeley, as illustrated in the Illustrated London News. *(Author's collection)*

Rugeley the next day, Stevens met Palmer on the train, Palmer having also travelled to London to see a moneylender.

Stevens informed Palmer that he wanted a post-mortem examination carried out on his stepson's body and that he had appointed a solicitor to investigate his son's financial affairs. Palmer did not seem unduly concerned by this news and the post-mortem examination was arranged for 26 November, to be carried out by Dr John Harland, a friend of Palmer's. (It had been Harland who had certified Walter Palmer as fit to be insured, receiving a dozen bottles of port from William for his trouble.)

In the event, Harland arrived without his medical instruments and two relatively inexperienced doctors, Mr Devonshire and Mr Newton, carried out the post-mortem under Harland's supervision. Palmer was present with Dr Bamford and, before the procedure commenced, offered brandy to the doctors. Once the examination was underway, Palmer deliberately jiggled the arm of one of the surgeons, causing some of Cook's stomach contents to be spilled. He also apparently tampered with the jars of samples that the doctors removed, using the excuse that he had moved them to give the doctors more room. At one point, Palmer turned to Dr Bamford and commented, 'They will not hang us yet.'

When William Palmer found out that the samples were to be sent to Home Office Pathologist Dr Alfred Taylor, he sought out the post boy who would be driving them to Stafford Station to be sent on to London and offered him £10 to upset the samples. Although the boy declined and later reported Palmer's attempt at bribery to the authorities, Dr Taylor received the samples in such poor condition that he demanded a second post-mortem. This was conducted on 29 November and a fresh set of samples was sent to London.

Meanwhile, Palmer tried to ingratiate himself with the coroner who would be conducting the inquest, William Webb Ward, sending him a number of gifts, including a barrel of oysters. He approached his old ally, postmaster Samuel Cheshire, and intercepted the coroner's mail before he received it. It was in this way that Palmer learned that Taylor had been unable to find any traces of Prussic acid, oxalic acid, morphia, strychnia, veratria (the poison of white hellebore), the poisons of tobacco, hemlock, arsenic, mercury or any other mineral poisons in Cook's remains, apart from traces of antimony. Palmer wrote to the coroner suggesting that 'death from natural causes' was the most likely verdict for the inquest, enclosing a £10 note with the letter.

Although Taylor had been unable to find any trace of strychnine in Cook's body, his symptoms led Taylor to believe that he had died from strychnine poisoning, the poison having been administered by William Palmer. Taylor attended the inquest and the coroner's jury eventually returned a verdict of wilful murder against Palmer, in spite of the fact that the inquest was described as 'most irregular' and the coroner was later officially censured. At the time, Palmer was supposedly ill in bed but was actually already under house arrest after one of the moneylenders he was indebted to took out a summons on his mother for the repayment of almost £2,000. Palmer had, of course, been forging his mother's signature as a guarantor to his loans.

As soon as he had recovered sufficiently to travel, Palmer was taken to Stafford Gaol. With the cause of death of John Parsons Cook now known, the authorities decided to exhume the bodies of Anne and Walter Palmer. When tested, large quantities of arsenic and antimony were found in both bodies and it was determined that both had died as a result of the administration of poison.

In March 1856, the Grand Jury at Stafford Assizes ruled that there was a case to answer as far as the deaths of Anne Palmer and John Parsons Cook were concerned but not on the death of Walter Palmer. Such was the depth of feeling locally against William Palmer that it was thought that it would be impossible to find a jury who had not already formed an opinion that he was guilty were he tried at Stafford. Hence he was committed for trial at the Central Criminal Court, or Old Bailey, in London. He was tried only for the murder of John Parsons Cook, to which he pleaded 'Not Guilty'. Lord Chief Justice Campbell presided over the proceedings, which opened on 14 May 1856. The Attorney General, Mr Edwin James QC, prosecuted, with the assistance of Mr Bodkin, Mr Welsby and Mr Huddleston, while Mr Serjeant Shee, Mr Grove QC, Mr Gray and Mr Kenealy defended Palmer.

Lord Chief Justice Campbell.
A pen and ink illustration from
the Illustrated London News.
(Author's collection)

The trial was to last for twelve days, with the opening speech for the prosecution alone taking the whole of the first day. Sixty-six witnesses were called for the prosecution and twenty-three for the defence and some of them had controversial evidence to recount.

One witness, a Mrs Anne Brooks from Manchester, told the court that she was a frequent race-goer and had attended Shrewsbury races on the day that Cook was first taken ill. According to Mrs Brooks, a large number of people had been stricken with exactly the same symptoms, including a member of her own party. There had been much discussion around the racecourse about whether the water was poisoned, since so many people had experienced severe vomiting and purging.

The testimony of medical witnesses took up much of the trial. Dr Jones, who had treated Cook in his final illness and had witnessed his death, had formed the opinion that Cook had died from tetanus. During the post-mortem examination of Cook, some small 'granules' had been found near to his spinal cord and the defence called doctors who stated that similar granules had been found in patients who were known to have died from tetanus. Several of the medical witnesses believed that these granules could have caused the type of convulsions experienced by Cook before his death.

The defence seized on this explanation, arguing that Cook could have contracted tetanus through some small and unnoticed wound. Both the defence and the prosecution called a number of doctors and nurses to argue the point, all of whom either specialised in tetanus and lockjaw or had treated patients poisoned by strychnine. It was stated that there were two types of tetanus –

The trial of William Palmer at the Old Bailey, London, as illustrated in the Illustrated London News. *(Author's collection)*

traumatic tetanus, arising from an external wound, and idiopathic tetanus, which was very rare and could be caused by an internal injury. The defence argued that Cook was known to suffer from an inflamed throat and was also believed to have a syphilitic sore or chancre on his penis. However, the general consensus of the medical opinions of the prosecution's witnesses seemed to be that the muscle stiffening caused by the ingestion of strychnine produced convulsions of a very different nature to those experienced as a result of tetanus. A Dr Todd described the symptoms of strychnine poisoning in animals as:

> …spasmodic action of the muscles, chiefly of the trunk and the spine—the spinal muscles produce a very marked opesthotonos, as it is called; the spine is drawn back, the head thrown back, and the trunk bowed in a very marked manner—the extremities are generally stiffened—there are violent jerks, and the muscles are all rendered stiff, and rigid, and hard from the spasm—that stiffness remains, once set in, it does not perfectly relax; fresh paroxysms come on, always accompanied by the peculiar curving back of the head and neck and spine—the movement of the muscles is a rigid jerk.

Another medical witness differentiated between the symptoms, explaining, 'Tetanus is a disease of days, strychnia of hours or minutes.'

Mr Serjeant Shee also made much of Cook's syphilis, suggesting that he had poisoned himself by taking mercury to try and cure the disease. He also suggested that Cook may have been an epileptic and the convulsions he experienced as he neared death could have simply been a fit and that the traces of antimony found after the post-mortem might have come from the tartar emetic used to make Cook vomit, in itself a dangerous poison in sufficient quantity.

Dr Bamford was suffering from English cholera at the time of the trial and was unable to testify until the later days of the proceedings. Initially, his own doctor, Dr Tweedie, read out a lengthy statement from him, detailing his treatment of Cook and his presence at the post-mortem examination. Bamford believed that Cook had died from apoplexy.

The defence then made a final attack on Dr Taylor, who had conducted the chemical analysis on Cook's viscera. Unfortunately, Taylor had been somewhat indiscreet about his findings, publishing a letter in *The Lancet* and allowing his picture to be used in conjunction with an article in the *Illustrated Times*. Taylor insisted that he did not know that he was being interviewed for an article in the newspaper, calling the actions of the editor '…the greatest deception that was ever practised on a scientific man'. According to Mr Serjeant Shee, Taylor's actions had prejudiced his client's chance of a fair trial.

As a parting shot, the defence called Dr William McDonald from the Royal College of Surgeons in Edinburgh. Much had been made throughout the trial of the fact that no strychnine had been discovered in Cook's remains. Dr Taylor had blamed the poor quality of the specimens he had received but Dr McDonald told the court that it was possible to detect the presence of strychnine in quantities as small as one fifty-thousandth of a grain.

The court had heard a stream of conflicting medical evidence throughout the ten days of the trial and it took a further day and a half for the presiding judge to summarise the evidence for the jury. In spite of the sheer volume and complexity of the evidence, the jury retired for less than an hour before returning with a verdict of 'Guilty'. (Among the multitude of spectators awaiting the verdict was official hangman, William Calcraft.) Asked if he had anything to say, Palmer enigmatically replied that he was '…not guilty of poisoning Cook with strychnine'.

Appeals for clemency, made on the grounds that the evidence against Palmer was circumstantial, were denied and thirty-one-year-old Palmer was hanged by George Smith at Stafford Prison on 14 June 1856. The path to the gallows was apparently very muddy and Palmer's main concern as he approached them seemed to be avoiding getting his feet wet. He maintained his innocence until the very end.

William Palmer is suspected of poisoning at least twelve people for financial gain and, as well as Cook, his victims are believed to have included his wife,

Above: *HM Prison Stafford, 1908.*
(Author's collection)

Right: *HM Prison, Stafford.*
(Author's collection)

his mother-in-law, his brother, two or three of his gambling acquaintances, his uncle and several of his children. As well as being a murderer, Palmer was not above stealing, committing fraud and forgery, doping horses, fixing races and bribery. Yet, when informed of her son's execution, William's mother's only comment was, 'They've hanged my saintly Billy.'

John Parsons Cook's grave in Rugeley churchyard, as illustrated in the Illustrated London News.
(Author's collection)

At the conclusion of the trial, the people of Rugeley wished to dissociate themselves from the man who had become known in the press as either 'The Rugeley Poisoner' or 'The Prince of Poisoners'. They petitioned the government to change the name of the town and the Prime Minister is said to have suggested that the town should be renamed after him – his name was Lord Palmerston.

Note: As might be expected in a case from this period, there are some discrepancies between various contemporary newspaper accounts. George Abley is alternatively referred to as Walter Abley and Palmer's mother-in-law is variously named Margaret, Ann and Mary. The amount Palmer inherited from his father varies between £7,000 and £9,000 and the anomalies with Anne's inheritance are discussed in the above account. There are so many rumours surrounding Palmer that it is difficult to determine exactly how many victims he actually killed.

8
'I wish you were dead and out of the way'

BURLEY, NEAR LEEDS, YORKSHIRE, 1856

The nature of the illness affecting twenty-eight-year-old Harriet Dove was proving a complete mystery to her medical advisers. Harriet's husband, William, first called in surgeon Mr George Morley in December 1855, after Harriet began to suffer from what was described as a 'functional disorder of the stomach and of the nervous system'. However, Mr Morley was unable to find out what was causing Harriet's symptoms and, having prescribed a general tonic for her, he could do little more than keep her under observation. Fortunately, her baffling symptoms soon eased and Harriet gradually regained her health and strength.

By February 1856 she was almost back to normal, able to move about the house freely and even take outdoor exercise – until the afternoon of 26 February, when she ate some jelly. After just one mouthful, Harriet complained that the jelly tasted very bitter and asked her husband if he had put anything in it. William admitted that he had put some of Harriet's medicine in the jelly. Harriet remarked that it was unkind of him to do so and, within minutes, was suffering from the all too familiar symptoms of an upset stomach and uncontrollable twitching.

This time her illness was thankfully brief and she had recovered sufficiently to attend church on the following morning. However, on 29 February, Harriet took breakfast with her husband and almost immediately went into severe spasms. Her body quivered constantly and she struggled to breathe, complaining of terrible pains in her legs. A neighbour, Mrs Jane Witham, was called in to help nurse her while William Dove went to fetch Mr Morley. Mrs Witham found Harriet reluctant to drink anything cold and when a cloth soaked in cold water was applied to her lips, Harriet's twitching and spasms increased in intensity and frequency.

William Dove found Mr Morley out on his rounds, so returned with Morley's assistant, Mr Scarfe, who prescribed a mixture of ether and henbane to alleviate Harriet's symptoms. By the time Mr Morley himself called at the house later that morning, he found Harriet much improved, suffering only an occasional nervous twitch. Thinking that the tics and spasms were symptomatic of a nervous hysteria, Morley prescribed yet more tonic. Yet over the following few days, Harriet continued to exhibit prolonged bouts of twitching, usually directly after having taken her medicine.

Mr Morley called on Harriet daily, bemused that his medicine seemed to be making her symptoms worse rather than better. By Wednesday of that week, Morley suggested to William Dove that it might be wise to seek a second opinion on his wife's illness. Dove wrote to Mr Morley on the following day, expressing confidence in the doctor's abilities to cure his wife and declining the offer of a consultation with another doctor:

> Dear Sir,
> Mrs Dove tells me that she has entire confidence in you and she thinks it would be going to needless expenses to have anyone else. Don't be deceived – I have entire confidence. I don't wish to grieve you to-day. Will you be kind enough to speak to Mrs Dove tomorrow on religion? For she says she wants some person to take her by the hand as she feels herself a sinner.
> I am, dear sir, yours respectfully WILLIAM DOVE

Just twenty-four hours later, Harriet was seized by a further violent attack during which her body went rigid, twitching convulsively and causing her to struggle to breathe. Once again, Mrs Witham was called in to help and once again Harriet's condition slowly improved to the extent that she was able to get out of bed and eat a mutton chop, at which point Mrs Witham felt that it was safe to leave her in her husband's care.

Later that day Mrs Witham called in to see Harriet, along with another neighbour, Mrs Wood. While they were there, Harriet asked William to give her some medicine and William crossed the bedroom to the washstand, where he poured a dose of medicine into a wineglass and gave it to his wife. As soon as Harriet had drunk the contents, William immediately rinsed out the glass.

Harriet pulled a wry face on drinking her medicine, exclaiming to her visitors that it was 'disagreeable and hot' and asking if there was anything to take the taste away. Mrs Witham fished in her pocket and produced a peppermint lozenge, which she gave to Harriet to suck. Within minutes, Harriet's whole body stiffened, her spine arching until just her head and heels rested on the bed. She gave a dreadful scream and clutched desperately at Mrs Witham's hands, her eyes rolling back in her head. William sent a servant to fetch Mr Morley and, when Harriet's condition worsened before Morley's arrival, William followed his servant to ask Morley to bring another doctor with him. Surprisingly, Dove made a point of telling Mr Morley that, should his wife die, she had a horror of being dissected.

Main Street, Burley, 1908. (Author's collection)

Burley Park, Leeds. (Author's collection)

By the time the two doctors reached the Doves home at Cardigan Place, Burley, near Leeds, Mrs Dove had already died. Both doctors noticed that her face bore an extremely fearful expression and Dove's immediate reaction to his wife's death was to go out and get blind drunk.

During the course of Mrs Dove's illness, Mr Morley had briefly considered that she might be suffering from the effects of poison but had dismissed the notion as ridiculous, given William Dove's apparent respectability and standing in the community. However, when he returned home after his final visit to Harriet Dove, Morley's apprentice informed him that William Dove had recently obtained strychnine from the surgery for the purpose of killing some stray cats. This knowledge, coupled with Harriet's hitherto unexplained symptoms, finally led Mr Morley to report his suspicions to the coroner, Mr Blackburn, who immediately requested that a post-mortem examination should be conducted.

Harriet's husband and his mother seemed determined to prevent the investigation from taking place and declined to give their permission. Eventually, Mr Morley assured William Dove that he was not under any suspicion of poisoning his wife and permission was reluctantly granted by her family for the post-mortem examination of Harriet's body to go ahead.

Mr Morley and a second surgeon, Mr Nunneley, examined Harriet's body less than forty-two hours after her untimely death and were able to find no evidence of any natural disease that might have accounted for her demise. On analysing the contents of the dead woman's stomach, the doctors discovered the presence of strychnine, which was also found to a lesser degree in Harriet's intestines. Thus both doctors concluded that Harriet had died as a result of the ingestion of strychnine.

Armley Gaol (Leeds Prison), 1920s. (Author's collection)

Town Hall, Leeds.

Town Hall, Leeds, c. 1910. (Author's collection)

As soon as this opinion was made known, the coroner ordered that William Dove be detained in Leeds Prison. Mr Blackburn stressed the fact that Dove's detention did not necessarily mean that he was implicated in his wife's death but the fact that his wife had died from strychnine ingestion, and that he had recently been in possession of the poison, had caused some suspicion.

Thirty-five-year-old Dove was brought before magistrates at Leeds Court House on the following morning and remanded in custody pending the results of the coroner's investigations into the death of his wife. Described in the contemporary newspapers as being '...of spare body, with a cadaverous countenance', Dove laughed several times during the petty sessions prior to his own hearing.

Mr Blackburn opened an inquest at Fleischman's Hotel in Leeds and in due course, the coroner's jury returned a verdict of 'wilful murder'. Dove was immediately charged with his wife's murder and committed for trial at the next Assizes in Leeds. The proceedings opened on 17 July 1856, before Mr Baron Bramwell. Messrs Overend, Hardy and Bayley prosecuted the case, while Mr Bliss, Mr Sergeant Wilkins, Mr Hall and Mr Middleton acted for the defence.

William Dove wore a new black suit in court, appearing cool and calm as he pleaded 'Not Guilty' to the charge against him. Mr Overend opened the case for the prosecution by describing the physical effects of strychnine on animals. He then went on to describe the tempestuous relationship between William and Harriet Dove for the court.

Both William and Harriet were the children of respectable parents, both having fathers who worked as leather merchants. One of Harriet's brothers was married to William's sister.

The couple had become acquainted in 1851 and William had courted Harriet until their eventual marriage at the end of 1852. At that time, William had been a farmer and had taken his bride to live on his farm. However, William's father had died at Christmas 1854, leaving his son a legacy of £90 a year. Then on the point of being evicted from his property, William immediately gave up farming and lived on this income.

Yet a large proportion of his money was spent on drink, even though this was against the strict religious upbringing experienced by both himself and his wife. William frequently got drunk and, although he could on occasions be kind to Harriet, he could equally be abusive and violent. Harriet's efforts to get him to stop drinking provoked even more quarrels between the couple and eventually Harriet turned to her mother for help.

Harriet's mother travelled from her home in Plymouth to visit her daughter and son-in-law and, realising that their marriage was beyond saving, consulted a solicitor on Harriet's behalf. It was agreed that William and Harriet should separate and that William would pay £20 a year towards her upkeep. Yet before the planned separation could take effect, some well-meaning friends of the couple intervened. They extracted promises from William that he would stop drinking and treat Harriet more kindly and Harriet agreed to give the marriage one more chance.

However it seemed that William Dove had no objection to ridding himself of his wife – what he actually objected to was paying £20 of his inheritance each year as maintenance. In the months before Harriet's death, William consulted a 'wise woman' about his problems and was thereafter happy to relate to all and sundry – including his wife – the woman's predictions that Harriet would die before February 1856. He also sought the services of a 'wizard', whom he requested to ensure that Harriet was tormented for refusing to share their marital bed. On occasions, William had punched Harriet in the face with his fist and once had to be pulled away from her by neighbours after attacking her with a carving knife. In the aftermath of his vicious attacks against his wife, during which William regularly accused her of being a 'damned whore', he was always contrite and solicitous towards her, although his caring attitude invariably evaporated with his next bout of drinking. 'I wish you were dead and out of the way,' he told her, complaining bitterly about the expense her illness was putting him to. On at least one occasion before her death Harriet called in the police and asked for protection against her husband.

Shortly before Harriet's death, William told a friend that she was about to die, promising him a 'regular jollification' once her death had occurred. The prosecution told the court that William was extremely anxious for Harriet to die, since he desperately wanted to marry their neighbour, Mrs Witham. The suggestion of any mutual desire between William Dove and Jane Witham was strenuously denied by Mrs Witham, who admitted only that Dove had asked if he could sit with her occasionally after the death of his wife and that she had turned him down because of what people might think.

Dove had apparently been inspired to murder his wife by the activities of William Palmer, 'The Rugeley Poisoner' (*see* chapter 7). Following accounts in the newspapers, Dove went to Mr Morley's surgery and initiated a discussion with Mr Boocock, his apprentice, on the methods used to test for the presence of different poisons. Days later, Dove went back to the surgery and talked another apprentice, Mr Elletson, into letting him have ten grains of strychnine for poisoning stray cats. Elletson was then persuaded to part with a further five grains after Dove told him that the first dose had been washed away by rain.

Two days before Harriet Dove's death, Mr Morley's groom, William Benton, saw William Dove sneaking into Morley's surgery. When the groom went to investigate, a flustered Dove told him that he had just popped in to light his pipe at the gas mantle.

A number of acquaintances and servants were called to give their accounts of Harriet's last illness and of the relationship between her and her husband. One of these was Mary Wood, who had been visiting Harriet on the day of her death. Mrs Wood told the court that she had known William Dove since he was five or six years old, having once been in service to Dove's father.

The prosecution asked Mrs Wood for her opinion on William Dove's sanity, a question that was immediately objected to by the defence lawyers. The question was rephrased several times, with the defence team objecting to every variation on the grounds that Mrs Wood was not qualified to offer a 'scientific' opinion. Eventually the question was put in a form that was agreeable to the court and Mrs Wood was allowed to relate some unusual incidents from William's childhood. The court was told that he had frequently chased his sisters with a red-hot poker. He had set fire to his bedroom curtains, placed lighted candles in baskets and locked the baskets in closets, and dangled a cat out of an upstairs window by its tail. As a child he had also frequently cut himself, writing his name in blood.

Mrs Wood also told the court that she had gone with a servant, Hannah Taylor, to clean Dove's house shortly after his wife's death. They had been accompanied by a little dog, which had found a spot of dried blood on the floor and licked it. The dog had died very shortly afterwards.

The court also heard from Henry Harrison, the 'wizard' consulted by William Dove who turned out to be merely a dentist with an interest in astrology. Harrison testified to the fact that William Dove had told him that he had sold his soul to the Devil. While living at the farm, Harriet had refused to share William's bed and consequently William had asked Harrison to conjure up demons to torment his wife and thus persuade her to return to the marital bed. Harrison and Dove had also had conversations about strychnine, with Dove asking Harrison whether he could manufacture or obtain it for him.

John Elletson, apprentice to surgeon Mr Morley, also told the court that he and Dove had discussed strychnine together. Dove had assured Elletson that strychnine could not be detected in the human body but Elletson had argued that it could, producing a medical textbook to support his argument. Dove had persuaded Elletson to let him have two separate packets of strychnine, having told him that he was plagued by stray cats. Elletson had asked him for a cat skin that he could make into a tobacco pouch should Dove be successful in killing any.

The prosecution concluded their evidence by producing a number of eminent chemists and doctors to support the medical evidence that Harriet Dove had died as a result of strychnine poisoning. The doctors who had conducted the post-mortem examination had experimented with samples taken from Harriet's body, injecting them into two mice, two rabbits and a guinea pig. All the animals had subsequently died, having first shown exactly the same symptoms as Mrs Dove in her last hours.

The defence then set about trying to prove that William Dove was insane at the time of his wife's murder and thus not responsible for his actions. They called a number of witnesses who were prepared to testify to Dove's manifestations of strangeness. He had told tall stories about his travels to America, during which he insisted that he had been appointed chief of the Red Indians and that he had killed a bear that had grasped him in its paws and was trying to kill him by breathing into his mouth. Since his incarceration he had also penned a letter to the Devil, written in his own blood.

There was much legal debate on the probable consequences of Dove's alleged insanity, which included testimony from Dr Smith, the proprietor of a lunatic asylum in Leeds. Smith believed that Dove was insane at the time of his wife's murder, although he qualified his opinion by stating that he believed that Dove was capable of distinguishing right from wrong, although incapable of preventing himself from committing the act of murder, regardless of the consequences. Other medical witnesses backed Smith's opinion, although the prosecution insisted that Dove had managed to live his life in a way that appeared outwardly normal, asking the jury to consider whether Harriet's mother would have consented to her daughter marrying a lunatic.

The jury retired to consider their verdict. It was widely reported in the local newspapers of the time that they were deadlocked, with two of their number strongly in favour of acquitting Dove. Eventually the newspapers reported that a compromise had been reached and the jury found Dove guilty, while recommending mercy to the judge on the grounds of insanity. The jury were later to speak to the newspapers, denying any split and stating that the guilty verdict and recommendation of mercy were the unanimous decision of them all.

Regardless of how the verdict was reached, it remained only for the judge to pronounce the death sentence on William Dove, which he received with the same jauntiness and indifference that he had displayed throughout his trial.

York Castle, c. 1920. (Author's collection)

The jury's recommendation for mercy came to nothing, as did appeals to Home Secretary, George Grey, and Her Majesty Queen Victoria. William Dove was executed on 11 August 1856 in front of York Castle. Shortly before his death, he made a full confession to the murder of his wife, Harriet, by the administration of strychnine in a glass of medicine. Although he expressed some remorse, stating, 'I execrate and abhor myself in dust and ashes for the crime I have committed,' he placed the blame for the poisoning of his wife squarely on the shoulders of 'wizard' Henry Harrison who, he maintained, had constantly told him that he would never be happy while Harriet was still alive. Harrison vigorously disputed this statement in the press, professing himself horrified at the very idea that Dove should accuse him of complicity in the murder of his wife, whom he described as a lovely and amiable woman who was far too good for the likes of a wretch such as William Dove.

Dove's execution was watched by up to 20,000 spectators. The condemned man's last words were, 'Tell my Mother I die happy' before walking to the scaffold with his customary indifference to his situation.

In the aftermath of the case, many newspapers printed editorials in which Dove's alleged insanity was indignantly discussed. It was written that, rather than demonstrating insanity, Dove's actions throughout his life simply showed that he was 'brutal, mischievous and malignant'. Meanwhile, other newspapers bemoaned the cost of the trial which, excluding the coroner's inquest and the actual execution, was said to have amounted to £2,476 16s, the implication being that good money had been wasted in defending a man who was so evil that he would kill his wife rather than simply separate from her and pay a proportion of his inheritance to maintain her.

9
'I won't be troubled long'

SOUTH HETTON / HENDON / PALLION / WEST AUCKLAND,

COUNTY DURHAM, 1860—1872

Mary Ann Cotton was born Mary Ann Robson in 1832, the daughter of a colliery worker and his wife. Her father died in a pit accident when Mary Ann was just fourteen years old and, when she was sixteen, she found a job as an under nurse at the home of Mr Edward Potter at South Hetton. Two years later, she returned home again to live with her mother and began an apprenticeship as a dressmaker.

At about this time she met a man named William Mowbray and the couple married at St Andrew's Church, Newcastle-on-Tyne. Mowbray's job took him to Plymouth and from there to various other towns in the South West but, after five years away, the couple returned to South Hetton, where they were to stay for several years. On her return to the North of England, Mary Ann told people that, since her marriage, she had given birth to four children, all of whom had died. Infant mortality rates in the nineteenth century were high and Mary Ann's story wasn't questioned.

On 24 June 1860, Mary Ann lost a fifth child, a four-year-old daughter, also named Mary Ann. Mr Broadbent, a local surgeon, certified the cause of the child's death as gastric fever. Soon afterwards, William Mowbray obtained employment as a fireman on board a steam vessel and moved his family to Hendon, where the Mowbrays lost yet another child, John Robert William, who died on 22 September 1864, aged about one year. He was attended in his final illness by Sunderland surgeon Mr Gammage and once again the cause of death was recorded as gastric fever.

Next to die was William Mowbray on 18 January 1865. William, aged forty-seven, was insured with the British and Prudential Insurance Office and, on his death, Mary Ann was paid the sum of £35. She received a smaller payout on the death of her four-year-old daughter, Mary Jane, whose death on 2 May 1865 was again recorded as resulting from gastric fever.

Sunderland Infirmary. (Author's collection)

Now Mary Ann obtained a job at the Sunderland Infirmary and, in the six-month period in which she worked there, she met and married a patient named George Ward, the couple taking a house in Grey Street, Sunderland. The marriage proved to be short-lived, since George Ward died on 21 October 1866, aged thirty-three. Just months earlier, Mary Ann's mother, Mrs Stott, had also died suddenly and unexpectedly, at which Mary Ann promptly removed everything she possibly could from her mother's house, much to the fury of her stepfather.

Following the death of her second husband, in December 1866, Mary Ann obtained a position as a housekeeper for James Robinson, a foreman in the ship-building industry at Pallion. Robinson became Mary Ann's third husband in June 1867. However, since the commencement of Mary Ann's employment with Robinson, death had been a frequent visitor to his house, claiming ten-month-old John Robinson on 4 January 1867, his brother, James, aged six, on 6 April, his eight-year-old sister Elizabeth on 13 April, nine-year-old Elizabeth Mowbray on 2 May and three-year-old Margaret Robinson in December. Again, all five of the children's deaths were attributed to gastric fever.

It was around this time that people began to voice their concerns about Mary Ann and the number of sudden, unexplained deaths occurring around her. Among them was Mr Thomas Riley, the assistant parish overseer of West Auckland, who was amazed by the unprecedented demand that Mary Ann was making on the parish for coffins. James Robinson's sisters also harboured suspicions about their sister-in-law, which they communicated to James, prompting him to look a little more closely at his wife's actions since their marriage.

Mary Ann had persistently asked James to insure his own life and those of his children, even trying to arrange an insurance policy without her husband's knowledge, but he had refused to do so. Now he found that his new wife had run up debts of almost £60 and that she had pawned some of his clothes, as well as items from the house. Trustingly, he had placed his bank-book and building society book in her charge and, on scrutinising them, he found that Mary Ann had frittered away almost £50 of his money, as well as recording non-existent payments into his building society account. When James taxed Mary Ann with his suspicions, both on her dishonesty and the premature deaths of the children, she waited until he had gone to work before sneaking out of the house, never to be seen by Robinson again. She took with her one of her children, but almost immediately abandoned the child in the street, having asked someone to keep an eye on it for a few minutes while she went to post a letter. It took Robinson some time to recover the child.

Mary Ann apparently spent the next few years living rough in Sunderland, Tynemouth and Newcastle until 7 July 1870, when, calling herself Mary Ann Mowbray, she obtained a position as a housekeeper to Frederick Cotton, a pitman from Walbottle, Northumberland. Just three months later, Mary Ann and Frederick married at the same church where she had wed her first husband, although since her last husband, James Robinson, was still very much alive, the marriage was bigamous.

It was while Mary Ann Cotton was living at Walbottle that some pigs belonging to the family died in suspicious circumstances. Mary Ann was quick to accuse her neighbours of poisoning them. The neighbours were equally quick to return the accusations and Mary Ann subsequently became so unpopular in the village that the family were forced to move. Frederick Cotton found another job at a colliery back in West Auckland but was not to work there long as on 19 September 1871, he too died from gastric fever, aged thirty-three. His death was quickly followed by those of his sons – ten-year-old Fred died on 9 March 1872 and Fred's fourteen-month-old half-brother, Robert, who was Mary Ann's own child, died on 28 March.

By now, Mary Ann had taken a lodger, Joseph Nattrass. Nattrass barely had time to become engaged to Mary Ann and to change his will in her favour before the widow found another job, caring for a smallpox sufferer, Mr John Quick-Manning. Quick-Manning was an excise officer with a pleasant cottage and was considerably higher on the social scale than Mary Ann or her fiancé, Joseph Nattrass. The two became lovers and Mary Ann fell pregnant. However, while Quick-Manning seemed perfectly happy to sleep with Mary Ann, he didn't seem keen on marrying her, particularly since she was still responsible for

Walbottle village, 1904. (Author's collection)

the upkeep of her one remaining stepson, seven-year-old Charles. Hence Mary Ann continued to live in the home she had shared with her husband, taking in additional lodgers to help pay her bills.

Joseph Nattrass made his own contribution to Mary Ann's finances, dying on 1 April 1872, after which Mary Ann Cotton was approached by her old adversary, assistant overseer Thomas Riley, who asked if she would be willing to nurse a second smallpox patient. Mary Ann told him that she was unable to help on account of having the responsibility of looking after her stepson.

She asked Riley if it were possible to send young Charles to the workhouse, but Riley told her that that could only happen if Mary Ann went there with him and Mary Ann didn't fancy that idea at all. Riley then asked her if she intended to marry Mr Quick-Manning but was told that she could not marry again while she had to care for her stepson. 'I won't be troubled long,' she added, half to herself, and sure enough, Charles Edward Cotton was taken ill the very next week. Dr Kilburn was called to the child, who was showing symptoms of a severe upset stomach, as well as fits and convulsions. Kilburn prescribed a mixture of bismuth, morphia and Prussic acid but Charles did not respond to the medication and died on 12 July 1872. All three of the ingredients of Charles's medicine were known to be poisonous, although in much larger quantities than in Kilburn's treatment.

Having been suspicious about Mary Ann in the past, Riley went straight to the police with his suspicions and also approached Dr Kilburn. Kilburn refused to issue a death certificate for Charles, without which Mary Ann was unable to claim the £4 10s life assurance money due to her on his death.

The coroner ordered Dr Kilburn to carry out a post-mortem examination, which revealed no obvious cause of death. Kilburn eventually attributed Charles's demise to gastric fever, leaving the inquest jury with no option but to record a verdict of natural death. Yet, unaccountably, Kilburn had taken it upon himself to remove some of young Charles Cotton's organs, which he took home with him and placed in a closet. The next day, having decanted the contents of the boy's stomach into a jar, he buried the child's organs in his garden.

The stomach contents remained untouched for several days before Kilburn decided to perform a Reinsch test to see if they contained arsenic. To his horror, the tests proved positive and, to Kilburn's credit, he immediately went to see Superintendent Henderson at Bishop Auckland police station to report his findings and no doubt to explain his actions.

The police began enquiries in the area and it was established that, roughly six weeks before Charles's death, Mary Ann had sent charwoman Mrs Dodds to the local chemist's shop to buy two-penny worth of arsenic and soft soap, commonly used to kill bedbugs. Mrs Dodds had then smeared the mixture liberally in the crevices of the iron bed in Charles's room and also around the skirting boards and on the cross hatches under the bed. This had accounted for most of the jar of arsenic and soft soap and what little remained had been placed in the lumber-room. The jar was not found when the house was searched after Charles's death.

Mary Ann was arrested for the wilful murder of her stepson and once she was safely in custody at Durham Gaol, the Home Office determined that the bodies of Joseph Nattrass, Frederick Cotton and his sons Robert and Fred should be exhumed and their remains tested for the presence of arsenic. Unfortunately, all had died during an epidemic of smallpox in the area and the greater than normal number of deaths had meant that burials in the churchyard at St Helen's had not been recorded as efficiently as they usually were. The police quickly located the bodies of Nattrass, Robert and Fred but, even though they searched all day, they were unable to find the body of Frederick Cotton senior. The church sexton was an elderly man whose memory was failing, and although he directed them to numerous graves where he thought Cotton's remains might be located, when the police dug down to reveal the coffin, it was invariably the wrong one. Thus they had to be content with the bodies of Nattrass and the two boys, from which samples were taken and sealed into jars before the bodies were reburied. The remains were sent to a doctor from Leeds for analysis, along with several items removed from Mary Ann's home.

Meanwhile Mary Ann Cotton had been committed for trial at the Spring Assizes in Durham, charged only with the wilful murder of Charles Edward Cotton, to which charge she pleaded 'Not Guilty'. The trial opened on 5 March 1873 before Mr Justice Archibald. Mr C. Russell QC, Mr Trotter, Mr Greenhow and Mr Bruce appeared for the prosecution, with Mr Campbell-Forster and Mr Pont defending.

The prosecution first established Mary Ann's relationship to the dead child and told the court that she had constantly complained that the boy was a tie and a burden to her and that keeping him cost her a lot of money. It was also pointed out that Mary Ann had insured Charles for the sum of £4 10s with the Prudential Insurance Office.

The prosecution then called medical witnesses, the first of which was Dr Kilburn, who related the details of Charles's final illness and the findings of his post-mortem examination. Dr Scattergood then entered the witness box to testify on the results of his analysis of Charles's remains. Scattergood first stated that he had found no arsenic whatsoever in any of the items removed from Mrs Cotton's home. However, he had found traces of arsenic in Charles's stomach, stomach contents, bowels, bowel contents, liver and kidneys and had estimated that a total of two and a half grains of the poison was present in the boy's body. In Scattergood's opinion, a fatal dose of arsenic for an adult would normally be between two and three grains and about half that amount would be sufficient to kill a child. Scattergood testified that he believed that Charles Cotton had been given repeated doses of arsenic, including a final dose shortly before his death, since arsenic had been found in his stomach. The doctor thus attributed Charles's death to arsenic poisoning.

The court then paused for some legal arguments as to whether Scattergood should be allowed to continue with his testimony on the results of his tests on the organs of Joseph Nattrass and Fred and Robert Cotton, given that Mary Ann was only charged with the murder of Charles. The defence objected to the inclusion of any further evidence from Scattergood on the grounds that it would not be admissible and would prove prejudicial towards their client. Defence counsel Mr Campbell-Forster cited previous similar court cases with relevant rulings, particularly mentioning two cases tried by Chief Justice Baron Pollock in his argument.

The judge took a break, during which he consulted with Baron Pollock, returning to court to say that having considered the legalities, he intended to hear Scattergood's evidence. The defence immediately asked him to reserve the case for consideration at the Court of Appeal, but Mr Justice Archibald declined to do so, saying that he had made up his mind on the point. Thus Scattergood's testimony resumed with the results of his analysis on samples from the exhumed bodies.

All three of the deceased had complained of vomiting and diarrhoea with stomach pains and ultimately convulsions and Mary Ann Cotton had nursed them all, preparing all their food and drink. Dr Kilburn had attended both of the children throughout their final illness, while Nattrass had been under the care of a Dr Richardson. Richardson believed that Nattrass was suffering from Bright's disease, which affected his kidneys. Nevertheless, Richardson recorded the cause of death as gastric fever. Fred's death had been attributed to typhoid and gastric fever and, according to Dr Kilburn, Robert had died from teething convulsions. All three bodies contained traces of arsenic and, in Nattrass's stomach alone, a massive seventeen and a half grains were found. Scattergood therefore concluded that all three had died as a result of the ingestion of arsenic.

By 7 March, the third day of the trial, it only remained for the counsels for the prosecution and defence and the judge to summarise the case for the jury. Mr Charles Russell began for the prosecution, telling the jury that the deaths from arsenic poisoning of Nattrass, Fred and Robert effectively precluded the defence of accidental death that Mary Ann Cotton's counsel intended to rely upon for the charge against her of the wilful murder of Charles. Mary Ann had ample motive for killing her stepson. She had been witnessed treating him cruelly in the past, often beating him with a leather belt. She viewed him as a tie and a nuisance, a needless expense, whose very presence prevented her from marrying the man of her choice. Not only that but on the boy's death, she would receive a payout from the insurance company.

She alone had looked after the boy, giving her ample opportunity to poison him. Mr Scattergood had already explained the ease with which the arsenic and soft soap mixture could be separated, knowledge that Mary Ann would most probably have gleaned from her past experience of working as a nurse. The fact that Charles Cotton had died from arsenic poisoning was undisputed, since a more than fatal dose of the poison had been isolated from his remains. Mr Russell told the jury that even though there was no actual proof that Mary Ann Cotton had administered the poison, taking all the circumstantial evidence against her into account, there could be little doubt that Charles's death had been at her hands.

Mr Campbell-Forster then addressed the court on behalf of the defence. He first asked the jury to put all prejudices behind them and focus solely on the evidence they had heard in court, rather than referring to the numerous newspaper accounts of Mary Ann's alleged activities, published way in advance of her trial and therefore likely to affect their perception of her. Of particular note was the view of the *Daily News*, which informed its readers 'Women have a natural turn for poisoning, usually by arsenic'.

He then went on to discuss the inclusion of evidence relating to the deaths of Joseph Nattrass, Fred and Robert, stating that, had Mary Ann been found guilty of poisoning these three victims in court, then the law would have prohibited any reference to her other victims to be made in this trial for fear of biasing the jury. With regard to Mary Ann's alleged cruelty to the child, Campbell-Forster maintained that he had only been beaten for the purposes of correction. Besides, the evidence that he had been beaten came only from three or four gossiping women, all of whom undoubtedly had an instrument of their own for chastising their children when necessary. Regardless of what had been said on the subject of Mary Ann beating the boy, Campbell-Forster reminded the jury that there had not been a mark on him at his post-mortem examination and that other witnesses had testified that Mary Ann had treated the child kindly. He dismissed the idea of a financial motive for the murder of Charles Cotton, pointing out that the payout from the insurance company would be totally swallowed up by the child's funeral expenses.

It had been established that Charles had died from arsenic poisoning, as had Joseph Nattrass and the two other children. However, Mrs Dodds had testified to buying arsenic and soft soap, which she used to deter bedbugs in the defendant's house. She had used nearly all the mixture she had purchased from the chemist's shop, which would have contained almost 300 grains of arsenic in total. Dr Scattergood had testified that, in the six weeks between the purchase of the mixture and the death of Charles Cotton, the soft soap would have dried out and hardened, so that every time the boy moved in bed, it was likely that an arsenic dust would be created. Not only that, but the boy's room was decorated with green wallpaper and the green colouring was known to be produced using arsenic.

Dr Scattergood himself had estimated that, in a room the size of Charles's bedroom, rubbing the wallpaper might release twelve grains of arsenic into the air, in the form of dust. If the arsenic and soft soap mixture was brought into the equation, then every time Charles ran about, played with his toys or got in and out of bed, he would be stirring up dust that was heavily impregnated with arsenic. This would be inhaled into his lungs and would also coat moist parts of his body, such as his tongue and mouth and would then be swallowed. Having spent five days ill in bed before his death, it was quite conceivable for his body to have absorbed sufficient arsenic to kill him.

Dr Kilburn had prescribed a medicine containing bismuth, morphia and Prussic acid for the child, which he had made up himself in his surgery. An inspection of Dr Kilburn's dispensary had shown that a bottle of arsenic was kept on the same shelf as the constituents of the medication. The defence contended that it was perfectly possible that a mistake had been made in mixing the medicine, or that the ingredients used had somehow come into contact with arsenic at the doctor's surgery and so become contaminated.

Could the jury really believe that Mary Ann Cotton had poisoned the child by design, then immediately called in a doctor to attend to him, laughingly watching the day-to-day agony that her actions had provoked, and then hypocritically throwing herself into the deepest distress when the child had finally succumbed to her mischief, asked Campbell-Forster? It was far easier to believe that the child had died through accident or mistake than to acknowledge that a woman capable of such conduct could exist.

The jury retired for more than an hour before making their beliefs known, returning a verdict of 'Guilty'. Mary Ann Cotton seemed stunned by the verdict, slumping into a faint as the judge pronounced the death sentence, after which she was carried from the court in a semi-conscious condition to await her execution at Durham Gaol. However, within a few hours she had fully recovered her normal cold, reserved demeanour and continued to assert her innocence.

Mary Ann Cotton's execution was delayed, as at the time of her trial she was pregnant by Mr Quick-Manning. On 7 January 1873 she gave birth to a baby girl, Margaret Edith Quick-Manning Cotton, and was allowed to care for her daughter herself, under the supervision of female prison warders. The delay gave plenty of time for petitions for clemency to be submitted to the Home Secretary, which were rejected, although it is said that Mary Ann herself firmly believed that Royal clemency would be forthcoming and that her life would ultimately be spared.

On 12 March she wrote a letter to her former husband, James Robinson. It is reproduced here verbatim:

> my dear frens. I so pose you Will mor then I can tell you con serning my Aful faite I have come I Wish to know if you will let me see the 3 Childer as soune as you possible you can. I should Like to see you Bring them if you can not Ask sum Won Else to Bring them…And i think if you have Won sparke of kindness in you Will Try to get my Life Spared you know your sealfe thare has been a moast dredful to hear tell of the Lyies that has been told A Bout me ie must tell you you Ar th Cause of All my trouble fore if you had not Left th house And so As i could have got into my house When I came to the dor I Was to Wandr the streets With my baby in my Armes no home for me no plase to lay my head…But When you closed the dore I had no Won fore you. Know your sealfe I am Knott guilty of the Lyies that has been tolde Consirnig me.

On 24 March 1873, Mary Ann Cotton walked bravely to meet executioner William Calcraft, still staunchly maintaining her innocence. Her execution was clumsy and she continued to writhe and twitch convulsively for almost three minutes after the trapdoor had fallen.

Although she was convicted only of the murder of her stepson, Charles, Mary Ann Cotton is thought to have been one of the most prolific killers in British history, having been implicated in causing the deaths of twenty or more people by poisoning them with arsenic, mostly for her personal convenience and financial gain. Her name was immortalised in a skipping song, sung by generations of little girls from the Sunderland area and still heard today:

> Mary Ann Cotton, she's dead and forgotten, she lies in a grave, with her bones all rotten. Sing, sing, oh, what can I sing? Mary Ann Cotton is tied up with string. Where, where? Up in the air, selling black puddings a penny a pair.

The ease with which she apparently murdered her nearest and dearest, while managing to remain undetected, also brought about a substantial change in the way that births and deaths were registered in the United Kingdom. Prior to her conviction, there had been a fee for registering births and deaths and thus many simply went unrecorded. Shortly after Mary Ann Cotton's death, this fee was abolished and replaced by a considerable fine for failure to register a birth and possible imprisonment for failure to report a death. From January 1874, it also became necessary to obtain a death certificate from a doctor before a funeral could take place.

10

'Don't cry, you hypocrite'

On 5 May 1863, a fire broke out in Berkeley Terrace in Glasgow, at the home of Dr Edward William Pritchard and his family. When it was finally brought under control, the charred remains of Elizabeth McGirn, one of the Pritchard's servants, were found in her attic bedroom. Dr Pritchard had neglected to pay the fire insurance on the property and it was rumoured at the time that the fire had been deliberately started specifically to kill the servant girl, who was reputed to be pregnant by the master of the house. However, no official investigations were made and the doctor subsequently moved his wife and five children to a

Sauchiehall Street, Glasgow, c. 1910. (Author's collection)

house in Royal Terrace. Only a year later, he purchased the house and practice of Dr Corbett in Clarence Place, part of Glasgow's famous Sauchiehall Street. The purchase was partly financed by Dr Pritchard's mother-in-law, Mrs Jane Cowpey Taylor, who loaned Pritchard £500 to complete the sale.

Pritchard's history is somewhat sketchy and unreliable, since much of what is recorded about him seems to be of his own invention. He was born in Southsea, Hampshire on 6 December 1825 and was educated in both London and Paris, before being apprenticed to two surgeons in Portsmouth. Having completed his apprenticeship, by his own account, he was admitted to King's College as a student of surgery, something that the college has since denied. Yet, however he ultimately achieved the qualification, he became a member of the College of Surgeons in May 1846 and immediately became a naval surgeon, passing the necessary examinations for entrance to the Society of Apothecaries in 1847. By some accounts, he resigned only a year later to become a private physician to a wealthy gentleman, by others he remained in the navy until 1851, having served on HMS *Victory*.

However, by 1850, he had met and married Mary Jane 'Minnie' Taylor and soon afterwards decided to settle in England, opening surgeries in first Humanby and then Filey in Yorkshire, receiving considerable financial assistance from his father-in-law in order to do so. However he soon found that English country life was not to his liking and, having purchased a medical degree from a German university, moved to Glasgow in 1861.

Contemporary photographs of Pritchard show him to be a pleasant-faced man, whose baldness is disguised by a 'comb-over' and compensated by a luxuriant, bushy beard. He appears to have had a very high opinion of himself, particularly of his prowess as a lover. Although he was unpopular with his fellow doctors, who described him as 'vain', 'ignorant, daring and reckless' and as 'a plausible liar', he published books and articles in respectable medical journals as well as becoming an examiner in Physiology, a freemason and a director of the Glasgow Athenaeum.

Shortly after his move to Clarence Place, Pritchard impregnated one of his servants, fifteen-year-old Mary McLeod. He was later to induce an abortion, having told Mary that he would marry her on the death of his wife. At the time, he suspected that both Mrs Pritchard and his mother-in-law, Mrs Taylor, were aware of his 'connexion' [*sic*] with Mary, particularly since Mrs Taylor had almost caught the couple together in the doctor's consulting room, forcing Pritchard to hurriedly bundle the girl into a cupboard and shut the door.

In October 1864, Minnie Pritchard became ill with severe sickness and diarrhoea. As soon as she was well enough to travel, she went to the home of her parents in Edinburgh to recuperate, returning to her husband in time for Christmas. Days after her return, she experienced a recurrence of her symptoms and this time her husband sent for her mother, who travelled from Edinburgh to Glasgow in order to care for her. Soon Mrs Taylor appeared to be afflicted by whatever illness was affecting her daughter and, on 25 February 1865, shortly after eating a tapioca pudding, she died.

Pritchard tried to persuade his neighbour, Dr James Paterson, to sign Mrs Taylor's death certificate but, when Paterson was unwilling to do so, Pritchard certified his mother-in-law's death himself, giving the causes as paralysis (twelve hours) and apoplexy (one hour). He then accompanied his mother-in-law's body to her home in Edinburgh and supervised her funeral and burial in Grange Cemetery.

When he returned home to Glasgow, he found that Minnie was still very poorly. On 17 March 1865, she complained of dizziness and cramp, at which her husband gave her something to drink. Minnie's condition then deteriorated alarmingly and Dr Paterson was called in, sadly too late to be of any help to the patient. Mary Jane Pritchard died at around midnight on 17/18 March. Once again, Dr Pritchard himself certified the death, giving the cause as gastric fever (two months).

Pritchard escorted his wife's coffin to the same cemetery where her mother had been buried just a short time earlier. While awaiting burial, the body was lodged at Mary Jane's father's home in Lauder Road and, before witnesses, Dr Pritchard asked for the coffin to be opened. He then kissed his dead wife gently on the lips, apparently exhibiting a great deal of emotion at her untimely death. Yet on returning to Glasgow by train after her funeral, Dr Pritchard was arrested as his train pulled into Queen Street Station.

While Pritchard had been away, the Procurator Fiscal – a Scottish legal official who acts as both coroner and public prosecutor – had received an anonymous letter, in which the writer expressed his suspicions about the deaths of Mrs Taylor and her daughter. (It was believed that the anonymous correspondent was Dr James Paterson.) The contents of the letter were sufficient to prompt an investigation into the deaths and it was found that Pritchard had recently purchased both antimony and a preparation called Fleming's Tincture of Aconite. This information led to the exhumation of both bodies. Analysis of both women's organs showed the presence of large quantities of antimony and, as a result, Dr Pritchard was charged with murdering both Mary Jane Pritchard and Jane Taylor by poisoning.

His trial opened at the High Court of Justiciary in Edinburgh on 3 July 1865, before Lord Justice Clerk the Right Honourable John Inglis, Lord Ardmillan and Lord Jerviswoode. The Solicitor-General of Scotland, Mr Gifford, prosecuted the case, with the assistance of Mr Crichton, while Mr Clark, Mr Watson and Mr Brand defended Pritchard, who pleaded 'Not Guilty' to both charges of murder against him. The proceedings began with some debate about whether the two cases should be tried separately. However, it was the court's opinion that it would be impossible to separate the two charges.

One of the first witnesses called to testify was Catherine Lattimer, who had worked as the Pritchards' cook. She had been due to leave their employ on 2 February 1865 but, due to Mary Jane's illness, had stayed on until 16 February. Catherine told the court that Mrs Pritchard had been severely afflicted with cramp on or about 14 February and that Mary McLeod had been sent to fetch a doctor to treat her. According to Catherine, Dr Pritchard had been in his wife's bedroom at the time and had been distressed and tearful at the apparent seriousness of her condition. Mary Jane had admonished her husband, saying, 'Don't cry, you hypocrite,' adding that doctors were all hypocrites together.

Next to testify was Mary McLeod, by now seventeen years old. Mary was on the witness stand for more than four hours, during which time she admitted to having an affair with Dr Pritchard, saying that he had promised to marry her should his wife die before him but that she had treated this remark as a joke. Dr Pritchard had given her gifts of a ring, a brooch and a locket containing his photograph, which she had since torn up. Mary McLeod admitted to engaging in 'improper familiarities' with Dr Pritchard, saying that Mrs Pritchard had once caught them kissing. She stated that she had become pregnant but had suffered a miscarriage. When asked if Dr Pritchard had done anything to her to bring about the miscarriage, the counsel for the defence objected to the question, saying that it would constitute a separate crime, one with which the defendant had not been formally charged and the judge immediately disallowed the question before the girl had a chance to reply.

Much of the trial was taken up by the testimony of the various medical witnesses. Professor Maclagan detailed the results of his post-mortem examinations on both bodies, after their exhumation. He had sent samples of the dead women's organs to Dr F. Penny, Professor of chemistry at the Andersonian Medical School in Glasgow. Penny had run a series of tests on the viscera and had detected mercury and antimony in Mrs Pritchard's remains and antimony alone in the remains of her mother.

In addition, he had tested various samples obtained from the Pritchards' home after the doctor's arrest and had found antimony, hemlock, digitalis or aconite in several of them, including some tapioca. He also found large amounts of aconite in a bottle of commercial medicine called Battley's Solution. Penny had given the solution to some rabbits, all of which had subsequently died, although genuine, unadulterated Battley's Solution had not killed them. It was known that Mrs Taylor, who suffered from neuralgia, was a long-term user of Battley's Solution, which acted as a sedative.

According to Professor Maclagan, the medical evidence pointed to the conclusion that Mrs Pritchard had taken a large quantity of tartar emetic and that the cause of her death could be reliably attributed to antimony poisoning. By the quantity of the poison found in her remains, it was evident that the poison had been taken consistently for some time, rather than as one large dose.

The presence of mercury in her body could be accounted for by the medicine she had been prescribed by Dr Paterson shortly before her death and was not in sufficient quantity to have been a contributory factor. There were no known natural illnesses that replicated her symptoms and she had definitely not died of gastric fever, as certified by her husband.

In respect of Mrs Taylor, Maclagan concluded that she too had been repeatedly dosed with antimony and had probably received an additional dose of aconite shortly before her death. Even though the analyst had found no trace of aconite in her organs, it was certainly found in the Battley's Solution that she was known to take regularly and it was suggested that the emetic properties of the antimony might have caused her to vomit up most of the aconite. Mrs Taylor's symptoms suggested a combination of antimony, aconite and morphine poisoning and were not consistent with death from apoplexy, as certified by her son-in-law. Furthermore, Maclagan had actually tasted the bottle of Battley's Solution given to him by the police and had been able to discern the presence of aconite.

Numerous witnesses were then called before the court to testify about Dr Pritchard's financial situation at the time of his wife's death. Most of his bank accounts were overdrawn and, on the death of her mother, Minnie Pritchard was due to inherit the sum of £2,000. According to the terms of Minnie's will, in the event of her predeceasing her husband, this money was to be paid to him for the benefit of their children until they attained the age of twenty-one, after which time, all of the money was his, for his own use.

Dr Pritchard showed no emotion as he watched the proceedings from the dock, until two of his five children were called to give evidence. Fourteen-year-old Jane had lived with her grandmother and told the court that Mrs Taylor had often spoken kindly about Dr Pritchard and likewise, him about her.

Eleven-year-old Charles had lived in the family home with his father and mother until his mother's death. He stated that they had all lived happily together and that his parents were very fond of each other.

Dr Pritchard continued to maintain his innocence. He admitted to having given his wife chloroform to help her insomnia, saying that it had disagreed with her and he had discontinued its use immediately. He also admitted to rubbing antimony on Mary Jane's neck to relieve a swollen gland and to giving her a little bottle of the poison for her to use externally on the gland. Other than that, he maintained that he had given his wife nothing apart from champagne, brandy and wine to increase her strength during her illness. With regard to Mrs Taylor, he continued to insist that she died from apoplexy, as he had certified.

The prosecution maintained that Dr Pritchard had cruelly poisoned both his wife and her mother. Pritchard's defence counsel insisted that the prosecution had not proven their case. They had shown no real motive for the murders and neither had they produced any conclusive proof that it had been Pritchard who had actually administered the poison to both of the victims. Indeed, Mr Clark pointed out that Mary McLeod had prepared or served food to both of the dead women and it could just as easily have been her who poisoned her mistress and Mrs Taylor in order to ensure that Dr Pritchard was free to marry her.

The circumstantial evidence against Dr Pritchard was too strong for the jury to ignore and they deliberated for less than an hour before finding him guilty. He was sentenced to be hanged on 28 July 1865. Awaiting his execution at Glasgow Prison, following a plea from his daughter, he made a partial confession to his crimes to clergyman Revd R.S. Oldham, in the presence of prison governor John Stirling and warder John Mutrie. He continued to declare himself innocent of the murder of Mrs Taylor, saying that he now believed that she had taken an overdose of Battley's Solution. Pritchard admitted to committing adultery with Mary McLeod, to 'producing a miscarriage' when she became pregnant, and to administering sufficient chloroform to his wife to cause her death, an act that he attributed to yielding to temptation in an evil moment, while under the influence of whisky.

Shortly before his execution, he made a second confession to the man he described as his 'present spiritual advisor', Revd T. Watson Reid. In the presence of John Stirling and warders Edward Geary and John Mutrie, Pritchard now admitted to killing both his wife and her mother, saying that he could attribute no motive for his conduct '...beyond a species of terrible madness and the use of ardent spirits'. He exonerated Mary McLeod of all culpability in the murders, stating that the facts presented at his trial were the truth. Pritchard went on to thank the judges, jury and legal personnel at his trial for their careful consideration of his case and the staff at the prison for their kindness towards him. Urging his 'fellow creatures' to pray for him, he expressed his penitence for his crimes and hoped that God would have mercy on his soul.

William Calcraft executed Dr Pritchard on 28 July 1865. The hanging coincided with the annual Glasgow Fair and was thus watched by a massive crowd of around 100,000 people. It was to be the last public execution to be carried out at Glasgow Prison and, according to witnesses, did not run smoothly. As Pritchard hung suspended from the noose, his body was seen to quiver violently for several minutes, his shoulders shrugging and his hands clenching and unclenching. The body having hung for the customary hour, Calcraft was left to lower the body into a coffin waiting at the bottom of the pit. However, in doing so, he momentarily lost his grip on the rope, leaving the body to plummet into the coffin from a height, knocking the bottom straight out.

Pritchard's body was buried within the confines of the prison walls, only to be exhumed forty-five years later in the course of some construction work at the prison. Although his body had become little more than a skeleton, the elastic-sided patent leather boots he was wearing at the time of his execution were found to be perfectly preserved and were immediately stolen by souvenir hunters.

11

'I don't like it. It tastes nasty'

BRIGHTON, SUSSEX, 1870—1871

Christiana Edmunds is perhaps best described as a frustrated and bitter old maid. Having reached her forties and never married, Christiana instead directed her affections towards an unattainable target – her doctor, Dr Beard.

Dr Beard, whose surgery was located in Grand Parade, Brighton, was a married man, although he was not above a little flirtation with his female patients. Somehow, in Christiana's mind, this harmless flirtation spawned the belief that the doctor was madly in love with her and, to his embarrassment, she began to bombard him with passionate letters. At a loss as to how to stop her, Beard showed the letters to his wife and the couple agreed that they were best ignored.

Royal Pavilion, Brighton, 1928. (Author's collection)

King's Road, Brighton, 1959. (Author's collection)

By 1870, Christiana had made up her mind that Mrs Beard was the only thing standing between her and happiness with the man of her dreams and in September of that year, she presented her unsuspecting love rival with a gift of chocolate creams. Having eaten them, Mrs Beard fell dreadfully ill, although she fortunately made a full recovery. Her furious husband accused Christiana of trying to poison his wife although, without proof, he did not feel that he could report his suspicions to the police.

Christiana was hurt by his accusations and devastated at having lost the affections of the man that she loved. She decided that, if she could prove to him that there was another poisoner at large in Brighton, she might regain his love.

With this goal in mind, on 18 March 1871, Christiana purchased ten grains of strychnine from Isaac Garrett, a chemist and druggist who had a shop on Queens Road in Brighton. She told Garrett that she intended to use the poison for killing stray cats, brushing aside his objections that this was cruel. When Garrett warned her of the dangers of the poison she was buying, she reassured him that she was a married woman and that only herself and her husband would be handling it. Garrett told her that she would need a witness in order to buy the poison, so Christiana persuaded a local milliner, Mrs Stone, to witness her purchases. Signing the Poisons Register 'Mrs Wood', she was to repeat her purchase on 15 April and, on 10 May she purchased a further ten grains, this time supposedly for the purpose of killing a dog. On that occasion, she told Garrett that she and her husband were about to leave Brighton for Devon and had an elderly, sick dog, which could not go with them.

*West Street,
Brighton, 1906.
(Author's collection)*

However, Christiana had a far more sinister purpose in mind for the poison than culling stray cats and elderly dogs. She began to buy quantities of cream chocolates from G. Maynard's, Confectioners, of West Street in Brighton, usually recruiting small boys to purchase the sweets on her behalf and later returning the chocolates to the shop, asking to exchange them for a different kind. Trustingly, the shop owner and his assistants were only too happy to oblige and would hand over replacement chocolates to one of her errand boys, replacing the returned chocolates in the display case to be sold again.

Soon, people all over Brighton began to fall ill after eating chocolates from Maynard's shop. To divert any suspicion from herself, Christiana also made a complaint to the shopkeeper, saying that a friend of hers had been violently ill after eating a chocolate cream.

On 12 June 1871, Charles Miller was on holiday in Brighton and purchased some chocolate creams from Maynard's, which he shared with his family throughout the day. Although most of the chocolates tasted fine, in the afternoon Miller gave one to his brother, Ernest, and one to his nephew, four-year-old Sidney Albert Barker. Ernest found the sweet tasted 'coppery' and spat it out. Miller himself ate two sweets and gave another to his nephew but within ten minutes, Sidney began to cry. 'I don't like it. It tastes nasty,' he sobbed. Soon Mr Miller began to feel dizzy, his limbs strangely stiff and his joints fused. Sidney's limbs also stiffened and a doctor was called urgently.

Dr Richard Rugg arrived within minutes and found Sidney convulsing violently. He administered an emetic but the little boy died before it could take effect. On the following day, Dr Rugg performed a post-mortem examination on the child but, other than the fact that the body was unusually rigid, he could find no reason for Sidney's death apart from changes to his brain normally associated with convulsions. However, at the request of the Brighton coroner,

David Black, Rugg removed the child's stomach and its contents, which were sent to analyst Professor Letheby.

Letheby found the boy's stomach to contain about a quarter of a grain of strychnine, which was more than enough to cause the death of a child so young. Letheby also tested some chocolate creams. He found strychnine in the remainder of the sweets in the bag bought by Charles Miller and also in an identical batch purchased from Maynard's after Sidney's death. Letheby concluded that Sidney had died from strychnine poisoning as a result of eating chocolates contaminated with the poison.

An inquest was opened, at which Christiana Edmunds volunteered to give evidence. She told the inquest that she had twice purchased chocolate creams from Maynard's and that, on each occasion, she and a friend had both been ill after eating them. She spoke of visiting the shop to complain and of telling Mr Maynard that she intended to get the sweets analysed. She took the chocolates to a local chemist, Mr Schweitzer who, she said, initially treated her complaint very lightly until he tasted one of the chocolates himself. He had analysed the chocolates and given Christiana a written report, which she stated that she had handed to Dr Rugg.

The inquest jury eventually found that although Sidney Barker had died from strychnine poisoning, his death could not really be blamed on anybody specific. Hence, a verdict of 'accidental death' was recorded, although the jury did issue a warning to Mr Ware, who made the chocolate creams sold at Maynard's, to revise his manufacturing processes. Ware was completely baffled by the warning, since he had never before received any complaints about his products and kept no strychnine on his premises.

Soon after the end of the inquest, Sidney Barker's father received three letters. The first, signed 'An Old Inhabitant and Seeker of Justice' urged him to take official action against Mr Maynard, saying that the inhabitants of Brighton would assist with the costs. The second, signed 'G.C.B.' was on the same theme, asking, 'Why should Mr Maynard be screened?' and the third letter, signed 'A London tradesman now in Brighton' again advised Barker to initiate proceedings against the seller of the chocolates. All three letters were very similar in style and content and Mr Barker handed them straight to the police.

Meanwhile, the anonymous poisoner continued to strike terror into the hearts of Brighton residents. Several more people were taken ill after eating chocolate creams and some residents – including Mrs Beard – received parcels containing cake or fruit, which made them ill when they ate the contents. In some cases, worried residents took the remains of the seemingly poisoned food items to chemist's shops in the town. They in turn contacted the police, who forwarded the samples to Professor Rodgers for analysis. Rodgers found all of the samples to be heavily laced with arsenic – in one cake alone he found more than eleven grains of the poison.

On 8 June, a boy delivered a note to Isaac Garrett the chemist, which purported to come from another firm of chemists, Glaisyer and Kemp of North Street. The note asked if Garrett could possibly supply them with half an ounce of strychnia. Garrett sent a note back with the boy, saying that he only had a drachm and, in due course, the boy returned saying that a drachm would tide them over until their own stocks arrived. The boy handed over 2s 6d and was given the poison and some change.

In July, Garrett received another note brought by a young boy, allegedly from David Black, the coroner. The note asked if Black could inspect the Poisons Register, promising to return it almost immediately. Garrett sent the book with the messenger and it was indeed promptly returned. It was not until he next went to use the book that Garrett noticed that several pages had been torn out.

On 19 July, another messenger arrived from Glaisyer and Kemp, this time asking for two or three ounces of arsenic. This time, Garrett checked with the chemists directly and learned that the request hadn't come from them.

The police were busy interviewing everyone who had been affected by chocolates purchased from Maynard's and, in due course, they came to Christiana Edmunds. Having interviewed her, Inspector Gibbs then sent her a note, to which she immediately replied. A handwriting expert, Mr Nutherclift, was asked by the police to examine the reply and found it to be written in the same hand as the three notes received by Mr Barker after the death of his son, the letters sent to Isaac Garrett supposedly from Glaisyer and Kemp and the coroner, and the signature 'Mrs Wood' in Garrett's Poisons Register. The police also traced another chemist, Samuel Bradbury, who had recently left Brighton and who, on or around 21 July, had supplied Glaisyer and Kemp with three ounces of arsenic having received a written request from them. The note had not come from the chemists and was written in the same handwriting as all the other correspondence.

Christiana Edmunds was arrested and charged with indiscriminate poisoning, the attempted murder of Mrs Beard and the murder of Sidney Barker. After appearing before magistrates at Brighton in September 1871, she was committed for trial.

She was eventually tried at the Old Bailey in London, since the depth of feeling against her in Brighton made finding an unbiased jury impossible. The trial was presided over by Baron Martin, with Mr Serjeant Ballantine and Mr Straight prosecuting and Mr Serjeant Parry, Mr Poland and Mr Worsley defending. Tried only for the murder of Sidney Barker, Christiana Edmunds pleaded 'Not Guilty'.

Just days before the opening of her trial on 15 January 1872, Christiana made a lengthy formal complaint to prison officials, complaining about having to share a cell with a bigamist, not being allowed to wear a bonnet to chapel and having been denied her velvet dresses and furs, which were most appropriate for the season.

The prosecution called a steady stream of witnesses including doctors, chemists, analysts, Mr Maynard and his staff, Mr Ware the sweet manufacturer, Sidney Barker's father and uncle, the handwriting expert, several Brighton residents who had been taken ill after eating supposedly poisoned chocolates or other foodstuffs and a series of young boys who had purchased or returned chocolates for Miss Edmunds or had delivered her notes to the chemists and collected poison in return. On the second day of the trial, the three letters sent to Sidney Barker's father were introduced into court as evidence before the prosecution rested and gave way to Christiana's defence counsel.

The defence focused mainly on trying to prove that Christiana Edmunds was insane. In his opening speech, Mr Serjeant Parry stated that he couldn't deny that Christiana Edmunds had purchased sufficient poison to kill sixty or seventy people. Neither could he deny that she had bought chocolate creams and returned them to Maynard's, having first doctored them in some way. He accepted that six or seven children had become ill after eating chocolates given to them by Christiana Edmunds. However, what he did dispute was that Christiana Edmunds had been in any way responsible for the death of Sidney Barker, a child she had neither known nor even seen before and against whom she could harbour no malice, hatred or dislike.

The prosecution had called eleven-year-old Adam May, who testified that he had bought and returned chocolates to Maynard's for Christiana Edmunds on an unknown date in May. Shop assistant Anne Meadows recalled Adam's visit, although she believed it had occurred at the beginning of June. Sidney Barker's death had occurred on 12 June and, in the interval between May returning the chocolates and Sidney's death, there had been no other reported incidences of any illness.

Maynard's kept the chocolate creams in a glass case in the shop and sold between 3lb and 4lb each week. The defence maintained that, in the time between the chocolates being returned by May and the purchase by Miller, the glass case would have been emptied and refilled several times. The sweets bought by Mr Miller had been the last of the chocolates in the case, which had been refilled after his purchase. Those bought by Mr Barker after his son's death and given to Inspector Gibbs for analysis were part of a new batch and had also contained strychnine. These facts alone suggested that Christiana was innocent of poisoning the chocolates eaten by Sidney Barker.

Professing himself to be baffled by the singularity of the case and at a loss as to how to present it to the jury, Mr Serjeant Parry then set out to demonstrate to the jury that his client was of 'impaired intellect'. The court was told that Christiana's father had suffered from suicidal and homicidal mania and had died in middle age in an asylum. Her brother, Arthur, had died in the throes of an epileptic fit while a patient in an asylum, her sister suffered from nervous hysteria and both of her grandfathers and a first cousin were of unsound mind.

Christiana herself had suffered from nervous paralysis and hysteria and, about twelve months ago, had changed in character and even now was sufficiently vain to deny her real age, claiming to be thirty-four and not forty-three years old.

Citing insanity as the cause of the destruction of her moral sense, the defence counsel pointed out the lengths she had allegedly gone to just to prove to Dr Beard that she had not tried to poison his wife and so regain what she saw as his affections. She had given poisoned sweets to children in broad daylight; she had torn pages from a Poisons Register – although not the pages relating to her own purchases – and had written incriminating letters in her own handwriting. Was this the behaviour of an imbecile or did it show soundness and clarity of mind?

Mr Serjeant Parry acknowledged the inconsistency of his arguments in first saying that the prisoner did not commit the murder with which she was charged, then asking the jury to believe that she should be found not guilty due to reasons of insanity, but said that he wanted the jury to have all the information and evidence on both sides.

The defence then called a series of witnesses to testify to Christiana's mental state. Her mother, also called Christiana Edmunds, with whom she shared lodgings in Gloucester Place, fully described the mental deficiencies of Christiana's father, siblings, cousin and grandparents. Mrs Edmunds also told the court how distressed her daughter had been on hearing Dr Beard's allegations that she had tried to poison his wife.

Mrs Edmunds was followed into the witness box by several doctors who corroborated her evidence of inherent insanity on both sides of Christiana's family.

The chaplain at Lewes Jail, the Revd Thomas Cole, believed that Christiana had been insane while she was incarcerated there after her arrest and two friends of hers testified that they had noticed a change in her about fifteen months previously. She had become unusually excited, given to rolling her eyes and frequently saying that she felt unhappy and that she was going mad.

Finally, several doctors who had examined Christiana while she was incarcerated at Newgate Prison gave their opinions on her sanity. All agreed that insanity was hereditary but some believed that she was on the borderline between criminality

and insanity, others that she was insane. Without exception, all of them found her unable to appreciate the seriousness of her crime and described her moral sense as deficient. In the midst of the medical evidence,

The female exercise yard at Newgate Prison. (Author's collection)

Broadmoor Asylum, 1906. (Author's collection)

Christiana suddenly stood up in the dock and began to speak. When told that she couldn't be heard at the moment, she calmly resumed her seat.

In summarising the case for the jury, the judge carefully went over all the evidence, as well as outlining in some detail the legal definition of insanity. The jury retired for exactly one hour before returning a verdict of 'Guilty'.

Once Baron Martin had placed the black cap on his head, the clerk of the court asked Christiana if she had anything to say before sentence was passed upon her. Christiana said that she wished she had been tried on the other charges that had been brought against her and that she also wished to be examined about the improper intimacy said to exist between herself and Dr Beard.

The judge responded that it did not rest with him and that the prosecution decided which charge she should be tried on.

'It is owing to my having been a patient of his and the treatment I received in going to him that I have been brought into this dreadful business,' Christiana insisted. 'I wish the jury had known the intimacy, his affection for me and the way I have been treated.'

The judge refused to be drawn into an argument, saying that he had wished Dr and Mrs Beard to be kept out of the proceedings as much as possible so that she might have a fair trial. He then pronounced sentence of death.

As was customary for female prisoners, Christiana was then asked if there were any reason why her execution should be stayed. Christiana obviously did not understand the question but when a warder explained it to her, she immediately announced that she was pregnant. A jury of matrons was promptly assembled from those attending the court and, with the assistance Mr Gibson, the prison doctor and another doctor, Dr Beresford Ryley, who just happened to be a spectator at the proceedings, were charged with trying the issue. They quickly determined that Miss Edmunds was not pregnant.

Ten days after the conclusion of her trial, it was announced that Christiana Edmunds had been found insane after all and that, rather than facing execution, she would be committed to Broadmoor Lunatic Asylum. She was to die there in 1907.

12
'See how easily they can be swallowed'

Percy Malcolm John had been a boarder at Blenheim House School for three years, having been placed at the school by his brother-in-law, Mr William Chapman, after the death of his parents. Percy was eighteen years old, expecting to celebrate his nineteenth birthday on 18 December 1881. Although otherwise a healthy young man, he suffered from a severe curvature of the spine and was consequently paralysed from the waist down, using a wheelchair and relying on help from his fellow students to get around the school.

On 3 December 1881, William Henry Bedbrook, the principal of the school, was passing through the hall when he spotted Percy's other brother-in-law, George Henry Lamson. At first, Bedbrook didn't recognise Lamson, who had lost a lot of weight since he had last seen him. However, when Lamson walked into the room where the school pupils normally entertained their visitors, Bedbrook realised who he was and immediately sent someone to fetch Percy. Another pupil brought the boy to the room and placed him in an armchair close to his visitor.

Lamson greeted his brother-in-law with the words, 'Why, how fat you look, old boy.'

'I wish I could say the same of you, George,' responded Percy.

Bedbrook offered Lamson a drink of wine and Lamson asked for a glass of sherry. When it was brought to him, Lamson took a sip before asking if he might have some sugar to 'destroy the alcoholic effect'. Although Bedbrook suspected that the addition of sugar to the sherry might have exactly the opposite effect, he rang for the school matron, who eventually brought a small bowl of powdered sugar. Lamson added a small amount to his drink, which he then stirred with the blade of his penknife. Seeming satisfied, he produced a newspaper-wrapped Dundee cake from his bag, along with some sweets that he claimed to have bought in New York.

Lamson, Percy and Bedbrook sat chatting for fifteen minutes or so, sipping sherry and sharing the cake and sweets. Then Lamson suddenly delved into his black bag again, pulling out two boxes of capsules. 'I thought of you and Percy while I was in New York,' he told Bedbrook, continuing to extol the virtues of the new capsules, saying how simple it would be for Bedbrook to use them when he had to give medicine to the boys in his charge.

Bedbrook took a closer look at one of the capsules, noting that it was in two halves, which could be pushed together. Lamson urged him to try one. 'See how easily they can be swallowed,' he remarked to the school principal, who found that the capsule slipped down without any difficulty. Lamson then spooned a little of the sugar into another of the capsules to demonstrate to Bedbrook just how easily they could be filled with medication. Pushing the two halves together, he handed the filled capsule to Percy, who obediently swallowed it without comment.

Minutes later, Lamson took his leave of his brother-in-law and Mr Bedbrook, saying that he was on his way to London Bridge to catch the eight o'clock train to Paris. From there, he intended to travel to Florence where he planned to spend the winter, before returning to England to settle down.

Once Lamson had left, Mr Bedbrook went off to do some singing practice. When he returned fifteen minutes later, it was to find Percy complaining of having heartburn. Bedbrook told him to sit quietly for a few minutes and left the boy looking at some newspapers that his brother-in-law had brought for him. Ten minutes later, Percy was complaining of pain in his stomach and told his headmaster that he believed that Lamson had given him a quinine pill, since he had suffered exactly the same pain once before after being given such a pill on the Isle of Wight. Ten minutes later, Percy was still feeling ill and asked to go to bed. When Bedbrook checked on Percy a little while later, he found the boy writhing in agony on his bed and vomiting, complaining of pain in his mouth, throat and stomach and a tight feeling in his skin.

The matron, Mary Ann Bowles, was sent for to look after the sick boy, along with Alfred Godward, one of the junior masters and the Classics master, Alexander Watt. However, Percy's condition gradually worsened and at a quarter to nine that evening, Bedbrook decided to send for the doctor. As he went down to the hall he happened upon Dr Berry, who coincidentally had just arrived at the school to visit another pupil. Bedbrook asked Berry if he would be kind enough to examine Percy and while Berry went upstairs to do so, Bedbrook sent for another doctor, Dr Little. The doctors fed Percy beaten egg whites in water and placed hot linseed poultices on his stomach, and, as his pain worsened, they twice injected him with morphine. By ten past eleven that evening, Percy was drifting in and out of consciousness, his pulse and heartbeat growing ever weaker. He was given brandy as a stimulant but sadly died at twenty past eleven that evening.

Apart from his disability, Percy had been in excellent health and spirits on the day of his death until the visit from his brother-in-law. The matron had seen him playing a lively game of charades with other students just half an hour before Lamson arrived. Hence, on the following morning, Mr Bedbrook went to the police station to report the boy's sudden death. Inspector John Fuller went to the school and removed various items, including the capsules brought to the school by Mr Lamson, the remains of the Dundee cake and sweets, the sherry and a sample of the sugar used to sweeten it, and some quinine powders and two letters from Percy's trunk.

On 6 December, Dr Berry, Dr Little and Mr Bond, a lecturer in forensic medicine at Westminster Hospital, conducted a post-mortem examination on Percy. As well as examining the boy's body, they also obtained samples of his vomit, which, along with the food items removed from the school by Inspector Fuller, were given to Auguste Dupré, the lecturer in chemistry at the Westminster Hospital. The doctors suspected that Percy had been poisoned with some kind of vegetable alkaloid, most probably aconitine, a derivative of the dried root of the monkshood or wolfs bane plant, also known as aconitia.

Dupré tested the samples, together with Thomas Stevenson, a doctor who was also a Fellow of the Royal College of Physicians, a Fellow of the Council and Institute of Chemistry, a lecturer on medical jurisprudence and chemistry at Guy's Hospital, and an examiner in forensic medicine at the London University. Using a test known as 'Stass's Process', the chemists isolated traces of aconitia from Percy's urine and vomit. No trace of poison was found in any of the foodstuffs or the gelatine capsules, although aconitia was found in three of the quinine powders and some quinine tablets that Percy had kept in his trunk in his room. Stevenson confirmed his results by injecting the samples into mice, resulting in the death of the animals. As a control, the chemists injected more mice with a known solution of aconitine, observing that the mice died after showing exactly the same symptoms as they had exhibited following the injection of the solutions derived from Percy's samples. Thus the doctors and analysts formed the conclusion that Percy's death had been caused by the ingestion of aconitine.

Their investigations were hampered by the fact that none of the doctors or chemists had ever come across a case of death by aconitine poisoning before. In fact, as far as they were aware, this was the only time it had ever been used as a poison in Britain, although there was one recorded case in Europe. Aconitine was not used internally, since it was so dangerous, although it had on occasions been used as an ingredient in ointments or liniments, applied externally for pain relief from such diseases as rheumatism and neuralgia.

Meanwhile, as soon as he had been notified of Percy's death, William Chapman had written to his brother-in-law George Lamson in Paris, receiving a reply almost by return of post:

Dec. 7, 1881.

My dear Will,

Your letter reached me on Monday night too late to catch any train except one, via Dieppe, and which I should have had to rush for. This doctor would not allow me to do. I was so prostrate at the sudden, awful, and most unexpected news that I became delirious very soon. I was obliged to remain in bed all day yesterday. Early this morning I saw the Evening Standard. I read therein the dreadful suspicion attached to my name. I need not tell you of the absolute falsity of such a fearful accusation. Bedbrook was present all the time I was in the house, and if there was any noxious substance in the capsule it must have been in his sugar, for that was all there was in it. He saw me take the empty capsule and fill it from his own sugar basin. However, with the consciousness that I am an innocent and unjustly accused man, I am returning at once to London to face the matter out. If they wish to arrest me they will have ample opportunity of doing so. I shall attempt no concealment. I shall arrive at Waterloo Station about 9.15 tomorrow (Thursday) morning.

The police had already identified George Lamson as the chief suspect in the death of Percy John and, on 8 December, a decision was made to send an officer to Paris to apprehend him. However, almost as soon as Sergeant Moser had departed for the continent, George Lamson and his wife appeared at Scotland Yard. There Lamson introduced himself to Inspector Butcher with the words, 'My name is Lamson; I am Dr Lamson, whose name has been mentioned in connection with the death at Wimbledon.'

From his demeanour at the police station, it was quite clear that Lamson fully expected to be asked a few questions and then allowed to go on his way. When he was charged with Percy's murder by Chief Superintendent Williamson, he was initially shocked, although quickly recovered his composure to ask about the possibility of bail.

Lamson had qualified as a doctor in Paris and after qualification had served in the French Ambulance Corps during the Franco-Prussian War. By 1876, he was in active service in the Balkans. However, along with decorations by both the Serbian and Romanian governments, his war service left him with an addiction to morphine.

When he married Percy's sister, Kate John, on 16 October 1878, she was in possession of a sizeable legacy from the death of her parents. Kate was the eldest of five children, each of whom had been equal beneficiaries in their parents' will. The premature deaths of two of Kate's brothers, Hubert and Sydney, had meant that their share of the inheritance had been divided between Kate, her sister, Margaret Chapman, and Percy. Yet George Lamson quickly frittered away his wife's inheritance buying a medical practice in Bournemouth, which his addiction prevented him from running successfully. At the time of Percy's death, Lamson was in dire financial straits. He owed money to numerous people and had resorted to passing invalid cheques and even to pawning his watch and his surgical instruments in order to raise money.

Lamson was tried for the murder of Percy John before Mr Justice Hawkins at the Central Criminal Court – the Old Bailey. His trial opened on 8 March 1882 and lasted for five days. The case was prosecuted by the Solicitor General, who was assisted by Mr Poland and Mr Smith. Lamson, who pleaded 'Not Guilty', was defended by Montagu Williams, Charles Matthews, R. Gladstone and W.H. Robson.

According to the prosecution, the motive for Percy's murder was his share of his parents' money, which amounted to more than £3,000. On his death, the sum would have been divided equally between his surviving siblings, sisters Kate Lamson and Margaret Chapman.

Several witnesses testified in court to having heard Percy say at the onset of his final illness, 'I have taken a quinine pill that my brother-in-law gave me.' Percy had said that his brother-in-law had given him a quinine pill once before in Shanklin, Isle of Wight, and that it had made him ill on that occasion too.

Members of staff from Messrs Allen and Hanbury, a wholesale and retail chemist, told the court that Lamson had bought two grains of aconitia from them on 24 November 1881. Staff from a chemist in Ventnor, Isle of Wight testified to Lamson having bought both quinine and one grain of aconitine in August of 1881.

At that time, Percy had come to stay with his sister and brother-in-law, Mr and Mrs Chapman, on the Isle of Wight, the family renting rooms from George and Sophia Joliffe. While Percy and the Chapmans were staying with the Joliffe's, George Lamson had visited and, shortly afterwards, Percy was taken ill, although he quickly recovered. It therefore seems as if George Lamson had made a previous unsuccessful attempt on Percy's life and had now doubled the dose of poison in the hope of achieving what would be, for him, a more favourable outcome on his second attempt.

The Old Bailey (Central Criminal Court), London. (Author's collection)

The trial of George Lamson.
(Author's collection)

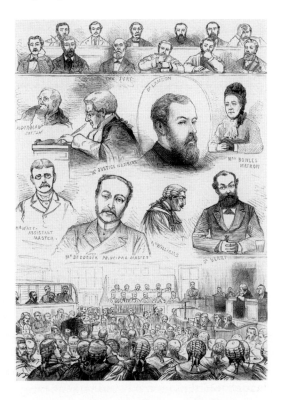

Much of the trial was given over to the evidence from the medical witnesses, Dr Little, Dr Berry, Mr Bond, Mr Dupré and Mr Stevenson. Although none of them had personally dealt with such a poisoning before, they were able to describe the meticulous tests they had employed, which included actually applying small amounts of the samples derived from Percy's urine, vomit and internal organs to their tongues. This produced the classic tingling and burning sensation known to be associated with aconitine.

The final day of the trial was spent hearing testimony from numerous witnesses to whom Lamson owed money, followed by summaries of the case from the prosecution, defence and the presiding judge.

Even though nobody had actually seen George Lamson administering a fatal dose of poison to his young brother-in-law, the circumstantial evidence against him was so strong that the jury returned a guilty verdict against him, leaving Mr Justice Hawkins to pronounce the mandatory death sentence. The doctor continued to protest his innocence, but, shortly before his execution by William Marwood at Wandsworth Prison on 28 April 1882, thirty-year-old George Lamson made a full confession of his guilt to the prison chaplain, acknowledging the justice of his sentence. It was said that Percy John idolised his brother-in-law George Lamson, a fact that makes his untimely death at the hands of his hero seem even more tragic.

13
'It's nauseous stuff, and as sour as vinegar'

PLUMSTEAD, LONDON, 1882

William Tregillis, aged eighty-five, rented the top half of a cottage in Plumstead with his wife, Mary Ann, who was nearly eighty-one years old. The couple survived on William's pension of £42 17s a year from the Royal Navy. It was a second marriage for William, who married his first wife in 1856. In the twenty-three years that they were together, the first Mrs Tregillis drove her husband literally out of his mind and he was sent to an asylum, where he spent seven months recovering. While he was an in-patient, his wife died. Released from the asylum, William married Mary Ann and by all accounts this marriage seemed to be a happy one.

Plumstead Common in the 1920s. (Author's collection)

On 27 July 1882, Mr and Mrs Tregillis received an unexpected visitor to their home. Thirty-six-year-old Louise Jane Taylor was the widow of an old friend and workmate of William's and she was to long outstay her welcome at the Tregillis' home. Having arrived for a visit, she explained to William and Mary Ann that she had been unwell recently and asked if she could stay with them for a few days for the benefit of her health. William and Mary Ann agreed that she could and, as they only had two rooms, William moved out of the bedroom and Louise moved in, sharing the only bed with Mary Ann.

On August Bank Holiday, Mary Ann and Louise went out for a walk together, during which Mary Ann fell and cut her eye. When they returned home, Louise suddenly fell to the ground in the throes of a fit. William lifted her from the floor and carried her to bed before sending for a doctor. By the time the doctor arrived, Louise was fully recovered, although she did get the doctor to leave some medicine for Mary Ann's eye.

From that day on Mary Ann's health gradually declined and Louise devoted herself to nursing her. First, Mary Ann complained of headaches and diarrhoea, which her doctor diagnosed as 'fever ague'. Within two weeks, Mary Ann 'looked like death' and the doctor was visiting her sometimes twice daily. Mary Ann's urine was dark red and her once white teeth had turned completely black. Her appetite deserted her completely and the only food she could be persuaded to take was a little beef tea. At night, Mary Ann frequently vomited and complained of a burning pain like fire in the back of her throat. Her illness exhausted her and she took to sleeping throughout the day, waking at night to more pain and sickness.

Her doctor, Dr Smith, and his locum, Dr Bliss, both prescribed medicines for her but she was reluctant to take them, saying that they hurt her throat. On one occasion, a frustrated Louise shouted at her, 'If you don't take it, I'll punch you.' Soon Mary Ann was complaining of constipation, stomach pain and vomiting, saying that everything she ate or drank made her sick. Dr Smith had never actually seen Mary Ann produce what Louise Taylor described as dark green vomit, with a yellowish shade. He repeatedly asked Louise to save him a sample of the vomit, but she insisted that it was too foul to save. As the weather at the time was unbearably hot and the vomit would have to be kept in a lodging with only two rooms, Smith didn't attach too much importance to her repeated refusals.

While Louise Taylor monopolised the invalid's care, she also found time to borrow small sums of money from William Tregillis, his landlady Sarah Ellis, and anyone else she could coerce into giving her a loan. She also pawned several items of Mary Ann's clothing. Louise seemed determined that William should come to live with her at her own house. Believing the offer to include his wife, William initially showed some enthusiasm for what would be cheap accommodation for them but Louise made it obvious that her offer was for William only and, when he protested, she told him that Mary Ann would be dead soon. She showed William an official-looking letter, which seemed to indicate that she had £500 in savings readily available to her. On one occasion she even packed William's clothes and ordered a cart to move his things to her house but William refused to go without his wife.

Throughout her stay with William and Mary Ann, Louise received frequent visits from a man named Edward Martin. Landlady, Sarah Ellis, disapproved of Martin's visits but after Louise untruthfully told her that he was a nephew of Mary Ann's, she didn't feel that she could protest. Martin, who was a watercress seller, visited Louise constantly, often staying for meals.

On 3 October, William went to collect his pension and, on his return, was immediately collared by Louise Taylor who said that Mary Ann wanted the money to be put under her pillow. He handed over £9 but the money vanished and both Mary Ann and Louise denied having seen it. By now, William felt he had suffered his guest long enough and, on 6 October, he made an official complaint to the police that Louise had been stealing from him. PC Ernest Glanville arrested Louise, charging her with stealing two dresses, a shawl, a petticoat and a pair of boots. Louise, however, insisted that she had pawned some of the items with William's consent.

On the walk to the police station with PC Glanville, Louise was approached by Rhoda Trice, a friend of Mary Ann's. Seeing Louise in custody, Rhoda assumed that she was being arrested for poisoning Mary Ann, something that had been the subject of gossip between many of the neighbours for some time. 'Why have you been trying to kill the old lady?' asked Rhoda and Louise replied that she had only bought sugar of lead to use for injecting herself. It was the first PC Glanville had heard of any attempted murder but, for the moment, he had to concentrate on the allegation of stealing made against his charge. When she arrived at the police station, Louise handed over thirteen pawn tickets and a further ten were found about her person when she was searched, totalling £4 9s. Louise still insisted that the items had been pawned with William's knowledge and consent and the money raised used for household expenses.

Meanwhile, Dr Smith continued to call at the house, sometimes finding Mary Ann comparatively well, sometimes finding her weak and trembling. By 6 October, she was at her weakest, her skin yellow and her fingers shaking so much that she could hardly lift her hand. Mary Ann's teeth had turned black almost at the onset of her illness yet now, when Dr Smith examined her, he noticed a dark blue line on her gums, close to her teeth. Smith instantly recognised the line as being characteristic of lead poisoning and believed that her inability to lift her hand was in fact 'wrist drop', also a known symptom of lead poisoning in its late stages.

Dr Smith ordered Mrs Ellis, his patient's landlady, to take charge of her care and, from then on, Mary Ann's health gradually improved. He also called in another doctor, Dr Sharpe, for a second opinion and, on seeing the blue line, Sharpe agreed that Mary Ann's illness was due to lead poisoning.

By now, the police had done some investigating and had found that Louise Taylor had purchased sugar of lead on a regular basis from a retail shop actually owned by Dr Smith. The first purchase had been made on 4 August 1882, supposedly for an injection for Louise Taylor. As this was at the time a recognised medical use, Mrs Smith, who served as an assistant in the shop, had no qualms about selling it to her. On at least one occasion, Edward Martin had purchased the poison on Louise's behalf.

With Mary Ann apparently fading fast, the police moved quickly to take a deposition from her. On 10 October, Louise Taylor, who had been incarcerated in Clerkenwell Prison on remand for the charge of stealing, was brought to Mary Ann's bedside in order to witness her statement. In the presence of police officers and magistrate Mr Marsham, Mary Ann dictated a deposition to the magistrates' clerk, John Glass Trotter, who wrote down her words and afterwards witnessed her marking it with her cross.

Mary Ann told the officials that Louise had been staying at the house, not as a servant, and that prior to Louise's arrival she had always enjoyed good health. When she became ill, Louise had nursed her and had always given her medicine. However, she had also seen Louise adding white powder to the medicine prescribed by the doctor, which made her very sick when she took it. 'I can't take that. It's nauseous stuff, and as sour as vinegar,' she protested when Louise had given her the medicine, but Louise had insisted she take it.

Once Mary Ann had given her deposition, Sergeant Charles Gillham turned to Louise Taylor and charged her with unlawfully and maliciously administering a certain noxious drug to Mary Ann Tregillis, thereby endangering her life and occasioning her actual bodily harm.

Sugar of lead is an alternative name for lead acetate and is so called because it has a sweet taste. Unfortunately, lead is a cumulative poison and, even though Mary Ann's general health improved, she had ingested too much of the poison for its effects to be reversed. Within a few days of her diagnosis, she slowly became paralysed, eventually dying on 23 October. Dr Sharpe conducted the post-mortem examination, watched by Dr Smith and another doctor. Sharpe found nothing of note, with the exception of the blue line and a general yellowing of Mary Ann's skin, both of which were characteristic of lead poisoning. Her organs were otherwise healthy and he could find no natural explanation for her death.

At the request of the police, Sharpe removed portions of Mary Ann's brain, lungs, liver and spleen, as well as the whole of her stomach and portions of her intestines, which he sealed in jars and sent to Home Office analyst Thomas Stevenson. Like Sharpe, Stevenson found no signs of any major disease in the organs that he examined. What he did find was lead. Mary Ann's stomach contained nearly half a grain of lead and Stevenson also found a quarter of a grain in her liver, a twentieth of a grain in her brain and traces of lead in her other organs. Having tested the water supply to the house and found no trace of lead whatsoever, Stevenson too came to the conclusion that Mary Ann Tregillis had died as a result of lead poisoning, although he stressed that it was impossible to state with any certainty how long before her death Mary Ann had taken the poison. Still, regardless of when it was ingested, Mary Ann's corpse now contained sufficient lead to poison three people.

An inquest was opened at the Railway Tavern at Plumstead before coroner Mr E.A. Cartier. On 22 November 1882, the coroner's jury returned a verdict of 'wilful murder' against Louise Taylor, who was tried at the Old Bailey before Mr Justice Stephen. Mr Poland and Mr Montagu Williams prosecuted the case and Mr Walton and Mr White defended.

The court first heard from William Tregillis, after which medical witnesses, police officers and other key witnesses such as landlady Sarah Ellis, Edward Martin and the friends and neighbours who had visited Mary Ann during her final illness took the witness stand.

The defence counsel strongly objected to the admittance of Mary Ann's deposition as evidence by the prosecution on the grounds that the magistrate had not signed it at the time at which it was taken but had instead signed it a few days later. Both counsels for the prosecution and defence cited numerous historic cases, which they believed had set a precedent supporting their argument, but eventually the judge ruled that the deposition was admissible and it was read out in court.

The defence made much of Louise Taylor's previous good character, informing the jury that this was the first time that '…the hand of accusation had been raised against her'. On the other hand, while he did not wish to make any accusations about an old man, William Tregillis had once been a patient in a lunatic asylum and, while in court he had given some evidence that had subsequently been proved to be incorrect. The defence counsel stopped short of accusing Tregillis of lying but suggested to the jury that, in view of his age, he may have become confused and given his wife the sugar of lead intended for Louise Taylor's injection rather than her own medicine.

The medical evidence was '…pregnant with matters which required explanation and raised doubts,' said Mr Walton. If Louise Taylor really had intended to poison Mary Ann, would she have mixed her concoctions in full view of her victim? And what was her motive? Could it really be possible that

Mr Montagu Williams QC, as illustrated in the Illustrated London News. *(Author's collection)*

Louise Taylor wished to dispatch Mary Ann Tregillis in order to marry her husband, a man with no means and with one foot in the grave?

In his summary for the jury, Mr Justice Stephen suggested that they must decide whether or not they believed that Mary Ann had taken the poison in one single dose. If they did, then much of the prosecution's evidence was weakened. He reminded them that several witnesses had testified that Louise always seemed to treat Mary Ann kindly throughout her illness and a crime such as that outlined by the prosecution involved deceit, treachery and hypocrisy, making the kindness apparently shown by the prisoner ambiguous to say the least. Was it real kindness, in which case the prisoner could not have committed the crime, or pretended kindness, designed to divert suspicion? The fact that the prisoner had sent for the doctor and had openly purchased the sugar of lead were points in her favour.

Thus, the jury should first decide whether they believed that Mary Ann had died from lead poisoning. If they did, they must ask themselves by whom it was administered. The evidence suggested that the prisoner had the means of administering poison to the deceased woman and, if she had indeed administered it in frequent doses, then it must have been done with the intention of taking life. This, said the judge, was a case of murder or nothing, with no element of manslaughter. The prosecution had suggested that Louise Taylor was in financial trouble and, if she could persuade William Tregillis to marry her, she would benefit from his regular pension for the rest of his life. Although this was a paltry amount, if a person were capable of murder, then he or she might easily kill for a small sum of money as well as a larger one.

The jury retired for just twenty minutes, returning with a verdict of 'Guilty'.

Asked if she had anything to say, Louise simply replied, 'I am not guilty.' Her statement did not prevent the judge from passing the death sentence and she was executed by William Marwood at Maidstone on 2 January 1883.

Note: In some accounts of the murder in contemporary newspapers, the name Tregillis is alternatively spelled Tregellis, Louise Taylor is also named as Louisa and Dr Sharpe is referred to as Dr Sharps.

14

'Can they tell if she has had mouse powder?'

Mary Ann Britland lived at Turner Lane, Ashton-under-Lyne with her husband, Thomas, and their teenage daughter, Elizabeth. Elizabeth worked in a local factory and her younger sister, Susannah, had already left home to go into service. Early in 1886, Thomas Dixon, his wife Mary, and Mary's parents, moved into a cottage about a hundred yards away from the Britlands' home. Before long, an intimate relationship developed between Thomas Dixon and Mary Ann Britland, with Dixon apparently sufficiently attracted to his neighbour to try to persuade Mary Ann to leave her family and go away with him.

Stamford Street, Ashton-under-Lyne, 1911. (Author's collection)

On 8 March, Elizabeth Britland was suddenly taken ill. Dr Thompson, the Ashton surgeon, was called in on the following day and found nineteen-year-old Elizabeth resting in bed, looking pale and complaining of pain in her right-hand side.

Thompson asked Elizabeth if she had eaten anything that had disagreed with her and Elizabeth told him that, as far as she was aware, she had not. She also told him that she had not been sick, although her mother reported that she had been vomiting and purging violently. Dr Thompson left a prescription for belladonna and colocynth but was called back to the house at three o'clock in the afternoon by Mary Ann, who told the doctor that Elizabeth had suffered a fit.

The doctor asked Elizabeth how she felt and the girl continued to complain of pain in her stomach, now saying that she felt a choking sensation in her throat. Thompson prescribed a homeopathic remedy of acacia. He returned to the cottage at nine o'clock that evening to check on his patient but found on his arrival that Elizabeth had just died.

Mary Ann Britland had bought a packet of powder to kill mice from a nearby chemist's shop on 8 March, although her purchase was not made until after her daughter was taken ill. On 9 March, shortly before the doctor was called back for the second time, Mary Ann visited her neighbour, grocer Mr Fielding Oldfield, who was also the Britlands' landlord.

'Oh, do come in and look at our little girl, she looks very funny,' Mary Ann asked Mr Oldfield, who immediately went into the house with his wife. Entering Elizabeth's bedroom, he described the sick girl as appearing 'composed' but breathing heavily. He had returned at between five and six o'clock that evening to find that the she was now very restless and complaining of pains in her legs and left side. Mrs Britland and Mrs Dixon were both present and were rubbing Elizabeth's legs to try and ease her discomfort.

Oldfield went back to the house again at about eight o'clock, taking with him some linseed meal, which he and Mr Britland heated and prepared into a poultice. At that time he didn't see Elizabeth, who was to die within the hour.

After his daughter's death, Thomas Britland turned to alcohol for comfort. Although his drinking was not seen as a major problem, it was widely agreed among his acquaintances that he 'took more drink than he ought to'. Britland still managed to work long hours as a carter and his employers complained on just one occasion about his over indulgence.

On the evening of Friday 30 April 1886, forty-four-year-old Britland was at his workplace, Heath's Vaults in Ashton, cleaning the harness ready for the following day. He finished the task and left to go home at about ten minutes past nine in the evening, at which time, according to his colleague, James Marsden, he was in his normal good health. At a quarter to seven the next morning, Marsden was in bed when he heard knocking at his door.

His wife shouted down to the caller, who identified herself as Mary Ann Britland.

Mary Ann told the Marsdens that Tom had been taken ill overnight and would not be well enough to go to work that morning. Marsden suggested that she called a doctor and Mary Ann replied that she would. James Marsden called on the Britlands on the following Monday to see how Thomas was. He found him lying in bed, complaining of pains in his legs. As Marsden and Thomas Britland chatted, Britland suddenly began to fit, his legs jerking convulsively and his fists clenching tightly. Within minutes, the fit had passed and Thomas was sufficiently recovered to ask Marsden about the horse he usually drove at work.

A number of neighbours were milling around Britland's bedroom, all trying to help. They included Thomas Dixon, whom Mary Ann Britland had apparently summoned from his work when her husband fell ill. Soon, Thomas Britland was fading in and out of consciousness, his waking moments punctuated by violent attacks of shaking and convulsions, after which he seemed lucid and able to converse with his visitors, asking them time and time again to rub his legs. Someone suggested that he should be given brandy and a bottle was fetched. Given a teaspoonful by a neighbour, Britland immediately began to foam at the mouth but then appeared a little better.

By four o'clock that afternoon, Britland was perspiring freely and breathing heavily, seemingly unaware of his surroundings. Thomas Dixon visited him again and suggested that he should be given more brandy. Once again, the brandy seemed to revive him and when his wife asked him, 'Tom, do you know me?' he nodded in assent.

At seven o'clock Britland was conscious, although his body was still twitching uncontrollably and he was complaining of severe cramp-like pain in his legs and feet. By eleven o'clock, Dixon thought that Britland appeared much better – it was to be the last time he would see his neighbour alive.

Once again, Mary Ann Britland had visited the chemist's shop, buying a different brand of mouse poison on 30 April and a further three packets on 3 May, her visits recorded in the shop's Poisons Register. On the latter occasion, neighbour William Waterhouse accompanied her, acting as her witness to the purchase. Waterhouse jokingly remarked, 'Now, missis, administer them scientifically, not in too large doses and then you'll secure the club money,' to which Mary Ann replied, 'Nay, master, if you think I would do anything of that sort, may God forgive you.' Even though Waterhouse was joking, Mary Ann had actually received cash payments on the death of both her daughter and her husband. Elizabeth's life had been insured with the Prudential Assurance Company for £10, while Thomas had an insurance policy for £11 7s, as well as £8 of club money with the Society of Odd Fellows, both of which were paid to his widow on 4 May.

After the death of her husband, Mary Ann Britland immediately went to live with the Dixons, a situation that suggests that Mary Dixon was blissfully unaware of any illicit relationship between her husband and the recent widow. On 13 May, Mary Dixon and Mary Ann Britland went out together, returning at twenty past ten at night, after which they sat down to supper. Mary Dixon cooked the meal herself and everyone else in the house ate the same food, but by midnight Mary Dixon was complaining of agonising stomach pains.

Hot flannels were applied to her stomach and Mary Ann made her a cup of tea but neither brought her any relief and the doctor was called at one o'clock. By now, Mary Dixon was experiencing fits of violent twitching every few minutes. The doctor left medicine for her but she died the following morning. In view of the suddenness of her death, it was necessary to hold a post-mortem examination, the very thought of which seemed to send Mary Ann into a state of near panic.

When neighbours called at the Dixon's house to pay their respects, Mary Ann showed them the body, asking them if they thought Mary Dixon had been poisoned. John Lord told Mary Ann that he had once seen someone who had been poisoned and that the man had swollen up and turned black. This seemed to reassure Mary Ann, although she was soon asking more questions. 'Can they tell if she has been poisoned?' she asked Lord several times. 'Can they tell mouse powder? Can they tell if she had it in her tea?' She eventually admitted to Lord that she had recently bought poison in the village but that she had not told Tom Dixon about her purchase.

Lord advised her to tell him straight away and when Mary Ann refused to do so, he called Tom into the room and told him himself. Tom Dixon immediately crossed the room and threw himself on his wife's body. 'If anyone has given you poison, do tell me,' he beseeched his dead wife. After a few moments, he recovered himself and asked Mr Lord not to mention poison to anyone else. 'It is through you they are having the post-mortem,' Mary Ann told Dixon. 'You ought to stop them.'

Mary Ann continued to fret right up until the time of the post-mortem, when she watched the doctors preparing to examine Mary Dixon's body. Seeing them taking a number of jars into the room, she asked Tom Dixon's mother what they were for. Mrs Dixon senior explained that they were to take away the contents of the dead woman's stomach.

'Can they tell if she has had mouse powder?' Mary Ann asked and when Mrs Dixon said yes, she persisted, 'But can they if she had it in tea? If she drunk as much tea as she had?'

The post-mortem examination was conducted by Dr Hamilton, who took portions of Mary's stomach and intestines for testing, exactly as Mrs Dixon had forecast. The samples were sent to analytical chemist Mr Charles Estcourt, who found on testing them that they contained one-tenth of a grain of strychnine and one-thirtieth of a grain of arsenic. Estcourt fed a tiny portion of the samples to a mouse, which died within two minutes. He concluded that Mary Dixon had been poisoned by strychnine and that the amount of poison found in her body was only a small proportion of the quantity she had actually taken.

Given Mary Ann Britland's concerns about the post-mortem examination, her accessibility to the victim and the rumours of her affair with the victim's husband, she was an obvious suspect, particularly as she had suffered a further two bereavements within the last two months. She was arrested on 25 May 1886 and charged with the wilful murder of Mary Dixon, and, not only that, but the police also applied to the Home Secretary to exhume the bodies of her husband and daughter.

Surgeon Thomas Harrison first conducted a post-mortem on the remains of Thomas Britland. Harrison found no evidence of any illness and no signs of any damage caused by excessive drinking. Britland's stomach and intestines seemed well preserved, which is characteristic of poisoning by arsenic and, when Mr Estcourt tested the contents of both organs, he detected one-tenth of a grain. Elizabeth's remains also contained arsenic, this time one-twentieth of a grain. Even though no strychnine was found in the bodies of either of the Britlands, on hearing a description of their symptoms, Mr Julius Dreschfield, the Professor of Pathology at Victoria University, determined that both had died from strychnine poisoning.

Initially, Tom Dixon had also been taken into custody, suspected of the murder of his wife, but had been released due to lack of any real evidence against him. Thus, Mary Ann Britland was left to stand trial alone. She appeared at the Manchester Assizes before Mr Justice Cave on 22 July 1886. Mr Addison QC and Mr Woodard prosecuted, while Mary Ann was defended by Mr Blair and Mr Byrne.

Manchester Assize Courts, early 1900s. (Author's collection)

Although Mary Ann Britland was charged only with the murder of Mary Dixon, the prosecution first detailed the deaths of Elizabeth and Thomas Britland, calling chemist's assistants William Arden and William Greenhalgh, as well as witness William Waterhouse, to testify to the fact that Mary Ann had purchased packets of vermin killer at around the time they died. Insurance agents David Niel and Richard Mortimer told the court that Mary Ann had received insurance payments for both her husband and daughter on their deaths.

As proof of the relationship believed to exist between Mary Ann Britland and Thomas Dixon, the prosecution called John Butterworth, a hatter, who had sold a hat to Thomas Britland shortly before he died. Two months later, Thomas Dixon had brought the hat back, asking if it could be changed for one that would fit him.

The court was told of Mary Ann's ill-concealed panic when she learned that there was to be a post-mortem examination on the remains of Mary Dixon and of her admission to John Lord that she had bought poison. The prosecution then called the medical witnesses, who spoke of the symptoms of all three of the alleged victims, their treatment and the results of the post-mortem examinations and analysis of their remains. As well as testing the victims' stomach contents, Mr Estcourt had also tested the two different brands of vermin killer that Mary Ann had purchased. He had found Hunter's brand to contain strychnine but no arsenic, while Harrison's Vermin Powder – the first purchased brand – contained both.

Although Mary Ann's defence lawyers called no witnesses for the defence, Mr Blair cross-examined all of the prosecution witnesses. Susannah Britland, who did not live at home, told the court that her parents had always lived together on excellent terms and treated both her and her sister with great kindness. Their neighbour and landlord, Fielding Oldfield, who had known the family for about eight years, echoed this view of the Britlands and testified that Thomas and Mary Ann were of good character and were always affectionate with each other and kind to their children.

Oldfield revealed that previous tenants of the Britlands' cottage had complained of an infestation of mice and that Mary Ann herself had approached him about the problem in the month before her daughter's death. He had advised her to get a cat but Mary Ann told him that Tom wouldn't allow her to as he had a canary. Thus it had been Oldfield who had first suggested that Mary Ann should purchase poison. However, Mary Ann Talent, who had helped Mary Ann Dixon clean her entire house from top to bottom in preparation for Tom's funeral, testified that she had seen neither any signs of mice, nor any mouse poison at the house.

The defence team did not challenge the medical evidence but focused instead on questioning how Mary Ann had administered the poison to her victims. Given that Mary Ann had seemed preoccupied with whether or not poison could be detected in tea and that she was known to have made some for Mary Dixon shortly before her death, it was generally assumed that the poison had been administered in a drink.

Dr Harrison had carried out some experiments with tea and strychnine and found that, even when the tea was sweetened with sugar, the addition of one single grain of strychnine to a quart of tea produced a bitter, foul tasting mixture. Harrison told the court that the taste was worse if the tea was drunk on its own, without any food to accompany it, although he conceded that an unsuspecting person might drink half a grain of strychnine in a pint of tea, which would constitute a fatal dose. However, strychnine was not readily soluble and if mouse powder had been added to the tea it was probable that a good deal of it would simply have floated on the surface. In addition, both brands of the mouse-killing powder known to have been purchased by Mary Ann Britland were coloured ultramarine blue and would cause the tea to change colour.

One of the last witnesses to testify was Ashton policeman Sergeant Joseph Nightingale. He told the court that he had been transporting Mary Ann from Strangeways Prison to Ashton for a hearing at the magistrates' court, when Mary Ann asked him if he thought that Thomas Dixon, who was in custody at the time, would be freed that day. When Nightingale told her that he didn't know but that some people believed that Dixon would 'get off', Mary Ann said indignantly that Dixon had no right to get off and would not do so if she could speak her mind. 'He ought to have been locked up all the time, the same as me,' she continued. 'It was him as led me into it.'

According to Mary Ann, Dixon had offered to run away with her before her arrest and had also said that he would go away with her when all the 'bother' was over. Mary Ann had refused. 'I have nothing to go away for. If I go away, people will think I am guilty whether I am or not.'

Once the prosecution and defence counsels and the judge had summed up the evidence, the jury retired to consider their verdict. It took four hours of deliberation for them to return with a verdict of 'Guilty', leaving the judge to pass sentence of death on Mary Ann Britland, who was executed at Strangeways Prison by James Berry on 9 August 1886.

Quite how she managed to persuade Mary Dixon to drink a poisoned cup of blue-tinted, bitter-tasting tea with a powdery topping was never satisfactorily explained.

15
'Oh, mama, I cannot drink it'

By 1887, thirty-one-year-old Elizabeth Berry had been a widow for five years. She had lost an infant son, who died while teething and, fourteen months after the death of her husband, Thomas, Elizabeth suffered yet another tragedy when a second son died, supposedly from an illness resulting from sleeping in a damp bed. Elizabeth was left with one surviving daughter, Edith, who was usually known by her middle name of Annie.

In July 1886, Elizabeth took a job as a nurse in the Infirmary at Oldham Workhouse, while her sister-in-law, Mrs Ann Saunderson, looked after Annie. Elizabeth paid Mrs Saunderson three shillings a week for the child's keep, with an additional seven pence a week for her schooling and insurance, as well as extra money for clothes and other necessities, a total sum that accounted for almost half of her annual wage of £25.

On 27 December 1886, Elizabeth went to visit Annie at Mrs Saunderson's home at Miles Platting. When she left on 29 December, Annie accompanied her back to the workhouse, along with another child, Beatrice Hall, who was a school friend of Annie's. The two girls spent the next couple of days playing around the workhouse and in Elizabeth's sitting room at the Infirmary, which was situated next to the surgery. The drugs used by the doctors and nurses were housed in the surgery, which was usually kept locked, although like all of the nurses, Elizabeth had a key to the door. Although the poisons were kept in a locked cupboard, there were plenty of substances within easy reach of a child that could be described as lethal.

On 1 January, Annie was seen in the surgery with her mother, who had a tumbler in her hand and was trying to persuade her daughter to drink the contents. Annie was heard protesting, 'Oh, mama, I cannot drink it,' and half an hour later she began to vomit. She continued to vomit at roughly five-minute intervals and before long the vomit contained streaks of blood.

The Infirmary at Oldham Workhouse, later renamed Boundary Park. (Author's collection)

The workhouse surgeon, Dr Patterson, was summoned and he put Annie to bed in her mother's room, giving her a mixture of iron and quinine. Annie continued to vomit throughout the day and, when Patterson saw her again at ten o'clock that evening, she was no better. Elizabeth declined offers of help nursing her child, saying that she intended to sit up all night with her and when Dr Patterson saw Annie again the following morning, she seemed better. Patterson reassured Elizabeth, saying that there was every chance that her daughter would make a full recovery. He wrote another prescription for more medicine and left promising to return later that day.

At two o'clock in the afternoon, Patterson noticed that Annie had a blister on her upper lip, which her mother explained by telling the doctor that she had given the child an orange and some sugar and that the orange had most probably caused the blister. By nine o'clock that evening, Annie was worse than ever. The blister had grown in size and the child was retching every few minutes and complaining of pain in her abdomen.

Patterson noticed a strong smell of acid in the room and began to suspect that Annie might have taken some corrosive substance. He called in another doctor, Dr Robinson, and the two men agreed to treat Annie with a mixture of morphia and bismuth, although both instinctively felt that any treatment at all would be futile. Annie's condition continued to deteriorate and Elizabeth sent an urgent telegram to Ann Saunderson, which read: 'Come at once: Annie is dying'. Mrs Saunderson and her husband rushed to the child's bedside and, when they arrived, they naturally asked her mother what had happened. Elizabeth told them that Annie had eaten too hearty a meal and was suffering from 'a stoppage of the bowels'.

Edith Annie Berry died at five o'clock on the morning of 4 January 1887, aged eleven years and eight months. 'I shall want a certificate of death,' Elizabeth told Dr Patterson, who was somewhat unsure of what to record as the cause of death. He asked Elizabeth's permission to carry out a post-mortem examination on her daughter and Elizabeth consented. When Patterson asked if Annie were insured, Elizabeth told him that she wasn't and that all the funeral expenses would have to come out of her pocket.

A post-mortem examination was carried out but although the child's organs were tested, no trace of any poison could be found and, aside from the blister on her lips, some whitening of her mouth and gums and some reddening, bleeding and slight corrosion of her intestines and stomach lining, there was very little to indicate what had caused Annie's death. No natural explanation presented itself and the doctors eventually concluded that Annie had died from drinking a corrosive, irritant poison, which had been ejected from her body by her constant vomiting. Although no trace of it was found in Annie's body, it was thought that sulphuric acid was the most likely culprit.

Elizabeth was arrested and charged on suspicion of causing the death of her daughter and held in custody pending the results of further analysis on Annie's remains. These proved inconclusive, as, although Annie's symptoms and the condition of her stomach were consistent with her drinking a corrosive liquid of some kind, analyst Mr Estcourt could find no trace of any poison remaining in her body. Dr Harris, a lecturer on pathology at Manchester University, confirmed his findings.

Elizabeth Berry was committed for trial at Liverpool, charged with the wilful murder of her daughter. Mr Justice Hawkins presided over the trial, with Mr McConnell and Mr F.H. Mellor prosecuting and Mr Cottingham and Mr T.F. Byrne defending. Elizabeth pleaded 'Not Guilty'.

The prosecution outlined the facts of the case and called a number of witnesses who testified that, on the morning of 1 January 1887, Annie Berry had initially been in excellent health. Several people then testified to seeing Annie in the surgery with her mother. Workhouse inmate Ann Dillon had seen mother and daughter in the surgery, then, thirty minutes later, had seen Elizabeth trying to persuade Annie to drink some milky white fluid from a tumbler. After Annie's death, Elizabeth had seemed upset to think that people suspected her of poisoning her daughter and Ann Dillon had asked her directly if she had given the child anything. 'Nothing but a "selditz" powder, which you saw me give her in the living room,' replied Elizabeth.

Beatrice Hall, the child who had accompanied Annie on her visit to Oldham, had also seen Elizabeth giving Annie a white powder, while another inmate, Ellen Thompson, told the court that, after Dr Patterson had called and prescribed medicine for the sick child, Elizabeth had not given it to her

Mr Justice Hawkins, as illustrated in the Illustrated London News. *(Author's collection)*

daughter. When Ellen remonstrated with her about this, Elizabeth said that she did not want to punish her daughter and that she would tip some of the medicine away so the doctor wouldn't know it hadn't been given according to his instructions.

Although Elizabeth had insisted that Annie hadn't been insured, the prosecution called James Pickford of the National Sick and Burial Association, who stated that the child had been insured for the sum of £10. Another insurance agent, Harry Jackson of the Prudential, told the court that in April 1886, Elizabeth had approached him for what was known as a mutual policy. The policy would have covered both her life and that of her daughter and, in the event of the death of one of the policyholders, the sum assured of £100 would have been paid to the survivor. In the event, the policy was never taken out although, at the time of Annie's death, Elizabeth was not thought to be aware of this.

The medical witnesses testified to their treatment of Annie and their findings at post-mortem. All were of the opinion that Annie had ingested some kind of corrosive poison, most probably sulphuric acid, and that the reason none was found after her death was that it had either been absorbed by her body or ejected by her violent vomiting. The defence counsel did manage to coax an admission from Dr Patterson that the sulphuric acid in the workhouse surgery was quite a weak solution and probably best described as an irritant rather than a corrosive substance.

The defence counsel then called analytical chemist Mr William Thompson, who disagreed with the evidence of the other medical witnesses. Based on experiments he had conducted, he told the court that, had Annie Berry been poisoned with sulphuric acid, he would have expected to see blisters similar to that on her lips on the inside of her mouth, throat and gullet. Not only that but he would expect to be able to find traces of sulphuric acid in Annie's body for several weeks after her death, even though she had been violently vomiting.

Annie was known to have vomited on a carpet and a towel and Dr Patterson had already testified that he had smelled acid both on a towel and in Elizabeth's bedroom. Thompson maintained that, had vomit containing sulphuric acid come into contact with a carpet then much of the colour would have been destroyed. He would also have expected the vomit to burn holes in the towel. The ingestion of sulphuric acid would also cause intense pain in the mouth, something of which Annie had never complained. Thompson suggested that creosote might conceivably have produced Annie's symptoms; a substance known to have been medicinally used as a disinfectant, a laxative and a cough treatment.

Under cross-examination by the counsel for the prosecution, Thompson acknowledged that he had never actually seen Annie's remains but that he was basing his conclusions on his personal examination of the viscera of someone who had died from sulphuric acid poisoning fifteen or so years earlier.

Mr Cottingham then addressed the court on behalf of the defence. He pointed out Elizabeth Berry's hitherto unblemished character and questioned what possible motive she could have had for killing her own child. There were two sides to the proof of poisoning, said Cottingham. The first of these were the symptoms shown before death, which largely depended on the testimony of Dr Patterson and Dr Robinson, and Cottingham asked the jury to consider Patterson's conduct in the case. When did he first suspect that Annie had been poisoned? Was it from the very first, in which case he gave no treatment for poisoning? Annie's condition had improved overnight and, on the following morning, he had told her mother that he believed the child would make a full recovery. Yet he had still not treated the child for suspected poisoning, nor had he taken any steps to ensure that any foul play was not repeated. Was this behaviour consistent with that of a doctor who suspected that a child's life had been tampered with? If Patterson believed that the child's mother was the culprit, how could he have left the child in her charge, knowing that she had easy access to a room full of poisonous substances?

How could a corrosive poison have entered the child's body without leaving blisters on the mouth, throat and gullet, only to disappear without a trace? Cottingham reminded the jury that not a trace of sulphuric acid had ever been found and that Elizabeth had consented to the post-mortem examination being performed. Annie's father had died from emaciation after a two-year illness and her brother had died from a disease of the bowels and lungs, having shown similar symptoms to Annie's. For two days before her death, Annie and Beatrice had been given free rein to wander around Oldham buying and eating chocolates and sweets, which could undoubtedly prove injurious to someone with a stomach disorder.

If Elizabeth Berry had intended to poison her daughter, why had she invited another child to accompany her on her visit to Oldham? During her stay, Annie had written to her aunt, Mrs Saunderson, and the contents of that letter demonstrated the affection between mother and daughter. Finally, what was Elizabeth's motive for the murder? It could hardly be financial since Elizabeth was earning a good wage and the payment of Annie's board was no real burden on her. If, as the prosecution suggested, the insurance money had been the motive, then the £10 Elizabeth received on her daughter's death would barely have covered the child's funeral expenses.

After listening to the judge's summary of the evidence, the jury retired for just over ten minutes before returning to pronounce Elizabeth Berry 'Guilty' of the wilful murder of her daughter. Asked by the judge if she had anything to say before sentence was passed, Elizabeth calmly rose to her feet and said, 'I may be charged but the whole world cannot make me guilty.'

Elizabeth Berry became the first ever person to be hanged at Walton Gaol on 14 March 1887. She maintained her innocence until the very end, telling the prison chaplain Revd David Morris that, if Annie had in fact been poisoned, it must have been by creosote, which she believed had been prescribed for her daughter by Dr Patterson. However, according to the prison governor, she had also petitioned the Home Secretary for her life, saying that if she had poisoned her daughter then she must have been insane at the time. Nevertheless, her last words were said to have been, 'May God forgive Dr Patterson.'

James Berry carried out the execution and there is anecdotal evidence that he may have met Elizabeth previously at a dance and that the two were instantly enamoured with each other. It was also rumoured that Elizabeth Berry murdered her husband, two sons and her mother.

Note: In contemporary newspaper accounts of the case, the doctor who consulted with Dr Patterson on Annie's illness is sometimes named as Dr Robinson and in others Dr Robertson.

16

'I will not die with a lie on my lips'

On 28 June 1887, Polish Jew Isaac Angel got up at six o'clock to go to his work as a boot riveter in Spitalfields. His twenty-two-year-old wife, Miriam, who was six months pregnant, watched as he said his morning prayers, then the couple talked for a few moments before Isaac left their lodgings in Batty Street, Whitechapel. He pulled the door to the bedroom closed as he left but didn't lock it, since the key was already in the lock on the inside of the room.

It was Miriam's habit to go to her mother-in-law's house for breakfast every morning, usually arriving between half-past eight and nine o'clock. When she didn't arrive on 25 July, Dinah Angel waited until late morning before setting off for Batty Street to check on her daughter-in-law. None of the other tenants in the house had either seen or heard anything of Miriam that day and she did not respond to knocks on the bedroom door, which was now locked. Another tenant, Mrs Leah Levy, managed to look through a small window into the bedroom and saw Miriam lying on the bed. 'Perhaps she is fainting,' suggested Mrs Angel senior. The two women managed to force the bedroom door and rushed across to where Miriam lay motionless on the bed. Sadly, it was quickly apparent that the young woman had not just fainted but was dead.

Both women screamed and suddenly people were rushing from all corners of the house and even the street outside to see what all the commotion was about. One of the first to arrive was general dealer and shopkeeper Harris Dywein, who met Dinah Angel rushing down the stairs, desperately looking for someone to help her.

Dywein ran to the bedroom, where Miriam lay on her back on the bed, her nightdress pulled up over her breasts and her heavily pregnant belly exposed. Dywein pulled the bedclothes up over the woman to preserve her modesty then barely had enough time to notice the marks on her face before William Piper came into the room. Piper was the assistant to the local surgeon, Dr John Kay, and, on his arrival, he established that the young woman was dead and then cleared the room of all bystanders and locked the door behind him. Dr Kay arrived about ten minutes later and immediately went to examine the dead woman.

Miriam's hair was dishevelled and her body was not quite cold, with no onset of *rigor mortis*. Dr Kay noticed a yellowish stain on the side of Miriam's mouth. Her hands were similarly stained and there were a couple of yellow splashes on her neck and breast. Dr Kay pulled down the bedclothes to see if there were any other injuries and noticed a few spots of blood and some small acid burns on the feather mattress.

Dr Kay immediately concluded that Miriam had died as a result of drinking nitric acid, otherwise known as aqua fortis. With the help of Mr Piper and Mr Dywein, he began to search the bedroom for a bottle that might have contained the acid but, although there was a half empty glass of beer on the bedside table, he could see no bottle. Eventually, he pulled the bed away from the wall slightly and, as he did, he revealed a man lying beneath it.

The man was in his shirtsleeves, his eyes half closed. Dr Kay felt for a pulse and, to his surprise, the man was still alive, although unconscious. The police had already been called to the house and Dr Kay asked them to help him remove the man from under the bed. Once he had been pulled from his hiding place, it was obvious to Dr Kay that he too had drunk nitric acid, since his face, shirt and hands bore the same characteristic yellow stains as those on Miriam's body.

PC Arthur Sack dragged the man to his feet, although he fell over straight away and had to be pulled upright again. Although unsteady on his feet, the man now seemed to be semi-conscious. He obviously was not in too much pain but, even though Dr Kay spoke to him in both English and German, he made no response.

The man was taken by cab first to Dr Kay's surgery and then to Leman Street police station, where Inspector David Final tried to rouse him, first by slapping his face, then by poking a finger in the man's eye. Police surgeon, Mr Phillips, was summoned and he ordered a draught of mustard and water to try and make the prisoner vomit. When this didn't work, he was sent to the London Hospital and placed under police guard.

Doctors noted yellow staining on the man's fingers, as well as some slight scratches on the backs of his hands, forearms and face. The inside of his mouth and throat had some white patches, consistent with the ingestion of corrosive fluid and there was an abrasion at the back of his mouth, as though something had been violently thrust into it, although doctors believed that this had been caused by the stomach pump used at the hospital to rid him of the poison he had taken.

Meanwhile, PC Alfred Inwood had been searching the bedroom at Batty Street and had found a man's hat and coat, along with a small empty bottle, the interior of which smelled unmistakably of acid. In the pocket of the coat was a card bearing the words 'J. Lipski, United Stick and Cane Dressers' Protection Society' and there was also a pawn ticket for a silver watch in the name of 'John Lipski, Merdle Street'.

On the evening of the murder, Inspector Final and Sergeant Thick went to the London Hospital with interpreter Henry Smedge, and questioned the man, who was now completely conscious and sensible. He was twenty-two-year-old Israel Lipski, who was also a tenant at Batty Street, renting the room on the top floor. He had recently adapted his lodgings as a workshop, where he intended to follow his trade as a walking stick maker. Just days earlier, he had employed two men to work under him – Simon Rosenbloom and Richard Pitman.

Lipski told the police that at seven o'clock on the morning of the murder, he had been approached by a man who wanted to work for him. Needing another vice for the man to work at, Lipski told him to wait at the lodgings, and set off to buy one. As it was so early, he had to wait for the shop to open and, when it did, Lipski found the vices too expensive. The shopkeeper wanted four shillings and Lipski offered him three but was turned down. While he was out, another man, Mr Schmusch, asked Lipski for work. Lipski told him to go to his workshop and he would find him some work after breakfast. Schmusch waited for some time but left when Lipski did not return.

Israel Lipski, 1887.

When Lipski finally got back to his lodgings, the first prospective workman was still waiting for him. Lipski gave the man a sovereign and asked him to go and buy some brandy, asking his landlady Leah Lipski (no relation) to fetch some coffee. He then went upstairs but, as he reached the first floor, he saw the workman with Simon Rosenbloom, in the act of opening a box in a bedroom. Realising that they had been seen, the men grabbed Lipski by the throat and forced him to the ground, with the obvious intention of robbing him. When he told them that he had nothing apart from the money he had just handed over for the purchase of brandy, the men made him drink acid. They then knelt on his throat, put a piece of wood in his mouth and pushed him under the bed, leaving him for dead. The next thing he knew was being pulled out by the police.

Asked if he knew the two men, Lipski said that he knew both by sight. One of them was called Simon but he didn't know his surname or where he lived.

A post-mortem examination had been conducted on Miriam Angel by Dr Kay on 29 June. Kay found no signs of violence on the lower part of Miriam's body but noticed that she had a black eye and had received at least four violent blows on her head, possibly from a man's fist. Her mouth and the back of her throat were charred from the acid, some of which had gone into her stomach but most into her lungs. To Kay, this indicated that the acid had been forced into her while she was unconscious as the glottis was open. Had she been awake, this would have closed reflexively, protecting the windpipe from the acid 'going down the wrong way'. Kay estimated that at least half an ounce of nitric acid had gone into Miriam's windpipe, resulting in death within two or three minutes as it swelled and so prevented her from breathing.

Kay believed that the blood on Miriam's mattress had come from her coughing. There was no evidence of recent intercourse and Miriam did not appear to have been sexually assaulted. The doctor had also examined Lipski's coat, which was found at the scene of the murder, and noted that it was extensively marked with acid burns. The bottle from the bedroom had yielded a few drops of nitric acid.

Having conducted interviews in the neighbourhood of Batty Street, the police found a shop manager, Charles Moore, who recalled selling a pennyworth of nitric acid (about an ounce) to a man on the day before the murder. The purchaser said he was a walking stick maker and wanted the acid for staining sticks. He had supplied his own bottle, which Moore filled and corked, warning him that it was poisonous. Moore was taken to the hospital where Lipski was still recovering and, after walking up and down the ward, pointed out Lipski to the police as the man who had bought the poison.

On 2 July, Israel Lipski was charged with the murder of Miriam Angel, responding in German, 'I have not murdered her. I have not done it.'

He was tried before Mr Justice Stephen at the Old Bailey on 25 July 1887, with Mr Poland and Mr Charles Matthews prosecuting and Mr McIntyre QC and Mr Geohegan defending. As most of the participants were either Polish or Russian Jews, who were not fluent in English, the services of an interpreter were used throughout the proceedings.

The prosecution first described the events of 28 June, saying that they believed that Israel Lipski had entered the bedroom with the intention of stealing and that Lipski had used the nitric acid on Miriam then attempted suicide when he realised that he had killed her. Mr Poland dismissed Lipski's statement to the police as 'improbable', since he had spoken to his landlady earlier that morning, asking to borrow five shillings, and was therefore unlikely to have a sovereign to spend on brandy.

They then called a series of witnesses who had been in the house that morning, along with William Piper and Dr Kay, shop manager Charles Moore, and Simon Rosenbloom, who categorically denied any part in Miriam Angel's murder.

The defence could call very few witnesses apart from the mother of Lipski's fiancée of six months. Although Lipski had repeatedly borrowed small sums of money from Anna Lyons and not paid them back, she generously gave him a good character reference, as did his landlady, Leah Lipski. The defence also managed to challenge Charles Moore's identification of Lipski at the hospital, although Moore swore that the fact that Lipski was the only patient in the ward to have a policeman standing by his bed had not affected his certainty in the slightest.

In spite of the best efforts of the defence, it was an open and shut case and the only possible result was that Israel Lipski was found guilty of the wilful murder of Miriam Angel and sentenced to death. However, as the date of his execution approached, Lipski's solicitors announced that they had new evidence. They had already made strenuous efforts to gain a reprieve for their client and now secured an interview with the Home Secretary at the House of Commons, after which it was announced that there would be a temporary respite for Lipski while the new evidence was considered.

It came from a chemist who remembered selling two ounces of nitric acid to a 'foreign Jew' just before the murder. The chemist described the bottle the man had brought with him, the details of which precisely matched the one found in the bedroom. He also gave an exact description of the purchaser as a rather square-built, dark man with dark brown hair – Israel Lipski was slightly built, with fair hair and a light complexion. Yet, having considered the new evidence, the Home Secretary still saw no reason for interfering with the due course of the law.

In the condemned cell at Newgate Prison, Lipski was suffering from a guilty conscience and, on the eve of his execution, he made a full confession to Mr E.S. Milman, the prison governor. 'I will not die with a lie on my lips,' he began. 'I will not let others suffer, even on suspicion, for my sin.'

Newgate Prison, 1905. (Author's collection)

Lipski stated that he had been feeling very depressed at the time of the murder and had purchased a bottle of nitric acid with the intention of committing suicide. Knowing that he owed money to his fiancée's mother and others, he had entered the Angels' room thinking that they had money there. Miriam had woken up while he was searching the room and had cried out. In order to silence her, he had hit her on the head and then thought of the nitric acid he was carrying in his pocket. Having poured some into her mouth and realised that she was dead, he had taken the rest himself. Lipski swore that he had never entertained any intentions of violating Miriam Angel.

As Dr Kay had suspected, Lipski had not taken sufficient acid to render him unconscious but had merely fainted from fear when people had burst into the room and he realised that he was bound to be discovered.

Lipski insisted that he had been alone and apologised to Simon Rosenbloom and Mr Schmusch for trying to implicate them in the murder. He also begged the forgiveness of Isaac Angel and acknowledged that his trial had been a fair one, thanking his solicitor for all of his efforts.

Israel Lipski was executed by James Berry at Newgate Prison on 22 August 1887. Unlike many condemned prisoners, who die protesting their innocence, having heard the recitation of the Hebrew prayer for the dying on the scaffold, Lipski died acknowledging his guilt.

17

'But all doctors are fools'

LIVERPOOL, 1889

E ven the death of an elderly recluse on 23 October 1941 at her home in South Kent, Connecticut, could not end the controversy that had been a defining feature of her life since her teenage years. Once a woman of some means, Florence Chandler died in poverty, alone apart from the colony of stray cats she had spent her final years nurturing. Among her pathetically few personal effects was a family Bible in which was hidden a handwritten scrap of paper bearing an old recipe for a cosmetic face wash. It was this handwritten note that had apparently been the catalyst for much of the strife that had dogged Florence's entire adult life.

Florence Elizabeth Chandler was born on 2 September 1862 in Mobile, Alabama. At the age of eighteen she met and quickly married a forty-two-year-old man, James Maybrick, who worked as a cotton trader in Liverpool. The newlyweds lived in Virginia before moving to Liverpool in 1884, where the prosperous Maybrick purchased Battlecrease House in the suburb of Aigburth and employed a number of staff including a cook, two housemaids, a nurse for the couple's son and daughter and a gardener.

The marriage was far from happy. James Maybrick was a hypochondriac who persistently dosed himself with quack remedies to counter a series of illnesses, both real and imagined. He kept Florence short of money and she was soon in debt with many of the local tradesmen. Worse still, he had a mistress.

When Florence found out about his longstanding affair in 1887 she turned to one of Maybrick's friends for comfort, beginning an intrigue of her own with Alfred Brierly. In March 1889, she contrived to spend a week at a London hotel with her lover, telling her husband that she was planning to care for an aunt who needed an operation. Yet shortly after their arrival at the hotel, Brierly confessed to Florence that he was in love with another woman and Florence immediately ended their relationship. Having spent the rest of the week staying with friends, Florence returned home to her husband on 28 March.

Liver Buildings, Liverpool. (Author's collection)

The following day marked the running of the Grand National at Aintree Racecourse and Florence accompanied her husband to watch the racing. Once there, she bumped into Alfred Brierly and walked around with him for some time, much to the annoyance of James, who believed that Florence was showing him up in front of his friends. The Maybricks left the race meeting separately and, when they met at home later that evening, a furious row ensued, culminating in James lashing out at his wife and giving her a black eye.

The next day Florence went to visit the family doctor, Dr Arthur Hopper, complaining of feeling unwell. When Hopper commented on her black eye, Florence told him that her husband had hit her and that she wanted a divorce. The doctor took it upon himself to try and mediate between the Maybricks and eventually James agreed to pay off his wife's housekeeping debts and the couple appeared reconciled.

On 27 April, James Maybrick complained of feeling sick and retired to his bed. Florence told the staff that he had taken an overdose of the medicine prescribed for him by his doctor but seemed unconcerned by her husband's illness. The following morning, when Maybrick was still unwell, she prepared a mixture of mustard and hot water to induce him to vomit and called out the doctor, who diagnosed dyspepsia.

Maybrick remained ill in bed for a further two days, after which he was sufficiently recovered to go back to his work. However, just three days later, he took to his bed again, complaining of a return of the sickness.

Once again, his wife seemed unconcerned by his illness, and, when Alice Yapp, the children's nurse, suggested that she should call a doctor, Florence told her that Mr Maybrick was already under the care of Dr Humphreys, who believed that his patient had a liver condition. 'But all doctors are fools,' added Florence, 'and say that because it covers a multitude of sins.'

On 6 May, Florence went into town and, hearing James Maybrick moaning in his bedroom, Alice Yapp went in to see if she could do anything to help him. Maybrick appeared very flushed and was constantly moving his head restlessly from one side of the pillow to the other and, when Florence returned, Miss Yapp again pleaded with her mistress to summon Dr Hopper. Florence told her that she wanted Dr Hopper to visit her husband but that James would not allow it and, even if Hopper were called, he would not take any notice of him or take any medication that he might prescribe.

James Maybrick's condition worsened until 8 May, when he was so poorly that his brother Michael was summoned by telegram to his bedside. One of James and Michael's other brothers, Edwin, was already staying at the house on a visit and was worried, not only by James's rapidly deteriorating condition but also by the behaviour of Florence Maybrick. Michael was far from satisfied with what he found on his arrival, telling Florence that she ought to have sent for another doctor and engaged professional nurses to care for her husband. Florence, who until then had been caring for her husband herself, complained bitterly to the staff about Michael Maybrick, saying tearfully that he had always disliked her and, if she had her way, she would throw him out of the house. She had done her best to care for her husband, said Florence, and this was the thanks she received. Michael overruled Florence's objections and sent for another doctor, Dr Carter, as well as engaging a team of nurses to care for his brother.

Florence was blissfully unaware that a letter that she had recently written had fallen into the hands of Edwin Maybrick. On 7 or 8 May, she had given a letter to Alice Yapp and asked her to post it for her. Alice walked to the post office, having allowed the Maybricks' young daughter to carry the letter and the child inadvertently dropped it into some mud. Alice bought another envelope at the post office, with the intention of re-addressing the soiled one. What she read when she opened the letter was enough to send her straight back to Battlecrease House to hand the letter to her master's brother.

Addressed to Mr A. Brierly and signed Florrie, the letter began 'Dearest' and went on to reassure the recipient that '...all fear of discovery, now and in the future' was gone. 'He is sick unto death' the letter continued. 'You need not, therefore go abroad on this account, dearest, but in any case don't leave England until I have seen you again.'

As well as handing over the letter to Edwin Maybrick, the staff voiced other concerns to James's brothers. They told them that they had seen Florence

Poison bottle from the turn of the century. (© Martin Latham)

soaking arsenic-coated flypapers in water and produced a chocolate box that contained several bottles of medicine, including a small packet with a red label reading 'Arsenic – Poison. For Cats'. Michael Maybrick called in his brother's next-door neighbour, solicitor Mr Steele, and, in his presence, sealed the chocolate box with his own private seal and hid it in the wine cellar.

James Maybrick died on 11 May and a post-mortem examination was conducted on his body two days later. Doctors could find no natural cause for his death although they noted 'rosy flushes' on his intestines and his stomach was much inflamed. Believing Maybrick to have died as a result of ingesting an irritant poison, doctors took samples from his body for analysis, finding traces of arsenic in his intestines, liver and kidneys. No arsenic was found in his stomach, blood or heart. In spite of these findings, the body of James Maybrick was released and was buried in a family grave at the cemetery in Anfield.

On the day after his brother's death, Michael Maybrick called the police to the house and voiced his suspicions about his sister-in-law to them. He told Inspector Baxendale that he had personally seen Florence tampering with her husband's medicine, apparently transferring it from one bottle to another. Baxendale removed a number of objects from the house including the chocolate box, a bottle of brandy, some Valentine's meat extract and several letters found in Maybrick's room. He also took samples from the lavatories and drains. Arsenic was later found in many of the items removed from Battlecrease House, including the meat extract, the samples from the drains, and James Maybrick's dressing gown pockets.

Meanwhile, Florence Maybrick was under virtual arrest at the couple's home, supposedly prostrate with grief. The police continued their investigations into the death of her husband and soon determined that they had sufficient evidence to arrest Florence and charge her with his murder. However, they found themselves with a dilemma since the doctors attending her believed that she was medically unfit to be charged. Superintendent Isaac Bryning consulted with Mr Swift, a clerk at the county magistrates' court, then went directly to Battlecrease House, taking Mr Swift and magistrate Colonel Bidwill with him.

Before the police were permitted access to Mrs Maybrick, Dr Humphreys and Dr Hopper went to her bedroom to assess her fitness to allow the formal proceedings to take place. With the permission of the doctors and two solicitors, Arnold and Richard Cleaver, who were present to protect Mrs Maybrick's interests, Bryning formally charged Florence with having caused the death of her husband by administering poison to him. It was decided that she should be transported in a carriage to Kirkdale Gaol to be remanded in custody, with the two doctors accompanying her. Yet when the governor of Kirkdale Gaol was contacted, he pointed out that the prison had no accommodation for female prisoners, hence Florence was taken to Walton Gaol.

Coroner Mr Brighouse opened an inquest into Maybrick's death at the Garston Reading Rooms and pronounced himself dissatisfied with the examination of the dead man's remains. Hence it was decided to exhume the body to allow further tests to be made. Even before the exhumation had taken place, the coroner's jury reached their verdict. The thirteen men were unanimous in their decision that Mr Maybrick's death had resulted from consumption of an irritant poison and ruled by a majority of twelve

St George's Hall, Liverpool, c. 1908. (Author's collection)

to one that the poison had been deliberately administered to the deceased with the intent to take his life. The coroner immediately asked for Florence to be brought to him and committed her for trial at the next Assizes for her husband's wilful murder.

The trial opened at St George's Hall, Liverpool, on 31 July 1889 before Mr Justice Stephen. Mr Addison QC MP, Mr McConnell and Mr T. Swift prosecuted and Florence Maybrick, who pleaded 'Not Guilty', was defended by Sir Charles Russell QC MP and Mr Pickford.

The prosecution opened by outlining the events leading up to James Maybrick's death. However, as each prosecution witness was cross-examined by the defence, the case against Florence Maybrick appeared weaker. Having said that James Maybrick was 'an average healthy man', Dr Hopper went on to admit that Maybrick had consulted him fifteen times between June and December 1888 for complaints connected to the liver, digestive system and nerves. He was aware that Maybrick was a hypochondriac who placed undue importance on the most minor of symptoms and that he was prone to dosing himself and taking double doses of his prescribed medicine. Maybrick had given the doctor a number of prescriptions from his doctor in America, which were mostly for nerve tonics containing strychnine. Hopper wasn't aware of Maybrick ever being prescribed arsenic, although he did tell the court that he believed that Maybrick had taken it in the past as an aphrodisiac. Hopper also told the court that Florence Maybrick had consulted him some months before her husband's death, concerned that he was taking strong medicines and asking him to talk to her husband about what she saw as dangerous habits.

Dr Stevenson, a physician and lecturer in forensic medicine at Guy's Hospital in London, related the results of the tests he had performed at the request of Inspector Baxendale on Maybrick's remains and items from Battlecrease House. Arsenic was known to accumulate in the liver and when Stevenson had tested Maybrick's liver he found the equivalent of 0.29 grains of arsenic.

Stevenson had no doubt that James Maybrick had died as a result of arsenic poisoning since his main symptoms of nausea, vomiting, diarrhoea, numbness, dryness of the throat, furred tongue and foul taste in the mouth mirrored those normally associated with its ingestion. The doctor had also tested flypapers, identical to those bought by Florence Maybrick, supposedly to make a cosmetic face wash, and found that soaking them in cold water allowed arsenic to be extracted from them in sufficient quantity to constitute a fatal dose.

Sir Charles Russell, the counsel for the defence, pointed out that none of the doctors treating James Maybrick had at any stage harboured any suspicions that he was being poisoned and even at the post-mortem examination, judgement on the cause of his death was reserved until the samples had been analysed and found to contain arsenic. Dr Stevenson had given diarrhoea as one of the defining symptoms, yet there had been no mention of Maybrick suffering from diarrhoea until shortly before his death. Indeed, he had exhibited a condition called tenesmus – a persistent, ineffectual straining to produce faeces. In short, James Maybrick had shown no symptoms whatsoever that could not also be attributed to gastroenteritis.

Arsenic in one form or another had been found all over the Maybrick's home, yet apart from the flypapers, there was no evidence whatsoever of Florence Maybrick ever having purchased any.

Russell then went on to call witnesses who had known James Maybrick during the time he had lived in America. All testified that he had been in the habit of taking arsenic, often in beef tea or meat extract. A retired chemist from Liverpool, Edwin Stanton, told the court that he had frequently sold Maybrick a pick-me-up containing arsenic, which he would drink in the shop, often several times a day.

The defence next called Dr Tidy, a professor of chemistry at the London Hospital, who was also employed by the Home Office as an official analyst. Tidy disagreed with both the diagnosis and the post-mortem results, insisting that Maybrick was more likely to have died from gastroenteritis from eating bad food. He criticised Dr Stevenson's techniques, suggesting that his calculation of the amount of arsenic in the liver was seriously flawed. Tidy had seen very similar symptoms shown by people who had eaten spoiled food such as cheese, sausage or lobster.

Tidy's conclusions were supported by an eminent Dublin surgeon, Rawdon McNamara, and by Frank Paul, an examiner in toxicology, the latter pointing out that arsenic could even leach from the enamel coating on saucepans, such as those in which Maybrick's food had been prepared.

Russell then called a chemist and a hairdresser, both of whom testified that arsenic was frequently used in cosmetic preparations. Before resting, the defence called on Florence Maybrick to make a statement.

She told the court that for many years she had been in the habit of using a facial wash made from tincture of benzoin, elderflower water and arsenic, which had been prescribed for her by an American doctor, Dr Grace. Unfortunately, she had mislaid Dr Grace's prescription and finding herself suffering from skin eruptions, had attempted to make a substitute, obtaining the arsenic from soaking flypapers.

Florence then addressed the matter of arsenic found in the meat extract taken from her husband's room, saying that her husband had begged her to give him some of his powder since he felt so ill. 'I had not one true or honest friend in the house,' claimed Florence and, having nobody to consult, she had taken the decision to comply with her husband's wishes, mixing the powder with meat extract. However, when she went to her husband's room, he was asleep and had consequently never taken the powder he had requested.

With regard to her extra-marital affair, Florence insisted that she had confessed all to her husband and that, for the sake of their children, they had made a mutual decision to put the past behind them and start afresh.

Russell then made his closing statement. He told the jury that they must decide whether or not James Maybrick had died as a result of poisoning by arsenic and, if they believed that he had, whether that arsenic had been administered by Florence. 'Moral faults in a man were often regarded as venial,' he continued, 'but in the case of a woman it was an unforgivable sin.'

There was evidence that on the day he had first become ill, James Maybrick had taken a double dose of his prescribed medicine, which contained *nux vomica*. When Florence had found out about this she had made up an emetic of mustard and water and sent for Dr Humphreys.

If, as Florence had testified, her husband knew the full extent of her affair with Mr Brierly and had decided to forgive her and give their marriage another try then there was no motive for her to murder him. Florence was independently wealthy and in no need of her husband's money. In addition, if Florence knew that her husband's brothers were dissatisfied with the way she had cared for her husband during his final illness, why had she made no attempt to cover her tracks if she was guilty of causing that illness?

Even if Florence had poisoned her husband, why had she resorted to buying and soaking flypapers when there was so much arsenic already present in the house? In all, nearly 140 bottles of assorted medicines had been removed from Battlecrease House, some of which had been legitimately prescribed by a total of twenty-nine different doctors. The arsenic that Florence was likely to obtain from soaking flypapers – which she had done openly, without any attempt at subterfuge – was of an unknown strength and therefore not reliable as a means of poisoning someone. On the same day as she had purchased the flypapers, Florence had also purchased the tincture of benzoin and elderflower water and, having bought everything from a chemist's shop where she was well known, she had quite openly had the order delivered to the house.

The medical evidence was contradictory, with many eminent doctors prepared to state in court that Maybrick's symptoms were more consistent with gastroenteritis than with arsenic poisoning. The total quantity of arsenic actually isolated during the post-mortem analysis was one tenth of a grain – hardly a fatal dose and, in the opinion of Dr Paul, more likely to be the result of the persistent ingestion of arsenic by Maybrick for medicinal purposes. Dr McNamara had never known a case of arsenic poisoning in which the three usual main symptoms were absent – Maybrick had made no complaint about pain in his calves, stomach pain or excessive vomiting and diarrhoea. Not only that but the doctors would have expected to see petechial spots in the dead man's stomach if he had died from poisoning by arsenic. In Maybrick's examination, these small patches of bleeding had been conspicuous by their absence. Russell reminded the jury that Maybrick had a long history of stomach troubles and hypochondria and a habit of dosing himself and of doubling up on the dosage of his prescribed medicines.

It was then left to the judge, Sir James Fitzjames Stephen, to summarise the case. Stephen had suffered a stroke in 1885 and, as a result, his physical and mental condition had declined considerably. His summary continued for two days and was later to be described as 'prejudicial and muddled', focusing mainly on Florence Maybrick's affair and consequent moral transgression. At the end of the judge's summary, the jury retired for forty-five minutes, returning to pronounce Florence Maybrick 'Guilty' of the wilful murder of her husband, at which she was sentenced to death.

The verdict and the mandatory sentence that followed caused a widespread public outcry and petitions for clemency were immediately initiated in Liverpool, Brighton, Wolverhampton, Manchester and many other cities throughout the country, eventually numbering more than half a million signatures. A petition from America was also sent to the American Ambassador and it was even rumoured that a petition was circulated in the House of Commons. Despite an announcement in the press stating that the Home Secretary would not, under any circumstances, consider deputations in Mrs Maybrick's favour, the case was eventually reconsidered by the Home Secretary, Henry Matthews, who came to the conclusion that although the evidence clearly established that Florence had administered poison to her husband with

Aylesbury Prison, 1929. (Author's collection)

intent to murder him, there were grounds for reasonable doubt as to whether the arsenic so administered had ultimately been the cause of his death. Matthews therefore commuted Florence's death sentence to one of life imprisonment and she was taken from Walton Jail, where she had been awaiting her execution, to first Woking, then Aylesbury Prison to serve her life sentence.

In 1891, an appeal was raised by solicitor Richard Cleaver, not for clemency for his client but for the proceeds of an insurance policy on the life of James Maybrick amounting to £2,000. The policy had been left to Florence Maybrick in her husband's will and she had signed it over to Cleaver to pay for her defence. The court ruled that, having been convicted of her husband's murder, Florence Maybrick was not entitled to benefit from the insurance policy.

Florence was released from prison on 25 January 1904, having earned remission for good conduct and travelled immediately to America, her country of birth. In 1908, she was jointly awarded with her mother possession of some two and a half million acres of land in a legacy, although it was reported that her share had been made over to another person by deed of gift shortly after the death of her husband.

Florence Elizabeth Maybrick lived quietly in America until her eventual death at the age of seventy-nine when, but for a collection of yellowing newspaper clippings found in her house after her death, her previous identity would have remained completely secret. She was buried in the grounds of South Kent School in Connecticut.

The Maybrick case was briefly revived in 1992 after a fitter, Mike Barrett, allegedly made an extraordinary find in a house that he was in the process of renovating. It was a handwritten diary, purporting to be that of James

South Kent School, Connecticut, 1988. (Author's collection)

Maybrick, in which Maybrick confessed to being the legendary serial killer Jack the Ripper. According to the diary, Maybrick had been motivated to kill by his wife's infidelity with Alfred Brierly. It later emerged that the diary had not been 'found', but had been given to Barrett by a family friend, in whose possession it had been for many years.

Arguments among experts in all fields about the authenticity of this diary continued for many years without reaching a definite conclusion, although the general consensus of opinion seemed to be that the sixty-four page document was a hoax. Shortly after the existence of the diary was revealed, a gold pocketwatch was found in Liverpool. Engraved on the back was the name J. Maybrick, along with the words 'I am Jack' and the initials of the five accepted victims of Jack the Ripper. Tests conducted at Bristol University in 2004 seemed to indicate that the markings on the watch were 'tens of years old', although the fact that it had recently been polished made it impossible to date the inscriptions more accurately.

So, many years after the conclusion of the Maybrick case, it is unlikely that Florence Maybrick's guilt or innocence of the murder of her husband will ever be satisfactorily proven. Perhaps the best outcome that can be hoped for is that the Maybrick family motto *Tempus Omnia Revelat* – Time Reveals All – will prove prophetic.

Note: Contemporary newspaper accounts exhibit some variations in the spelling of the names of some of the key figures in the case. Alice Yapp is alternatively named Alice Japp and Dr Hopper is also referred to as Dr Hooper. I have used the most common variations for this account.

18

'I have evidence strong enough to ruin you forever'

London, 1891—1892

Thomas Neil Cream was born in Glasgow on 19 May 1850, the eldest of eight children. His family moved to Canada when he was just four years old and, in 1867, following a short spell as an apprentice shipbuilder, Cream was enrolled at McGill College in Montreal where he studied medicine. It is believed that his first foray into crime occurred while he was a student, when he set fire to his room at college with the intention of claiming the insurance.

Known as a ladies' man, Cream managed to impregnate Flora Elizabeth Brooke, the daughter of a wealthy hotelier. Cream subsequently performed a botched abortion on Flora, who was lucky to escape with her life. Forced into marrying Flora by her irate father, Cream quickly deserted his new wife, fleeing to London on the day after the wedding, where he enrolled himself into medical school. However, he proved a poor student and, having failed his exams, moved to Edinburgh where he finally qualified at the Royal College of Physicians and Surgeons.

On 12 August 1877, Flora died in suspicious circumstances, having taken some medicine sent to her by her husband. Cream then returned to Canada where he specialised in performing illegal abortions. One of his clients, Kate Gardener, was found dead in a shed, her body smelling strongly of chloroform. At her inquest, Cream managed to persuade the coroner that Kate had pressured him for an abortion and that, in carrying out the procedure, he had only been trying to help her. He was eventually released without charge and immediately moved to Chicago, where he was soon under suspicion of causing the death of a prostitute after another bungled abortion. Once more, Cream managed to talk his way out of trouble and was not charged with any offence.

As well as performing abortions, Cream also devoted himself to the manufacture and supply of anti-epilepsy drugs. One of his patients was Daniel Stott, who became suspicious about the frequency with which his wife, Julia,

Left: *Thomas Neil Cream.*
(By kind permission of
Scotsman Publications)

Below: *Illinois State*
Penitentiary, 1900s.
(Author's collection)

Illinois State Penitentiary, Joliet, Ill.

visited the doctor to collect his medication. Stott died suddenly in June 1881 and Cream immediately wrote to the local coroner accusing the pharmacist who had dispensed the drugs of poisoning him. Stott's body was promptly exhumed and found to contain traces of strychnine. However, it was Cream rather than the pharmacist who was ultimately charged with his murder. Tried and found guilty, he was sentenced to life imprisonment at the Illinois State Penitentiary but was released in 1891 for good behaviour, largely due to the efforts of one of his brothers, Daniel. Having inherited $16,000 on the death of his father and by now a drug addict, Cream immediately fled the country for London, where he was known as Dr Thomas Neill.

On 13 October 1891, Cream met Ellen Donworth, also known as Ellen Linnell. Nineteen-year-old Ellen had worked in a bottle factory but, having become pregnant, had been sacked from her job and was forced to turn to prostitution in order to support herself. Several people saw Ellen in the company of a man in a top hat and later that evening she was found slumped in the street, obviously in great agony. She was rushed by cab to St Thomas's Hospital but died before arriving. Before her death, she managed to tell bystanders that a tall, dark man with distinctive crossed eyes had given her something to drink. A later post-mortem examination attributed her death to strychnine and morphine poisoning.

Days later, East Surrey Deputy Coroner George Percival Wyatt received a letter dated 19 October, which read:

> I am writing to say that if you and your satellites fail to bring the murderer of Ellen Donworth alias Ellen Linnell, late of 8 Duke Street, Westminster Bridge Road, to justice that I am willing to give you such assistance as will bring the murderer to justice provided your government is willing to pay me £300,000 for my services. No pay unless successful.
> A O'Brien, Detective.

The coroner's jury recorded a verdict of murder by poisoning with strychnine and morphine by person unknown and, on 5 November, Mr Frederick Smith, a member of the family of W.H. Smith & Son, received a letter. The writer, who signed himself H. Bayne, purported to have in his possession two documents that implicated Smith in the murder of Ellen Donworth. He enclosed one of the documents – a letter allegedly received by Ellen Donworth, in which she was warned that Smith intended to poison her – and suggested that Smith retain Bayne as his legal adviser, placing a notice in one of his shop windows if he agreed to do so.

On 21 October, a prostitute named Lou Harvey, also known as Lou Harris, spent the night with a man in a hotel. In the morning, the man commented on some spots on Lou's forehead and offered to give her some medicine to get rid of them. Harvey told her boyfriend about the encounter and when she went to meet her companion of the previous night at a pre-arranged place to collect the promised tablets, he accompanied her, standing in the shadows a short distance away while Lou spoke to the man.

The generous stranger told her that he was a doctor at St Thomas's Hospital and produced some pills. Lou only pretended to swallow them, discarding them unseen on the pavement. The man asked to see her hands, which she opened for him to show that they were empty. She then asked the doctor to accompany her to a music hall but he pleaded a prior appointment at the hospital, although he did promise to meet her at eleven o'clock that night. He did not keep the appointment.

When Lou Harvey bumped into him by chance a few days later, he did not recognise her. Indeed, he was later to tell a man named Haynes that she had been poisoned and had dropped down dead outside the music hall. Haynes communicated this information to the police who checked and, having found that Lou Harvey was still very much alive, took no further action.

Yet although Lou Harvey was alive, unbeknown to the authorities, another young woman had been poisoned. On 6 October 1891, Cream met Eliza Masters in the street and went with her to her home. They later went out to Gatti's Music Hall and, when they eventually parted company, Cream promised to write to Eliza.

She received a letter from him on 9 October, telling her that he would call on her at home between three and five o'clock that afternoon, and asking her to keep the letter as he wished to have it back when they met. As the appointed hour for their meeting neared, Eliza Masters and her friend, Elizabeth May, sat looking out of the window of the house for the first signs of their visitor.

As they watched, they saw a young woman walking along the street, wearing an apron, a basket over her arm. Both Elizabeth and Eliza knew the woman by sight, although not by name.

She was Matilda Clover, a twenty-seven-year-old alcoholic prostitute with one illegitimate child. On 21 October her landlady found Matilda convulsing and screaming in agony in her room, her head wedged between the edge of the bed and the wall. A doctor was summoned but, although he tried to help her, his treatment had no effect and she died four hours later. In view of her lifestyle, the primary cause of her death was determined to be delirium tremens due to alcoholism, with syncope (fainting) given as the secondary cause. She was buried in a pauper's grave at Tooting and her death would have gone unnoticed but for the receipt a month later of a letter by an eminent doctor, Dr W.H. Broadbent.

The letter was dated 28 November 1891 and signed 'M. Malone'. The writer informed Dr Broadbent that Miss Clover had died from poisoning by strychnine and that he had in his possession written evidence that Broadbent had been hired to kill her and had been personally responsible for administering the fatal dose. Malone offered to hand over the evidence for the sum of £2,500, warning Broadbent, 'I am not humbugging you and I have evidence strong enough to ruin you forever.' Broadbent was instructed to respond by taking out a personal advertisement on the front page of the *Daily Chronicle* newspaper. Instead, Broadbent took the letter straight to Scotland Yard who placed the advertisement as requested, in the hope of trapping the author of the letter. Unfortunately the writer did not take the bait and the letter was eventually filed, its author unidentified.

In November 1891, Dr Cream met Laura Sabatini, a respectable young woman from Berkhampstead and, after a whirlwind courtship, proposed marriage to her and was accepted. By now, Cream was in contact with the Harvey Drug Company in America and expressed a wish to become an agent for their products in England. Accordingly, in January 1892, Cream travelled to America and Canada where he purchased a large quantity of medicines, returning to London in April 1892.

While abroad, he made friends with a Mr John Wilson McCulloch, a commercial traveller in coffee and spices, and confided in him about the life he had been leading in Britain. He told McCulloch that he frequently associated with women of the 'unfortunate class', saying that he had 'lots of fun' with them and admitted to disguising himself on occasions with false whiskers. He showed McCulloch some of the pills he had purchased, telling him that he used them for the purpose of preventing childbirth and he also showed McCulloch a large bottle, which he said contained strychnine.

In the early hours of the morning of 12 April 1892, PC Comley was patrolling his beat in Stamford Street when the front door of No. 118 opened and he saw two young women letting a man out into the street. Roughly an hour later, PC Eversfield was summoned to the same address by the landlord, arriving to find two young women, Alice Marsh and Emma Shrivell, writhing around in agony. Both women were experiencing severe tetanic convulsions, accompanied by rigidity of the muscles and paralysis.

The women were placed in a cab and transported to hospital, Alice dying on the way and Emma surviving until 8.45 a.m. the following morning. Before she died, she was able to give a description of a man who had allegedly given the two girls some pills. Her description closely matched that of PC Comley's account of the man he had seen leaving the house shortly before the women were taken ill. An inquest was held and the two women were found to have died following the ingestion of strychnine, the coroner's jury returning a verdict of wilful murder by person or persons unknown.

Soon afterwards, Dr Cream began asking questions of his landlord's daughter about a fellow boarder in his lodgings, whom he had never met. Mr Walter Harper was a recently qualified doctor, a doctor's son from Bear Street in Barnstaple, Devon. Soon afterwards, Dr Joseph Harper received an all too familiar letter, dated 25 April 1892 and signed 'W.H. Murray'. The writer accused Joseph's son, Walter, of murdering Alice Marsh and Emma Shrivell by the administration of strychnine and threatened to take the evidence in his possession to the coroner unless he received a payment of £1,500. Dr Harper was instructed that, if he wanted to save his son from being hung and protect the reputation of his family, he should take out an advertisement in the *Daily Chronicle* stating, 'W.H.M will pay you for your services. Dr H.'

When there was no response from Dr Harper, letters were sent to Coroner Wyatt, 'The Foreman of the Jury' and Detective George Clarke making similar allegations. The letters were written by Laura Sabatini, dictated by her fiancé, Dr Cream.

They were brought to the attention of the police, who, having seen the letter received by Dr Broadbent, were already harbouring suspicions about the death of Matilda Clover. If Matilda had indeed been poisoned, then it was obvious that the writer of the letter was a strong suspect, since her death had officially been attributed to her alcoholism and there had been no previous mention of strychnine poisoning. The police arranged for her body to be exhumed and the remains analysed. Tests on her organs by Dr Stevenson revealed the presence of strychnine and the cause of her death was amended accordingly. At an inquest before Mid-Surrey Coroner, Mr A. Braxton-Hicks, it was revealed that both Elizabeth May and Eliza Masters had observed Matilda Clover through their window. Not only that, but they had seen Matilda being followed at a short distance by a man that they knew as 'Dr Neill'.

Because Eliza and Elizabeth were actually expecting a visit from Dr Neill at the time, they had thought it strange when he walked straight past their house in pursuit of Matilda Clover. Hence they had followed him and seen him approach Matilda on the doorstep of her home at 27 Lambeth Street and, after engaging in a brief conversation with her, follow her into the house. They waited for about half an hour to see if he would come out again, returning home when there was no sign of him.

On 12 May, Sergeant Ward was patrolling in Lambeth Palace Road when he saw someone who fitted the description of the man PC Comley had witnessed leaving the home of the two prostitutes Marsh and Shrivell before their suspicious deaths a month earlier. The man seemed to be walking up and down the street closely observing female passers-by. Ward immediately sent for PC Comley, who was able to positively identify the suspect. The man was placed under observation and was later to make a complaint to the police that he was being followed.

Cream was eventually arrested on 3 June 1892 but charged only with sending a threatening letter to Dr Harper. 'You have got the wrong man. Fire away!' Cream said indignantly on his arrest. Between 22 June and 13 July, an inquest was held on the death of Matilda Clover and Cream, who was present throughout the proceedings, was given every opportunity to answer questions from the coroner. However, he declined to do so and, when the jury returned a verdict of 'wilful murder' against him, Cream was committed for trial.

On his arrest Cream was found to have in his possession a number of tiny, sugar-coated pills, each containing between one sixteenth and one twenty-second of a grain of strychnine, a fatal dose being between half and one grain. He was known to have purchased empty gelatine capsules and, on the evidence of Lou Harvey, who had described the medicine given to her by Cream as 'long pills', it was concluded that he had administered strychnine to Clover and his other victims by placing the pills in the gelatine capsules, each of which was capable of holding a maximum of twenty of the pills. Also found in his room was an envelope on which was written a series of initials and dates which corresponded to the initials of the murdered women and the dates of their deaths. A scrap of paper was found in the fob pocket of his trousers, which apparently bore the handwriting of murder victim Alice Marsh.

Cream's trial began at the Central Criminal Court on 17 October 1892 before Mr Justice Hawkins. He was charged under his assumed name of Thomas Neill with the wilful murders of Alice Marsh, Ellen Donworth, Emma Shrivell and Matilda Clover and also with sending letters demanding money with menaces to William Henry Broadbent and Joseph Harper and with attempting to administer strychnine to Louisa Harvey with intent to murder her. He pleaded 'Not Guilty' to all the charges against him and the court then proceeded to try the charge of the wilful murder of Matilda Clover.

Attorney General Sir Charles Russell QC MP prosecuted the case with the assistance of the Hon. Bernard Coleridge QC MP, Mr Sutton and Mr C.F. Gill, while Mr Geoghegan, Mr Warburton, Mr Luxmore-Drew and Mr Scrutton defended.

Much of the case for the prosecution involved carefully teasing out the facts of the four different murders and establishing a connection between the murdered women and Dr Cream. The court heard from various doctors who had performed post-mortem examinations on the bodies and it was stated that all four women had ingested a fatal dose of strychnine. Comparisons were also made between Cream's handwriting and that of the writer of the various letters. Although Laura Sabatini had admitted writing some of the letters at Cream's bequest, others were judged to have been written by the defendant himself, including the list of dates and initials found at Cream's lodgings after his arrest.

A key witness for the prosecution was John Haynes, who had become acquainted with Dr Cream after the latter visited his lodgings to be photographed by Haynes's landlord, a professional photographer named Mr Armstead. Haynes and Cream had become friendly and, as he had done with McCulloch in Canada, Cream soon began to confide details about the murdered women to Haynes, who had made notes of some of the conversations. When Mr Justice Hawkins heard about the notes, he adjourned the trial, sending Haynes home in the company of Inspector Harvey to fetch them and bring them to court.

The defence counsel then argued that it was up to the prosecution to prove three things beyond reasonable doubt. The first of these, stated Mr Geoghegan, was that Matilda Clover had actually died from the effects of strychnine poisoning. The second was that 'the brain and hand concerned in such an infernal murder as that they were inquiring into was that of the prisoner'. The third was that the strychnine had been administered feloniously.

If the jury were convinced of the first two points beyond any reasonable doubt then it followed that his client was guilty. However Geoghegan pointed out that Clover was known to have quarrelled with the father of her illegitimate child shortly before her death. Matilda had received a letter and it was this letter that had lured her out on the evening on which she died. She had returned in the company of a man described by another lodger, Lucy Rose, as being about forty years old, having a thick brown moustache and wearing a silk hat. If this man was Matilda's murderer, then he could have been any one of about 30,000 to 40,000 men in London and even though Lucy Rose had seen Dr Cream at the coroner's inquest and the magistrates' court, as well as at the present proceedings, she had been completely unable to identify him as the man who had accompanied Matilda home on the night of her death.

The defence also challenged the identification of Dr Cream by May and Masters as the man they had seen following Matilda in the street. They would have caught little more than a fleeting glimpse of his face, after which they had put on their coats and followed him, able only to see his back. It had then been six months before they had been called upon to identify Cream as the man they had seen following Matilda.

Geoghegan admitted that his client had written letters in an effort to obtain money but suggested that these were simply opportunistic demands resulting from his medical knowledge and did not mean that he had personally killed Matilda Clover.

The defence concluded by reminding the jury that the onus was on the prosecution to prove the facts of the case beyond all reasonable doubt. Geoghegan concluded his closing speech with the words:

Between you and the prisoner at the bar, between the bench and the prisoner, there stands a figure and that figure is the genius of the law of England. It is the best protector an accused man can have in his hour of need. It demands that the guilt of the accused shall be brought home to him as clear and bright as the light of heaven streaming into this court now; and it is to the protection of this figure that I leave my client Mr Thomas Neill.

In his summary for the jury, Mr Justice Hawkins reminded them that the murder of Matilda Clover was the case under consideration. He acknowledged the impossibility of separating her murder from those of the other victims but suggested that, were the court trying a case of robbery, the fact that the defendant had committed other robberies did not necessarily mean that he had committed this particular robbery. The other cases should be considered only in as far as their circumstances could legally and legitimately throw light on the murder of Matilda Clover.

With regard to the identification of Cream made by Masters and May, the judge told the jury that he had seen nothing that led him to believe that the girls had any other motive than honesty. He also believed that Lucy Rose's failure to identify the prisoner as the man she had seen returning home with Matilda Clover on the night of her death was due to the fact that she had seen him only briefly by the dim light of a paraffin lamp.

As Matilda Clover's death had initially been attributed to her intemperance, it was reasonable to assume that the writer of the letter signed 'M. Malone' was privy to information that only the person who had administered strychnine would be aware of. The judge read the letter aloud, reminding the jury that the letter had been proven to have been sent by the prisoner. Fortunately its recipient, Dr Broadbent, was not the kind of man to be easily intimidated and had passed the letter to Scotland Yard. They had attempted to find out who had sent the letter by inserting the advertisement as requested by the writer but there had been no response.

Next the judge addressed the matter of the cause of death, originally thought to be alcoholism then amended to strychnine poisoning. He conceded that people suffering from delirium tremens might experience fits but that these were of a totally different nature to those experienced by someone who had ingested strychnine. Describing Mr Stevenson as 'a gentleman of great scientific attainments, of vast experience and untiring perseverance in discovering the truth of all matters entrusted to him', the judge reiterated that it had been Stevenson who, after analysis of Miss Clover's remains, had determined the true cause of her death.

Finally the judge reviewed the murders of the other women, asking the jury if, having heard all the evidence presented in court, they were satisfied beyond reasonable doubt that the prisoner had committed the diabolical crime of poisoning Clover. If they were, then it was their duty to fearlessly say so but if they were not entirely satisfied then the prisoner was entitled to be acquitted.

It took the jury just twelve minutes to find the defendant 'Guilty' of the wilful murder of Matilda Clover.

Cream was sentenced to death for the murder of Matilda Clover and a subsequent appeal to the Home Secretary for clemency was denied, although Cream's execution was stayed for a week to allow papers to be sent from Canada and America. Whatever was contained in these documents did nothing to alter the final outcome, which was that Cream met his death at the hands of executioner Billington within the walls of Newgate Prison on 15 November 1892.

It is recorded that Cream faced his death calmly, making a short statement before his death thanking officials for their kindness toward him during his incarceration. There is anecdotal evidence that in the seconds before he dropped to his death, he suddenly cried out, 'I am Jack...' a statement thought by many to be a claim to being the infamous Jack the Ripper, who had murdered several prostitutes in the East End of London between 1888 and 1891. Unfortunately for those seeking Jack, whose true identity is still unknown to this day, many of the gruesome murders he is said to have committed occurred while Cream was imprisoned in America, effectively removing his name from the list of suspects.

19

'I never murdered the dear'

In 1902, an unplanned pregnancy was a matter of great shame for an unmarried woman and servant Ada Charlotte Galley of Finchley was mortified to find herself in such an unenviable predicament. In August of that year, she happened to read an advertisement in *Dalton's Newspaper*. 'Accouchement, before and during. Skilled nursing. Home comforts. Baby can remain.'

Charlotte, as she was usually known, wrote to the advertiser and received a reply inviting her for an interview at Claymore House, East Finchley. There she met a woman named Amelia Sach who offered to let Charlotte move into the house to await the birth of her child. The women agreed terms of one guinea a week, rising to three guineas a week during the actual confinement.

East Finchley, 1904. (Author's collection)

High Road and Congregational Church, East Finchley, 1920s. (Author's collection)

Charlotte had not been at Claymore House for long when Amelia approached her and asked if she would like to have her baby adopted once it was born. Charlotte agreed that she would, asking Amelia how much it would cost to arrange. Amelia told her that it would be between £25 and £30, a sum of money well beyond the means of the young servant girl. Eventually, Sach agreed to reduce the price to £25 and Charlotte wrote a letter to her baby's father, asking him for assistance. The necessary money was promised and, in the knowledge that her child would be spending his or her life with 'a lady of good position', Charlotte was able to relax, spending the weeks before the birth sewing clothes for her baby.

On 15 November 1902, Charlotte gave birth to a baby boy after a difficult and painful labour, attended by Amelia Sach and Dr Alexander Wylie. She saw her son only momentarily before Sach whisked the child away. At Charlotte's request, Amelia Sach sent a telegram to the baby's father and he came to visit Charlotte that evening. He was allowed to see the baby and handed over £25 in bank notes to Sach, for which he was given a signed receipt.

When Dr Wylie called the next morning to check on Charlotte, Sach told him that the baby had been sent to Charlotte's sister in Holloway. She later informed Charlotte that the baby had already been placed with his adoptive mother.

There were other young women staying at the house at the time, one of whom, Rosina Pardoe, had given birth to a daughter three days before the birth of Charlotte's baby. Like Charlotte, Rosina had agreed to have her baby adopted, paying Amelia Sach £30 to make the necessary arrangements for her, a sum she obtained from her married lover.

Meanwhile, on 29 October 1902, a fifty-four-year-old woman named Annie Walters had taken lodgings in the home of Mr and Mrs Seal in Islington. Henry Seal was a police officer and while Annie was staying at his home, she twice appeared with a different baby, telling her landlady and other lodgers that she was working for Amelia Sach and had agreed to deliver the infants to their new homes.

Walters asked her landlady if she might keep the babies in her room overnight but Alice Seal noticed that the children were exceptionally quiet and did not cry at all. When Alice commented on this, Annie admitted to giving the babies a couple of drops of chlorodyne to keep them quiet. Mrs Seal was horrified, telling Annie to be careful that she didn't kill the babies but Annie ridiculed the idea that medicating them in this way could be dangerous, saying that chlorodyne was so safe that she could take a whole bottleful herself without any adverse effects.

On 12 November, Annie was summoned by telegram to collect a baby from Claymore House. When she returned to her lodgings, she allowed her landlady to hold the infant briefly, at which time Alice observed that the newborn baby appeared to be healthy and thriving.

Annie sent another lodger, Minnie Spencer, off on an errand, giving her a £1 note and a shopping list that included a baby's bottle, a small tin of Nestlé's milk, a teat, a bottle of chlorodyne and a pennyworth of carbolic fluid. Minnie too was allowed to hold the baby and remarked on how red faced and healthy it seemed. However, when she returned with the shopping and the change, Annie refused to let her see the baby, telling her that it was asleep. The baby was kept at the Seals' house throughout the following day and although Minnie Spencer saw Annie several times and even ran some more errands for her, she was not allowed to see the baby again. Annie left the house with the baby on Friday 14 November, at which time it had not been seen or heard by any of the other occupants of the house since its arrival two days earlier.

Annie was next seen at Lockhart's Coffee Rooms in Whitechapel, nursing a tightly wrapped bundle. As Annie sat at a table enjoying some refreshments, the blanket in which the bundle was wrapped fell away slightly, revealing the pale face of a baby to waitress Ethel Jones, who first thought it was a life-sized doll. She questioned Annie about her package and was told that Annie was a nurse and that the baby had just undergone surgery for a double hernia and was still under the influence of chloroform. The explanation seemed perfectly plausible to Ethel at the time, although with hindsight she later came to realise that the baby had actually been dead while Annie Walters sat nursing it in the café.

Annie arrived back without the baby in the evening, at which time she was clearly intoxicated. She tossed some baby clothes to Alice Seal, telling her that she had taken the baby to a rich lady. 'You should see the little baby with its laces and muslin,' she told Mrs Seal, describing how beautiful the child had looked and how delighted its new mother had been to receive it.

On the following morning, one of the Seals' sons took a telegram for Annie Walters who read it and announced that she was to collect another baby, which was to go to a coastguard at Kensington. That evening Annie went out, returning with a baby girl, which she left in Mrs Seal's care for about an hour while she went out.

Mrs Seal called in her next-door neighbour, Mrs White, and together the two women undressed the baby, finding it to be a boy rather than a girl. When Annie Walters returned, she was most anxious, asking Mrs Seal if she had 'undone' the baby. Alice denied having examined the child, who spent the night in Annie's room. Once again, the infant was surprisingly quiet, although Minnie Spencer did hear it making a strange croaking noise when she went to Annie's room, having been out to buy some calico at Annie's request.

'The mother must have been frightened by a dog, the way it coughs so,' remarked Annie, although she would not allow Minnie to approach the baby, who lay on her bed under a pile of bedclothes.

By now, the Seals were becoming suspicious and Henry Seal asked his son, Albert, to try and get a look at the baby. Albert had already surreptitiously followed Annie Walters when she went out to collect the child, and seen her getting into a cab with a well-dressed woman by the Archway Tavern in Highgate. At that point, Albert had lost sight of Annie and returned home. Now he went to Annie's room and tried to look at the baby but saw no more than a heap of bedclothes on the bed. Annie cautioned him that the baby was asleep and would not allow him to disturb it.

Henry Seal communicated his suspicions about his lodger to his superior officers and a police guard was placed outside the house with the purpose of following Annie when she left with the baby. On 18 November, Detective George Wright tailed Annie, who was carrying a large bundle. With the police officer on her heels, Annie walked from her Danbury Street lodgings to Knowles Street and onto Duncan Terrace, where she stopped and spoke to somebody. At Rosebery Avenue, Annie boarded a bus, still carrying her bundle, disembarking at South Kensington Station, where she went into the ladies' lavatory.

Wright made his presence known to the stationmaster and, when Annie Walters came out of the toilet, he approached her, identified himself as a police officer and demanded to see the baby.

'Why?' asked Annie.

'I have reason to believe it is not as it should be,' replied the detective, before escorting Annie back into the ladies lavatory and unwrapping her bundle.

Annie Walters slumped resignedly into a chair, saying, 'I suppose you will take me to the station now.'

'I want to see the baby first,' said Wright. The blankets were removed from the bundle that Annie had been carrying, revealing the dead body of a newborn baby boy, his tiny hands tightly clenched into fists.

'Is it dead?' Annie asked.

The policeman confirmed that it was and announced his intention of arresting Annie on suspicion of the baby's murder.

'I never murdered the dear,' Annie insisted.

Wright cautioned her, reminding her that anything she said could be used in evidence against her. 'I won't say anything, then I cannot say wrong,' she responded.

Annie and the dead baby were taken to the police station at Kings Cross Road and police surgeon Dr Caunter was called to perform a post-mortem examination on the infant, along with Augustus Pepper, a Master in Surgery. The two doctors concluded that the baby was full term and only a few days old, well nourished and free from any disease. There were no visible external marks on the tiny body apart from some slight bruising and swelling on the right-hand side of his face and on the back of the head, which the doctors attributed to the use of obstetrical forceps during delivery.

The fact that the child's hands were clenched and its toes were also curled under suggested to the doctors that it had been asphyxiated, as did congestion in the baby's larynx and brain membranes and small spots of bleeding on the surface of its lungs. They determined that the most likely cause of death was the administration of a drug that contained either opium or morphine which, in so young a baby, would have acted on the nerve centre of the brain and reduced the circulation of blood to the heart and lungs. This would have severely compromised the baby's ability to breathe, resulting in its death from asphyxia.

When Annie Walters' room was searched after her arrest, a partially used bottle of Dr J. Collis Browne's Chlorodyne was found. A patent remedy of the time containing both morphine and chloroform, Dr Collis Browne's was advertised as being a general cure-all, recommended for treating coughs, consumption, bronchitis, asthma, diphtheria, croup, fever, diarrhoea, dysentery, cholera, epilepsy, hysteria, cancer, gout, rheumatism, meningitis and a host of other illnesses. The doctors were naturally familiar with the medicine and suggested that a dose of two drops would prove fatal for so young a baby. Unfortunately, the baby's stomach was completely empty when the post-mortem examination was conducted and Pepper found no traces of either milk or indeed chlorodyne.

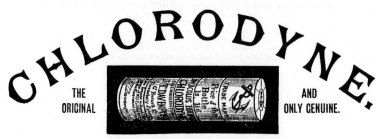

This page and opposite: *A contemporary advertisement for Dr J. Collis Browne's Chlorodyne Solution.* *(Author's collection)*

TESTIMONIALS.

Earl Russell has graciously favoured J. T. Davenport with the following:—"Extract of a despatch from Mr. Webb, H.B.M. Consul at Manilla, dated Sept. 17, 1864.

" 'The remedy most efficacious in its effects (in Epidemic Cholera) has been found to be CHLORODYNE, and with a small quantity given to me by Dr. Burke I have saved several lives.' "

*** Earl Russell communicated to the College of Physicians that he had received a despatch from Her Majesty's Consul at Manilla to the effect that Cholera has been raging fearfully, and that the ONLY remedy of any service was CHLORODYNE.—See *Lancet*, Dec. 31, 1864.

Extracts from the GENERAL BOARD OF HEALTH, LONDON, as to its efficacy in Cholera.

1st Stage, or Premonitory.—In this stage the remedy acts as a *charm*, one dose generally sufficient.

2nd Stage, or that of Vomiting and Purging.—In this stage the remedy possesses great power, more than any other we are acquainted with, two or three doses being sufficient.

3rd Stage, or Collapse.—*In all cases restoring the Pulse.* So strongly are we convinced of the immense value of this remedy, that we cannot too forcibly urge the necessity of adopting it in all cases.

From DR. THOMAS SANDIFORD, Passage West, Cork.

I will thank you to send me a further supply of Chlorodyne. It is the most efficacious remedy I ever used, affording relief in violent attacks of Spasms within a minute after being taken. One patient in particular, who has suffered for years with periodical attacks of Spasms of a most painful nature, and unable to obtain relief from other remedies, such as opium, &c., finds nothing so prompt and efficacious as Chlorodyne.

From W. VESALIUS PETTIGREW, M.D., formerly Lecturer at St. George's Hospital, London.

I have no hesitation in stating that I have never met with any medicine so efficacious as an Anti-spasmodic and Sedative. I have used it in Consumption, Asthma, Diarrhœa, and other diseases, and am perfectly satisfied with the results.

From SYMES & Co., Pharmaceutical Chemists, Medical Hall, Simla.—*January* 5, 1880.

To J. T. DAVENPORT, Esq., 33, Great Russell Street, Bloomsbury, London.

DEAR SIR,—Have the goodness to furnish us with your best quotations for Dr. J. Collis Browne's Chlorodyne, as, being large buyers, we would much prefer doing business with you direct than through the wholesale houses. We embrace this opportunity of congratulating you upon the wide-spread reputation this justly-esteemed medicine has earned for itself, not only in Hindostan, but all over the East. As a remedy of general utility, we much question whether a better is imported into the country, and we shall be glad to hear of its finding a place in every Anglo-Indian home. The other brands, we are happy to say, are now relegated to the native bazaars, and, judging from their sale, we fancy their sojourn there will be but evanescent. We could multiply instances *ad infinitum* of the extraordinary efficacy of Dr. Collis Browne's Chlorodyne in Diarrhœa and Dysentery, Spasms, Cramps, Neuralgia, the Vomiting of Pregnancy, and as a general sedative, that have occurred under our personal observation during many years. In Choleraic Diarrhœa, and even in the more terrible forms of Cholera itself, we have witnessed its surprisingly controlling power. We have never used any other form of this medicine than Collis Browne's, from a firm conviction that it is decidedly the best, and also from a sense of duty we owe to the profession and the public, as we are of opinion that the substitution of any other than Collis Browne's is a deliberate breach of faith on the part of the chemist to prescriber and patient alike. We are, Sir, faithfully yours,

SYMES & CO.,

Members of the Pharm. Society of Great Britain, His Excellency the Viceroy's Chemists.

From J. M'GRIGOR CROFT, M.D., M.R.C.P., London, late Staff-Surgeon to H.M.F.

November 26, 1859.

SIR,—After prescribing Dr. J. Collis Browne's Chlorodyne for the last three years, in severe cases of Neuralgia and Tic-Douloureux, I feel that I am in a position to testify to its valuable effects. Really, in some cases it acted as a charm, when all other means had failed. Without being asked for this report, I must come forward and state my candid opinion that it is a most valuable medicine, and I have recommended several chemists in this neighbourhood not to be without it for prescriptions.

From JNO. E. GOULSTONE, M.D., late Principal Surgeon to the Steam Ship *Great Eastern*.

I can confidently state that Chlorodyne is an admirable Sedative and Anti-spasmodic, having used it in Neuralgia, Hysteria, Asthma, and Consumption, with remarkably favourable results. It relieved a fit of Asthma in four minutes, where the patient had suffered eleven years in a most distressing manner, no previous remedy having had so immediate and beneficial an effect.

From DR. B. J. BOULTON & Co., Horncastle.

We have made pretty extensive use of Chlorodyne in our practice lately, and look upon it as an excellent direct Sedative and Anti-spasmodic. It seems to allay pain and irritation in whatever organ, and from whatever cause. It induces a feeling of comfort and quietude not obtainable by any other remedy, and it seems to possess this great advantage over all other Sedatives, that it leaves no unpleasant after-effects.

The doctors offered two possible explanations for this – either the baby had vomited the contents of his stomach or it had been manually asphyxiated. They suggested that the croaking sounds heard by Minnie Spencer were consistent with the dying gasps of a baby poisoned by the administration of a narcotic such as Dr Collis Browne's Chlorodyne.

The doctors then dismissed Annie Walters' story about the child she had been seen carrying in Lockhart's having had an operation for a double hernia. It was doubtful that an operation would have been performed on so young and small an infant unless the hernia was strangulated. After such an operation, the child would be confined to bed for between two and three weeks and any suggestion that a baby would have been allowed to be taken out of hospital while still under the effects of anaesthetic was ludicrous and nonsensical.

The dead baby taken from Annie at the station had been dressed in a nightgown, which bore a laundry mark 'F236'. The police managed to trace the mark to the Scottish Laundry at Finchley and, when they spoke to manageress Eva Brooksby, she confirmed that the number was written in her handwriting and identified the customer it represented as Amelia Sach of Claymore House.

The police went to Claymore House to interview Sach, who initially denied knowing Annie, insisting to Inspector Andrew Kyd that she had never given any babies for adoption. She told the Inspector that mothers were merely confined in her house but when she was asked if she could show Kyd any babies born there recently, she replied that the most recent mother was too ill to be disturbed. Kyd sent for a doctor and when Dr Russell arrived, requested that he examine the mother. As the doctor was about to do so, Sach suddenly told the Inspector that the baby was no longer on the premises and had been taken away. She expressed shock and surprise to learn that a baby born in her house was dead and that the police also strongly suspected that a second baby had been murdered.

Amelia Sach was arrested and charged with being an accessory to the murder of the baby found with Annie Walters at the station. Taken to the same police station as Walters, she caught sight of her on arrival and admitted that Walters had once worked for her but continued to deny having given her any babies. With Sach in custody, her room was searched and found to contain almost 300 items of baby clothing, a Post Office Savings Book with £20 credit, business cards, letters and several bank notes, two of which could be traced back to the father of Miss Galley's baby, who had noted down the serial numbers of the notes with which he had paid Sach for arranging the adoption of his son. Also found was an unopened letter, sent to Amelia by a woman in Woking, asking if there were any babies available for adoption, since she was unable to bear children of her own.

Amelia Sach and Annie Walters were both formally charged with the murder of the baby now identified as baby Galley. Later that evening, Annie Walters called guard Joseph Nespa over to her cell and indicated that she wanted to talk to him. Nespa cautioned her but Annie insisted on making a statement, which Nespa wrote down.

Annie told Nespa that the baby had been cross and that she had put two drops of chlorodyne in its milk to soothe it. She had then fallen asleep and, when she woke up, the baby was dead. Annie swore that she had never intended to kill the baby and, had she not been apprehended, had planned to drown herself. If the police went to East Finchley post office, they would find telegrams from Sach requesting that Annie meet her at Finchley Station to collect a baby. 'I can see now that I have been a foolish woman,' Annie said ruefully.

When the case reached court, both Annie Walters and Amelia Sach pleaded 'Not Guilty' to the charge of the wilful murder of baby Galley. Although Sach and Walters were charged with the murder of just one baby, the police now believed that they had killed considerably more children, possibly as many as twenty.

The trial opened on 15 January 1903 before Mr Justice Darling, with Charles Matthews and Mr Bodkin prosecuting and Mr Leycester and Guy Stephenson defending.

The court heard from a number of people who had known Annie Walters by a different name – some as Mrs Laming, others as Mrs Merith – and had been aware that she worked with Amelia Sach. She had complained to one landlady, Elizabeth Lowe, that she did all the hard work, while Sach reaped most of the benefit from placing the babies, saying that she was dissatisfied with her situation and wished to leave her job if she could find alternative employment.

The police officers and doctors concerned with making enquiries into the activities of Walters and Sach testified, as did the entire Seal family, Minnie Spencer, waitress Ethel Jones and laundry manageress Eva Brooksby. The court also heard from Ada Galley and Rosina Pardoe, as well as the fathers of their respective babies, who were allowed to remain anonymous. Another young unmarried mother, 'Miss Harris', told the court that she had given birth to a baby boy at Claymore House on 28 August 1902 and that Amelia Sach had arranged for the child to be adopted by a lady in Sevenoaks, Kent. After her baby had been taken to his new mother, Miss Harris remained at Claymore House until 23 October. Whenever she asked for news of her child, Sach told her that he was fine and growing into a big boy. Theresa Edwards, another resident at the house at the time, testified to seeing baby Harris being collected and taken away by Annie Walters.

While at the magistrates' court, Annie had submitted a handwritten statement in which she gave her account of what had happened to baby Pardoe, which was now submitted in her defence. Part of the statement read:

I had to take to Aldgate Staishin to meet a lady at ten minets to four I was to
soon so I went to Lockhart's to get some Refreshment I got that and left at
four I ment the lady, she was in a Brougham she said you have come. I said yes
I am could get in give me the baby I gave it to her she said untye the parcell
I untied it then she in Dress the baby and gave me the closes and drest it in
fine lase Robes and a boutful colke and Lace Vale she said it will be a lovly
baby I said it is good little sole it never cry had it at hall she said I am going
to Ireland or Scotland, I don't know wich but I am going to Pickidlley I will
Drop you at St James Street the baby was Dress and still asleep she said to me
I have a bottle of Shampain in my bag poor me out a glass she Drank that
and then she gave me one I said only a little I am not house to that she said it
wont hurt you then I got out she gave me ten shilling I said let me know how
you get home goodnight a title lady was going to adopt it. [sic]

The statement continued with Annie's account of what happened to baby
Galley, ending with, 'I gave the baby two drops of Chlordine, not intenthin to
arm it only to mak it sleep.' [sic]

It was thus the contention of the counsel for the defence that there had been
no intent to harm baby Galley and that the charge against Annie Walters should
therefore be one of manslaughter at the most, while Amelia Sach had played
no part whatsoever in the killing. The judge disagreed. In his summary of the
evidence for the jury, Mr Justice Darling told them that Amelia Sach had been
the instigator of Annie Walters in the actual taking away of life as part of the
business that she carried on and that the verdict had to be one of murder or
nothing at all.

The jury deliberated for around forty minutes before returning with verdicts
of 'Guilty' for both Amelia Sach and Annie Walters, although with a recommendation for mercy on account of the fact that they were women. With both
still claiming their innocence, Mr Justice Darling sentenced them to death by
hanging.

In spite of the jury's recommendation, Sach and Walters became the first
women ever to hang at Holloway Prison when they faced William Billington
and his assistant Henry Pierrepoint in a double execution on 3 February 1903.

Twenty-nine-year-old Amelia Sach was given a drop of 6ft and 1in, while the
drop for lighter fifty-four-year-old Annie Walters was calculated at three inches
less. In his diaries, Henry Pierrepoint wrote that both women had to be carried
to the scaffold and that both continued to protest their innocence to the very
end.

20

'If I had not got all this bastard lot to keep, I could get on better by myself'

HARLESDEN, LONDON, 1905

Ellen Gregory shared a close relationship with her daughter, Beatrice Ellen Maud, which continued even after Beatrice married Arthur Devereux, in November 1898. Just over nine months later, the Devereuxs' first child was born – a baby boy named Stanley. Both parents doted on him, as did his grandmother, who was always on hand to help her daughter with the new baby, even living for a while at the Devereux family home. Her constant presence annoyed her son-in-law and Ellen's relationship with Arthur gradually deteriorated until Arthur eventually told Beatrice that he would 'blow her mother's brains out'. Ellen moved out of his home after that and confined her visits to her daughter to the times when she knew Arthur would be at work.

On 5 April 1903, Beatrice went into labour with the couple's second child. Much to everyone's surprise, the expected new baby turned out to be twins, who were named Lawrence Rowland and Evelyn Lancelot.

Arthur Devereux was most unhappy. The babies irritated him with their crying and, although he remained very fond of Stanley, he completely ignored the twins, telling Beatrice that she should have been satisfied with having just one child. As the twins grew older, both developed rickets, which prevented them from walking normally. Beatrice was a devoted mother but, much to her husband's disgust, most of her time was taken up with looking after the babies.

On 28 January 1905, Beatrice and her mother met to go shopping together. Ellen was expecting to go away for a while and, when she said goodbye to her daughter that evening, leaving her in good spirits, they agreed to write to each other while Ellen was away. However, Ellen heard nothing so, on her return in mid-February, she went straight round to her son-in-law and daughter's home in Milton Avenue, Harlesden, to see why.

To Ellen's surprise, the house was deserted. The next-door neighbour, Mrs Wells, thought that the family had moved out, although she had no idea where they might have moved to. Ellen made extensive enquiries in the area and discovered that a removal firm run by Thomas Bannister had collected the Devereuxs' furniture. Ellen visited Bannister several times over the next few weeks but he remained tight-lipped, believing it was not his place to reveal his clients' business. However, after three visits from the very determined Ellen, he did weaken slightly, telling her that he was storing a trunk for Arthur Devereux and that Arthur would probably contact him about it in due course. When he did, Bannister promised to ask him to let his mother-in-law know his new address.

'My daughter is probably in that trunk,' Ellen told Bannister, who said that she was a wicked woman for thinking such terrible thoughts. Nevertheless, when she left, Bannister went to take a closer look at the trunk.

It was a large tin trunk, which had been bound with strong straps, padlocked and sealed with red sealing wax. Devereux had told Bannister that it contained books and chemicals and that he was expecting to sell it shortly, asking Bannister to store it until the buyer came to London in a few months time. Now Bannister examined the trunk as best he could without opening it, even sniffing round it, to see if he could detect any smell coming from within. When he couldn't, he dismissed Ellen's concerns as hysteria.

Ellen was nothing if not persistent. Days later, she was back at Bannister's premises, this time having spoken to Susan Flint, a dealer in second-hand clothes. Mrs Flint told Ellen that Arthur Devereux had visited her, wanting to sell some women's and toddler's clothes, which he said belonged to his sister. Mrs Flint purchased a bundle of garments, paying Devereux £2 or £3 for them. Ellen now told Bannister that her son-in-law had been selling her daughter's and grandsons' clothes, asking him if he didn't find that suspicious.

Privately, Bannister did, although he was still not prepared to give Ellen her son-in-law's forwarding address, particularly after questioning the two employees who had actually performed the removal and finding that Devereux had given them five shillings not to tell her where he was living.

Bannister had not known Devereux's real name until Ellen first visited him, since the removal had been booked under the name of Egerton and, although his men could remember the location of the house where they had taken Egerton's goods, they could not recall the address. Bannister sent one of his men, George Willoughby, with a letter for Devereux but he received no reply.

On 14 March, realising that she was getting nowhere with her attempts to locate her daughter and grandsons, Ellen finally took her concerns to the police at Harlesden, telling them her suspicions about the sealed trunk. Detective Inspector Edward Pollard visited James Bannister, who told him that he didn't believe that there was anything untoward about either the trunk or its contents. Bannister did reveal Devereux's last known address to the police, who made some enquiries and eventually traced him to Coventry, where he was working as an assistant to chemist Frederick Bird, of Spon Street. Pollard contacted the Chief Constable of Coventry, and asked him to make a discreet investigation and, when it was revealed that Devereux was living in Coventry alone and had told Bird that he was a widower with one son, the police went back to Bannister's on 13 April, with the intention of opening the trunk.

Pollard first gave the trunk a little shake, expecting its contents to move around. When they didn't, he opened the trunk and found that it had a ledge running around the inside, close to the top. Resting on the ledge was a wooden lid, which had been tightly screwed down. A thick line of glue had been piped along the edges of the wood, hermetically sealing the seams around the lid.

Pollard unscrewed the screws and then pried up the lid with a jemmy. Underneath were a tablecloth and a quilt, both of which had been soaked in glue and, when the policeman managed to peel back a corner of the stiffened fabric and push his hand beneath it, he felt a child's head in the depths of the trunk.

Pollard immediately stepped back to avoid disturbing the contents of the trunk further. He arranged for telegrams to be sent to the coroner and also to the Chief Constable at Coventry, asking for Devereux to be detained. Then, as the trunk and its gruesome contents were taken to the Kilburn Mortuary for examination, Pollard and Sergeant George Cole set off by train to collect Devereux and bring him back to Harlesden for questioning. (Fortunately, the Coventry police had located Stanley Devereux, who was safe and well at a boarding school in Kenilworth.)

When the trunk was fully opened, it revealed the bodies of a woman and two small boys, each about two years old. The woman lay on her left side, with her legs bent upwards, and wore rolled down stockings, a black silk bodice, corsets, white cotton drawers, a vest and a chemise with a lace trim. Other than some faint bruises, there were no marks of violence anywhere on her body. The two boys each wore a nappy, a vest and a flannelette nightgown, although one of them had a calico nightdress over the top of his other garments. Like the woman, their bodies were also unmarked.

A post-mortem examination was performed on all three bodies by Dr Augustus Joseph Pepper, who was assisted by police surgeon George Robertson. Pepper believed that the bruises on the woman's body could have occurred when she was placed in the trunk shortly after her death and, since there were no external signs that could explain the three deaths and their internal organs all appeared relatively normal, the doctor's first thought was that they had been poisoned. All three victims had died of asphyxia – an inadequate intake of oxygen. What had caused that asphyxia would only be determined by further testing and samples of internal organs and flesh were sent to Home

Office analyst Sir Thomas Stevenson, along with samples of the glue and some cloths and dusters that had been found in the trunk.

Stevenson found that the glue contained minute traces of arsenic and had also been treated with boric acid, an antiseptic and anti-fungal preparation. The cloths and dusters showed little more than a few blood and mucus stains, along with cells that Stevenson believed had come from the mouths of the deceased. He theorised that the cloths may have been used to wipe the mouths of the women and children, either before or after their deaths.

Stevenson then analysed the organs from the woman's stomach, kidneys and liver, and he isolated a total of 1.125 grains of morphine. Most commonly combined with acid or salts, morphine was generally injected hypodermically. However, the morphine salts found by Stevenson were usually only used for testing in chemist's shops and not used as a medicine.

The analyst estimated that a residue of 1.125 grains of morphine in the woman's body would indicate that she had actually ingested about four grains. Initially, this would have led to mild euphoria then heavy sweating, quickly followed by a deep sleep, from which it would have been difficult to arouse her. Gradually, respiratory failure would have overtaken the victim, leading to death within three to six hours. Typically, people who died from morphine poisoning showed signs of asphyxia, along with congestion of the heart and lungs, exactly as observed by Dr Pepper at the post-mortem.

Stevenson then examined the samples taken from the two children and was able to isolate the residue of a fatal dose of morphine from both.

Meanwhile, Pollard and Cole confronted Arthur Devereux at Coventry police station and, after cautioning him, informed him that they intended to take him to Harlesden police station on suspicion of causing the deaths of his wife and twin sons by administering poison to them. Devereux took the news very calmly, saying, 'Very well; I wish to make a statement, but will do so later on.'

It wasn't until he was safely on the train to London that he told the policemen, 'I think I will make my statement now.' Pollard handed Cole his fountain pen but the sergeant managed only a few words before the ink ran out. That did not stop Devereux chatting cheerfully, even though his words could not now be recorded. He asked the officers if the trunk had been opened and, when they told him it had, wanted to know if there had been any smell. He boasted that he had read about a recent case in which a dead body had been sealed into a trunk with cement but was convinced that his method of mixing glue with boric acid was a far better way of preventing the smell of decomposition, since the acid would inhibit the growth of fungus within the trunk. All the while he was bragging about his efficiency, Devereux was tucking into the luncheon basket thoughtfully provided for the journey by the police. His behaviour so sickened

Pollard that he eventually went to sit on the other side of the carriage, leaving Cole on his own with the prisoner.

Once Devereux arrived at the police station, he made a statement, saying that, one evening at the end of January or beginning of February that year, he was out with his son, Stanley. He and Beatrice had quarrelled before he left and when he returned, the house smelled strongly of chloroform and his wife and the twins lay dead in their beds. Devereux kept chloroform and morphine locked in his desk '...in the event of my wishing to end my own life rather than face starvation.' He assumed that Beatrice had used them to kill the children then commit suicide and, not wishing to endure the formalities of an inquest, he had concealed their bodies in the trunk.

Stevenson found no evidence that either Beatrice or the children had swallowed chloroform, saying that had they done so, he would have observed the effects on their stomachs. He could not rule out the possibility that the children had inhaled chloroform but believed it impossible for Beatrice to have administered chloroform to herself. The effects of the morphine would have prevented her from doing so and, had she inhaled sufficient chloroform to cause her death, the morphine would not have been found in so many different parts of her body. In addition, chloroform was a very volatile substance, which evaporated quickly. The only way for Beatrice to inhale a large enough quantity to kill her was for her to keep replenishing the drug on a pad or cloth held to her nose, which would have been impossible, given that she had ingested so much morphine.

An inquest was opened into the three deaths by Dr Gordon Hogg, the coroner for West Middlesex. Having heard the medical evidence, along with the testimony of various witnesses, the coroner concluded that Beatrice had been an excellent mother, who had been known to deny herself in order to feed her children. There was no evidence to suggest that she had ever contemplated suicide and, indeed, she was a great believer in homeopathy, which led to her shunning the use of orthodox medicines.

Arthur Devereux, on the other hand, had a history of minor deceptions and had even served a nine-month prison sentence for cheque fraud. He habitually used false references to obtain jobs and was frequently fired for laziness. Shortly before the deaths of Beatrice, Lawrence and Evelyn, Arthur had been dismissed from his job as manager of a chemist's shop in Kilburn because of poor sales. One of his favourite cons was to reply to newspaper advertisements for domestic servants in the guise of a young girl, asking for travelling expenses for an interview. When the expenses were sent, he would forward a fake doctor's certificate, saying that the girl was ill and now unable to travel. Needless to say, the fares were never returned. Between the deaths of his family members and his arrest, he had plenty of time to concoct an explanation for concealing their bodies.

After a short deliberation, the coroner's jury decided that the three victims had died as a result of morphine poisoning at the hands of Arthur Devereux, who had administered the poison with malice aforethought. He was therefore committed to stand trial on three counts of wilful murder.

His trial opened before Mr Justice Ridley at the Central Criminal Court on 24 July 1905, with Mr Matthews and Mr Bodkin prosecuting and Mr Elliott, Mr Fitch and Mr Hutton acting in Devereux's defence.

The court heard from William Garfarth, the agent who had let the property in Milton Avenue to Arthur Devereux, who had given his name as Egerton on signing the lease. Devereux had moved out unexpectedly owing a week's rent on the property, which he promised to pay when he had sold his furniture, which he later did. In conversation with the agent, Devereux complained about the expense of feeding the twins, saying that they cost him half a sovereign a week in milk alone. He also asked the agent not to reveal his whereabouts to his mother-in-law if she came looking for him and Garfarth was under the impression that Devereux's main reason for moving was to hide from her.

Ellen Gregory did indeed come looking and would not be satisfied until Garfarth had shown her round the house. Later Garfarth entered the house to clean it for the next occupier and found a large bottle on the mantelshelf, labelled 'Prussic Acid – Poison'. Garfarth threw the bottle away and the prosecution now maintained that it had been deliberately left by Devereux to muddy the waters of any future investigation into the deaths of his family.

Various neighbours of the family and numerous tradesmen who called at the house were called to give evidence, including Thomas Bannister and his employees, as well as those who had bought clothes and furniture from Devereux at around the time of his move. Included among these items was the twins' perambulator and the prosecution argued that Devereux had been well aware that they would never need it again.

Ellen Gregory testified at length and told the court that Arthur hated the twins and had once said of them, 'If I had not got all this bastard lot to keep, I could get on better by myself.'

The police recalled their investigations into and arrest of Arthur Devereux and the medical witnesses, including Dr Pepper and Thomas Stevenson, reported their findings. Devereux's latest employer, Mr Bird, also gave evidence, saying that Devereux gave him 'every satisfaction' and that he considered him to be a clever chemist and a good businessman.

The counsel for the defence then focused on a succession of Devereux's relatives who had been treated in various asylums, including his father, James, who had attempted to commit suicide by taking rat poison in 1891. Arthur's brother told the court that he considered his brother mentally weak and '…not in a normal condition' and a vicar who had known the family in

'If I had not got all this bastard lot to keep, I could get on better by myself'

Mr Justice Ridley (Author's collection)

Arthur's childhood considered him 'wanting in many things'. However, since most of the relatives now appeared to be cured, their impact on the jury was dulled, particularly when the prosecution forced an admission from Detective Inspector Pollard, who stated, 'I have found nothing as to the prisoner's mental history except that he was of sound mind and understanding – every person that I have asked said he was perfectly sane, and all his employers said that he was the best chemist they ever had.'

Dr Forbes Winslow, who had examined Devereux in custody at Brixton Prison, stated that he considered him to be a man of very weak intellect, suffering from partial mental disease, as opposed to total insanity. Other doctors concurred with Winslow's observations. Curiously, Winslow and others noted the presence of 'lunatic's ear' – a swelling behind both ears, normally associated with mental degeneration.

The defence then tried a different approach, looking for insanity in Beatrice's family, which might have led her to commit murder and suicide. Ellen Gregory had previously admitted that more than thirty years earlier, she had suffered from puerperal fever after giving birth to premature twins and that Beatrice's brother, Sidney, who was also a chemist, had been depressed following a bout of suspected meningitis. Sidney had vanished from his home and his clothes had later been found on Plymouth Hoe. Everyone but his mother believed that he had drowned himself.

Devereux spoke in his own defence, insisting that he had simply found his wife and children dead and was guilty only of concealing their bodies. Unfortunately, the jury did not believe him and, after deliberating for just ten minutes, found him guilty as charged.

He was hanged at Pentonville Prison on 15 August 1905 by Henry Pierrepoint, who was assisted by John Ellis. Thirty-four-year-old Arthur Devereux maintained his innocence until the very last.

Note: Devereux's employer in Coventry is named both as Mr Bird and Mr Baird.

21

'I am innocent and some day evidence will prove it'

Hawley Harvey Crippen was born in 1862 in Michigan, USA and studied medicine both in America and on a visit to England in 1883. The medical qualifications he gained in America were not sufficient to allow him to practice as a doctor in the United Kingdom but, in 1900, he returned to England and began working for The Munyon Company, a purveyor of patent homeopathic medicines.

Crippen had married while living in America and the marriage had produced a son. However, his wife died and the child was sent to live with his maternal grandmother in California. On 1 September 1892, Crippen married for the second time. His new wife was a seventeen-year-old girl named Kunigunde Mackamotski, the daughter of a Russian-Polish father and a German mother. Kunigunde had adopted the name Cora Turner purely for convenience, since her given name was almost unpronounceable.

The new Mrs Crippen had ambitions to become an opera singer and, while her husband worked at various locations in America, he paid for her to have voice training in New York. She also adopted yet another stage name and now became known as Belle Elmore.

When Crippen became manager of the Shaftesbury Avenue branch of Munyon's offices, Belle joined him in London. Her opera training had come to nothing since her ambitions were actually far greater than her talent. However, while living in London, she took to performing in the music halls. Although her stage career was not a great success, it did allow her to make friends in a new country and she eventually became Treasurer of the Music Hall Ladies Guild. She became particularly close to a fellow American music hall artiste, Bruce Miller, who frequently visited her at home during the six months that her husband was on a work-related trip to Philadelphia.

The Crippens lived at a number of rented properties around London before finally moving to 39 Hilldrop Crescent, Camden Town in September 1905.

Although it was a larger house than the couple really needed, their marriage was in serious trouble and they deliberately chose a big house to permit them to have separate bedrooms. The Crippens took in lodgers at Hilldrop Crescent to earn an extra income but that abruptly ceased when Crippen came home unexpectedly and caught his wife in bed with one of them. Crippen was later to state that sexual relations between him and his wife ceased in 1907 and in compensation for the lack of marital affection, he took a mistress, a young typist named Ethel le Neve.

While Belle might not have had any vestige of affection for her husband, she was furious when she learned of his extra-marital affair and threatened to leave him. While this arrangement might have suited Crippen, the fact that his wife was also promising to empty their savings account certainly did not. Although Crippen earned a good wage of £3 a week, Belle had notoriously expensive tastes and liked to buy fur coats and jewellery, as well as throwing extravagant dinner parties for her friends.

Matters came to a head in December 1909. At that time, Crippen was slightly overdrawn at his bank, although he and Belle held a savings account with a balance of £600. On 15 December, she gave written instructions to the bank of her intention to withdraw this money after the obligatory period of twelve months notice. In January 1910, Crippen visited Lewis and Burrow's shop on Oxford Street and placed an order for five grains of hyoscine hydrobromide, a poison used in ophthalmic clinics to dilate the pupils of the eyes and by injection in small quantities as a sedative for the treatment of nervous diseases such as delirium tremens, mania and meningitis. It was later discovered to be very effective for the treatment of motion sickness.

On 31 January 1910, Crippen and Belle gave a dinner party at home for two friends, Paul and Clara Martinetti. They passed a pleasant evening dining and later playing a few hands of whist and, when the Martinettis left Hilldrop Crescent in the early hours of 1 February, the Crippens seemed to them to be on good terms. However, according to Crippen, as soon as their guests had departed, Belle, who was known to have a ferociously bad temper, rounded on him and accused him of being ill mannered.

During the course of the evening, Paul Martinetti had excused himself to visit the lavatory. Belle believed that Crippen should have escorted him upstairs to show him where it was and she cited this apparent breach of etiquette as the final nail in the coffin of their marriage. She announced that she was leaving him and, from that moment on, she seemed to disappear off the face of the earth.

Two days later, Melinda May, the secretary of the Music Hall Ladies Guild, received two letters dated 2 February, one addressed to herself and one to the committee as a whole, saying that Belle had been unexpectedly called overseas as a relative in America had been taken ill and that she was resigning her position as the Treasurer of the Guild as a consequence. The letters, which were not in Belle's handwriting, were signed 'Belle Elmore per pro HHC', and were delivered to Mrs May by Ethel le Neve, who also brought Belle's Guild bank pass book, paying-in book and chequebook.

Over the next few days, Crippen pawned several items of Belle's jewellery and, on 20 February, he took Ethel to a ball organised by the Music Hall Ladies Benevolent Fund. Notwithstanding the fact that Crippen took another woman to a ball where he could expect many of the guests to be closely acquainted with his wife, it was also noted that Ethel was wearing Belle's jewellery.

Throughout February, Ethel spent several nights away from her lodgings and eventually moved into Hilldrop Crescent with Crippen, who, on 16 March, gave his landlord three months notice that he would be leaving the house. Nobody had either seen or heard from Belle Elmore since 1 February and, by mid-March, Crippen was telling their mutual friends that his wife had been taken ill with bronchitis and pneumonia in America and was not expected to pull through. He would take a holiday in France if she died, Crippen told Mrs Martinetti and, on 24 March 1910, she received a telegram from Victoria Station saying simply, 'Belle died yesterday at 6.00 pm'. A notice of Belle's death was inserted in *Era* newspaper on 26 March, on the instructions of her husband.

By the time Crippen and Ethel returned from a week's holiday in Dieppe, most of Belle's friends had heard the news of her death and several of them visited Crippen to ask about sending tokens of remembrance. Crippen told them that Belle had died in Los Angeles and that her body was to be cremated there and the ashes returned to London. He then carried on going about his normal day-to-day business while, unbeknown to him, a tide of gossip swelled among Belle's circle of friends, all of whom believed that Ethel le Neve had moved in with Crippen with indecent haste and that the fact that she was openly wearing Belle's jewels and furs was in bad taste, at the very least.

In late June, Mr John Edward Nash and his actress wife, who was professionally known as Lil Hawthorne, returned from a trip to America and learned about Belle's death for the first time. Thinking it strange that none of their mutual friends in New York had mentioned her passing, they went to visit Crippen who was still at Hilldrop Crescent, having informed his landlord that he would in fact be staying on until 29 September.

Having spoken to Crippen, Mr and Mrs Nash were far from happy with the answers they received and took their suspicions straight to Scotland Yard, where, on 30 June, they saw Inspector Walter Dew. Having made some enquiries of his own, Dew went to Hilldrop Crescent on 8 July with Sergeant Mitchell but found only Ethel le Neve at home. At Dew's request, she escorted them to Crippen's office, where Dew told Crippen that his wife's friends were not happy about the circumstances of her sudden disappearance and that, having made some enquiries himself, he too was not satisfied.

Left: *Lil Hawthorne (Mrs Nash).*
(Author's collection)

Below: *New Scotland Yard.*
(Author's collection)

'I suppose I had better tell the truth,' Crippen said wearily, admitting to the Inspector that, as far as he was aware, Belle was still alive and well. Crippen then dictated a statement to Sergeant Mitchell in which he told the officers that she had left him and that he believed she had gone to Chicago to join Bruce Miller. The tissue of lies Crippen had told since 1 February had merely been an effort to cover the scandal that her leaving him for another man would have caused.

At Dew's request, Crippen accompanied him back to Hilldrop Crescent where he willingly allowed the Inspector to search the house from top to bottom.

'Of course, I shall have to find Mrs Crippen to clear this matter up,' Dew told Crippen, who seemed unconcerned and even suggested placing an advertisement in the American newspapers asking for news of his wife. When Dew agreed that this would be a good idea, Crippen immediately sat down and drafted an advertisement, which he agreed to arrange to be inserted immediately. However, when Dew went back to the house three days later, the advertisement still lay on the kitchen table and Crippen and Ethel le Neve had vanished.

Dew circulated a description of the two fugitives, both in the United Kingdom and abroad. Crippen was described as an American doctor, aged fifty, with thinning light brown hair, inclined to sandiness, false teeth and a long, straggly, sandy moustache. He had 'a rather slovenly appearance' and threw his feet outwards when walking. Ethel was twenty-seven years old with a pale complexion, large grey eyes and light brown hair. She was apparently quiet, reticent and subdued in her manner and had a habit of looking at the speaker intently when in conversation.

Dew and a team of police officers spent the next two days searching the house at Hilldrop Crescent with a fine toothcomb, even going to the extent of digging up parts of the garden, but they found nothing suspicious. It was not until 13 July that Dew happened to notice what looked like a couple of loose bricks in the cellar floor. When he placed a poker in the joints between the bricks, they lifted easily and before long Dew had removed several bricks

A contemporary press cutting: Crippen's solicitor reviews the evidence against his client. (Author's collection)

DR. CRIPPEN.

The cellar at 39, Hilldrop-crescent, beneath the floor of which were found the remains alleged to be those of Mrs. Crippen, was on Thursday inspected by Mr. Arthur Newton, the solicitor acting for Dr. Crippen, who is under remand on the charge of murder.

Mr. Newton, who was accompanied by Inspector Dew and Sergeant Mitchell, of Scotland Yard, afterwards made an examination of the whole house. An interview with Dr. Crippen in Brixton Prison followed. Mr. Newton stated on Thursday evening that his client was in good spirits and anxious for the proceedings to begin as soon as possible.

A police constable stands guard outside No. 39 Hilldrop Crescent, Camden Town, following the discovery of human remains there in 1910. (Author's collection)

and begun to dig up the soil beneath them. At a depth of nine inches, he struck what appeared to be human remains.

Dew immediately stopped digging and sent for Dr Marshall, the Divisional Police Surgeon, and Sir Melville Macnaghten, the chief of the Criminal Investigation Department. Marshall arrived the next day in the company of Mr Augustus Pepper and supervised the removal of the remains to Islington mortuary, where a post-mortem examination could be conducted.

The remains were only part of a human body and comprised some hair, a piece of flesh from the buttock and thigh, some internal organs and another small piece of flesh. There was no head or bones. As the search of the cellar continued, two more pieces of the body were located – a large piece of skin with a little fat attached to it, which measured eleven inches by nine inches and came from the upper abdomen and lower chest, and a second smaller piece of skin from the lower abdomen. When Master of Surgery Augustus Pepper examined the smaller piece of skin, he noticed what he believed to be an old surgical scar on it. Bernard Spilsbury, then the pathologist at St Mary's Hospital, agreed with Pepper's observation, as did police surgeon Dr Marshall.

No sexual organs had been found with the remains but Pepper believed that the position of the scar might indicate that the body was that of a woman whose ovaries and / or womb had been removed in life. There was nothing to indicate the gender of the body but Pepper based his conclusion that it was female on the fact that the long hair found with it had been bleached and a section of it was still wrapped around a hair curler. Pepper believed that the body had been buried for between four and eight months and that it had been dissected by someone who had previous experience in the evisceration of either humans or animals.

The body parts had been liberally sprinkled with lime in an attempt to accelerate decomposition and there was nothing to suggest that the person hadn't been perfectly healthy in life or indication of any natural disease in the internal organs. Pepper theorised that the remains were those of a young to middle-aged woman, who had been rather stoutly built.

With no sign of any disease that might explain the woman's death, samples of her internal organs were sent to William Wilcox, a lecturer on forensic medicine at St Mary's Hospital and the senior scientific analyst to the Home Office. He was also sent some of the hair that had been found buried in the cellar, along with some fragments of clothing. On analysis of the organs, Wilcox found traces of arsenic and carbolic acid but dismissed these as insignificant since disinfectant containing both had been used by the police near the area of the body. When the remains were analysed for alkaloid poisons, the preliminary results indicated that one was present. Further testing eliminated the more common alkaloid poisons such as morphine, strychnine and cocaine and Wilcox was able to narrow the type of poison down to a mydriatic vegetable alkaloid, of which there are three types – atropine, hyoscyamine, and hyoscine.

Wilcox was eventually able to extract almost two-fifths of a grain of hyoscine, which he calculated to show the deceased having ingested about half a grain of hydrobromide of hyoscine. Since a fatal dose for an adult would be between a quarter and half a grain, Wilcox concluded that, in this case, death had occurred as a result of poisoning by hyoscine and, as far as he was aware, this was the first known case of murder by administration of that particular poison. Arthur Pearson Luff, who also worked as a Home Office Analyst, repeated some of the tests and agreed with Wilcox's conclusions.

Both analysts felt that, after ingestion of the poison, the victim would initially be excited and delirious. The pupils of the eye would be paralysed and the mouth and throat would become very dry. Soon the victim would feel drowsy, before lapsing into unconsciousness and dying within a few hours.

On 16 July, a warrant was issued for the arrest of Hawley Harvey Crippen on suspicion of the murder of his wife and Inspector Dew redoubled his efforts to locate the American doctor and his probable companion, Ethel le Neve. On 20 July, Scotland Yard advertised a reward of £250 for information leading to the arrest of Crippen and Ethel le Neve, stating that Crippen was wanted for 'murder and mutilation'. Soon afterwards a telegraph message was received at Scotland Yard from Captain Kendall, who was currently sailing his ship SS *Montrose* from Antwerp to Quebec: 'Have strong suspicions that Crippen London cellar murderer and accomplice are among saloon passengers. Accomplice dressed as a boy. Voice manner and build undoubtedly a girl.' [*sic*]

The two passengers were sailing under the names of John Robinson and John Robinson junior, purporting to be father and son. However, Captain Kendall felt sure that John junior was actually a woman dressed in ill-fitting boys' clothes, with her hair cut short in a masculine style. The Robinsons seemed strangely affectionate towards each other and had even been observed on deck holding hands.

Inspector Dew caught a faster boat, *Laurentic*, and set out to race the *Montrose* to Canada. Meanwhile, Captain Kendall was careful to make sure that there were no newspapers on board his ship, since Crippen's story was big news all around the world.

On 31 July, SS *Montrose* docked at Father Point in Canada. Dew and Canadian detectives boarded the ship in the guise of pilots and arrested Crippen and Ethel le Neve. Crippen was walking on the promenade deck when Dew approached him and actually seemed quite relieved to see the police officer. 'I am not sorry. The anxiety has been too much,' he said as Dew charged him with the wilful murder of his wife, although he immediately denied the charge, insisting that Belle had died in America.

Ethel le Neve's arrest did not go as smoothly. Approached in the ship's state room, she immediately fainted when told about Crippen's arrest. The ship's doctor, Dr Stewart, was called for but Ethel came round before he arrived and was seen by a stewardess to take a small paper packet out of her pocket. Believing the packet to contain poison, the stewardess reacted quickly to try and stop Ethel taking it but Ethel 'fought like one demented', raking at

DR. CRIPPEN'S RETURN.

TO SAIL ON THURSDAY FOR BRISTOL.

MONTREAL, Sunday.

Sergeant Mitchell, of Scotland Yard, with the necessary documents for the return of Dr. Crippen and Miss Le Neve, and the two wardresses, who will take charge of the girl, are expected to arrive in Quebec at midnight to-night. Inspector Dew and Chief Detective McCarthy went yesterday to Rimouski to meet the Lake Manitoba, in which they travelled.

Crippen and Miss Le Neve will be formally handed over to the English police to-morrow (Monday), but will remain in gaol till the Royal Edward sails for Avonmouth on Thursday. It is officially stated that they will go by the first boat after to-morrow, and the Royal Edward is the first.

The prisoners spend their time reading and chatting with the warders. Crippen seems quite unconcerned. Miss Le Neve is anxious to get back to England. Her appearance has been quite changed since she bought a wig to hide her close-cropped hair. "I do wish I were back in England," she said to-day; "life is so wearisome here. I want to get home."—"Daily Mail."

Above and right: Contemporary press cuttings (Author's collection)

REPORTED CONFESSION BY CRIPPEN.

It is reported at Quebec that Crippen has confessed to having murdered his wife in consequence of a quarrel.

NEW YORK, Aug. 3.—The "Evening Sun's" Quebec correspondent says it is an absolute fact that Crippen has made a full confession to Inspector Dew of the murder of his wife.

QUEBEC, Aug. 3.—Dr. Crippen has sent the following telegram to Mr. Newton, the London solicitor, who, on behalf of the prisoner's friends, has offered his services for the defence: "Accept your offer. Secrecy will be observed."

"Dr." Crippen is much changed in appearance since his arrival. The four days' growth of his beard has not improved his looks, and he is not allowed to shave. Mr. Morin, the governor of the prison, said the precautions taken against the possibility of the suicide of "Dr." Crippen were so strict that he was not even trusted in the hands of the gaol barber.

The rumoured statements of "Dr." Crippen in connection with the crime have sent correspondents scurrying from one provincial officer to another, and although nothing in confirmation has been learned, it is variously reported that "Dr." Crippen admitted having had a scuffle with his wife, after which she was seized with a fatal illness. He is also said to have explained that the death was accidental. To all such stories the police reply that, so far as they know, neither "Dr." Crippen nor Miss Le Neve has made any statement regarding the crime.

the stewardess with her fingernails and tearing the woman's arms and wrists. When she was eventually subdued, Ethel too was arrested and changed out of her boys' clothes into some women's garments, loaned to her by the stewardess.

Crippen and his lover were led from the ship onto Canadian soil, where they were greeted by an excitable crowd of more than 800 people, all of whom had been avidly following Inspector Dew's pursuit in the newspapers. There was a delay in transporting the two fugitives back to London, since the necessary paperwork for their extradition had to be brought from England to Canada and then considered by a magistrates' court. Therefore it was 20 August before Inspector Dew finally set sail for England with the two suspects in his custody.

Crippen was tried for the murder of his wife at the Old Bailey before Lord Chief Justice, Lord Alverstone. The case was prosecuted by Richard D. Muir, Travers Humphreys and S. Ingleby Oddie and Mr A.A. Tobin, Huntley Jenkins and H.D. Roome handled the defence.

Mr Alfred A. Tobin, defence counsel. (Author's collection)

The trial of Dr Crippen at the Old Bailey, 1910. (Author's collection)

Crippen's only defence was that the body found in the cellar of the house at Hilldrop Crescent was not that of his wife. Taking the stand he assured the court, 'I did not at any time administer hyoscine to my wife. I have no idea whose remains were found at my house in Hilldrop Crescent. I knew nothing about them until I came back to England.' He admitted that his wife had a scar on her abdomen arising from the removal of her ovaries twelve years previously and he also agreed that she had bleached her hair blonde, saying that he had helped her to do so on occasions. Yet, as far as he was concerned, his wife had simply walked out on him and he believed that she had run away with Bruce Miller. He had invented the story of her death in America to avoid the scandal her actions would provoke.

The prosecution's evidence was persuasive. The medical witnesses testified that the woman had died as a result of poisoning by hyoscine and Crippen was known to have bought a large quantity of the poison, supposedly on behalf of Munyon's. The medical witnesses stated that hyoscine was not used as an ingredient in homeopathic medicine but Crippen countered by describing its use for the treatment of nervous diseases, going into great detail about the formula he used to prepare the medication, which was eventually made into small sugar discs to be sent out to his patients.

The one aspect of the case that Crippen didn't have a ready explanation for was the small pieces of cloth found buried with the remains of the body in the cellar. They had been identified as remnants of a man's pyjama jacket, which Crippen insisted was not his. The police had managed to trace the garment to its manufacturer, Jones Brothers Ltd, and a representative of the firm told the court that the particular cloth and pattern had not been used until late in 1908. This meant that the body must have been buried after that time, when Crippen and his wife were renting the house.

It took the jury less than half an hour to find Crippen 'Guilty' and he was given the mandatory death sentence by the judge.

Twenty-seven-year-old Ethel le Neve was tried for perversion of justice, the charge against her being:

> On February 1, 1910, Hawley Harvey Crippen having feloniously and unlawfully and of his malice aforethought murdered Cora Crippen, she, Ethel Clara le Neve, well knowing the said Hawley Harvey Crippen to have committed the said felony, did on that day and on divers days there-after feloniously receive, comfort, harbour, assist, and maintain him. [*sic*]

Although Ethel obviously knew that Crippen's wife had disappeared, there was no evidence to suggest that she had not been taken in by his story that his wife had died in America and she was acquitted.

Hawley Harvey Crippen maintained his innocence until the end. He was executed by John Ellis at Pentonville Prison on 23 November 1910, having made a last request for a photograph of Ethel le Neve and her letters to be buried with him.

Within hours of Crippen's execution, Ethel le Neve fled to New York aboard the SS *Majestic*. Travelling under the name Mrs Allen, she dressed in mourning and wore a veil over her face at all times. From New York she travelled to Canada, where she took a job as a typist. Three years later and now calling herself Miss Harvey, she returned to London and began working as a typist at Hampton's Furniture Store. There she met a clerk, Stanley Smith, and they married in January 1915, settling in Croydon.

Ethel gave birth to two children but, when she died from heart failure in 1967, neither her son nor her daughter had any idea about her past life.

The house at 39 Hilldrop Crescent, which had been the focus for a steady stream of sightseers since the discovery of the body, was destroyed by enemy bombs during the Second World War. However, a tissue sample from the remains excavated from the cellar was stored at the Royal London Hospital and, in the light of advances in forensic medicine, it was recently subjected to testing by a team of American scientists. At the conclusion of several years work, David Foran, a forensic biologist from Michigan State University made a startling announcement. According to Foran, the remains were not those of Mrs Crippen.

The scientists reinvestigating the case were initially puzzled by the dismemberment of the body. In an article in the *Guardian* of 7 October 2007, toxicologist John Trestrail stated that normally the aim of the poisoner was to convince doctors that the victim had died a natural death and, in his database of more than 1,100 cases, Crippen's was the only one in which the victim's body had been cut up. Researchers had spent many years tracking down and testing known descendants of 'Belle Elmore' and arrived at their conclusion after comparing the mitochondrial DNA from the original tissue sample and from living descendants of Crippen's wife.

Intriguingly, a check of the census records of the time showed that, ten years after Crippen's execution, a singer named Belle Rose was registered as living with Cora's sister in New York. The woman had entered America from Bermuda in 1910, shortly after the disappearance in England of Belle Elmore.

Whether Belle Rose and Belle Elmore were one and the same person will probably never be known but before his death, Crippen is reputed to have written a letter from the condemned cell in which he stated, 'I am innocent and some day evidence will prove it.' Almost one hundred years after his death, could it be that Crippen's prophecy might come true?

Note: There are some discrepancies in contemporary newspaper accounts of the case. Cora's age when she married Crippen is variously given as seventeen, nineteen and twenty-one years. The aliases used by Crippen and Ethel le Neve on board the SS *Montrose* are variously given as John Robinson and George Robinson. Crippen's son, who lived with his grandmother in America, is sometimes referred to as his stepson. There are also suggestions that Crippen may have actually shot his wife after giving her poison, some sources saying that the hyoscine had made her too excitable, others saying that having poisoned her, Crippen could not bear to watch her prolonged suffering. There is no mention of shooting in Crippen's trial.

22

'If you interfere with her money you will be in a rough corner'

Eliza Mary Barrow, a forty-nine-year-old spinster, died on 14 September 1911. The cause of her death was certified as acute enteritis and she was buried two days later. And there the matter might have rested had it not been for Frank Ernest Vonderache, who called to visit his cousin at her lodgings in Tollington Park, Islington on 20 September.

'Don't you know she is dead and buried?' asked Mary Chater, the servant who opened the door to him.

Vonderache certainly didn't know. The last time he had seen his cousin she had been in good health, living with a little boy, Ernie Grant, who she had informally adopted after his mother's death.

Tollington Park, Islington, c. 1910. (Author's collection)

The servant suggested that Vonderache waited to see the owner of the house, Frederick Henry Seddon, although eventually Vonderache was to call at the house several times before he was finally able to talk to his cousin's landlord.

Vonderache was aware that his cousin had been a woman of some means and asked Seddon if he might see her will. Seddon prevaricated, saying that since Vonderache was not the oldest member of the family, he didn't think he should show it to him. He reassured Vonderache that the will was perfectly legal.

As well as owning numerous shares, Miss Barrow had also owned the Buck's Head, a large public house, along with the barber's shop next door. When Vonderache asked Seddon who now held the leases to these premises, Seddon told him that Miss Barrow had signed everything she owned over to him, in exchange for an annuity of £1 a week. In addition, Seddon had taken over some India stock owned by Miss Barrow, for which he gave her an additional weekly payment of £2 2s. Seddon produced a copy of a letter that he had supposedly sent to Vonderache, notifying him of his cousin's death and telling him that all her property had been left to her ward, Ernie Grant and Ernie's sister, Hilda, with Seddon as the sole executor of her will.

When Seddon eventually produced the will, Vonderache noticed that it had been drawn up and signed the day before his cousin's death and witnessed by members of Seddon's family. Vonderache was shocked to find that all his cousin's property now belonged to her landlord. He was also disturbed to learn that Miss Barrow had been swiftly and cheaply buried in a public grave in Finchley, rather than in her family vault. Vonderache realised that, with Seddon paying Miss Barrow a weekly annuity in return for ownership of her property, the shorter her life, the more profit Seddon was likely to make. He took his concerns to the Director of Public Prosecutions and consequently the police were asked to investigate Miss Barrow's death.

Miss Barrow was known to be rather deaf. She was also somewhat eccentric, an extremely parsimonious woman, who could be awkward and difficult to get along with at times. She had lived with her cousin and his wife for eleven months until July 1911, at which time she left following a minor disagreement about how her food was cooked, then renting rooms with Seddon and his wife and family at 63 Tollington Park. An engine driver from St Austell in Cornwall, Robert Hook and his wife also took lodgings there on the same day, on the agreement that they would care for Miss Barrow. Hook and Miss Barrow were former sweethearts who had remained good friends, although they were no longer romantically involved. Miss Barrow had previously lodged with Hook's mother and, after her death, had moved to lodge with Hook's sister, Mrs Grant, the mother of Ernest and Hilda. When Mrs Grant died from the effects of alcoholism, Hilda was sent to an orphanage, while Miss Barrow agreed to care for Ernie.

Hook therefore knew Eliza Barrow well and was aware that she was distrustful of banks and usually kept large amounts of cash in her room. On one occasion in 1906, Hook had even helped her count her money and knew that, at that time, she had £420 in gold alone, not including bank notes, her India Stock, the ownership of the leases of the pub and barber's shop and some nice pieces of jewellery.

Within two weeks of Hook moving into his lodgings, landlord Mr Seddon served a notice to quit on him and his wife, saying that it had come from Miss Barrow. According to a letter from Miss Barrow, she wanted the Hooks to leave because Robert had treated her badly, even though, as far as the Hooks were aware, they had been on friendly terms with her right up until the moment that the notice was served. Hook was suspicious of Seddon, accusing him of trying to get his hands on Miss Barrow's money but Seddon insisted that he was only trying to protect his lodger's interests. 'If you interfere with her money you will be in a rough corner,' Hook told Seddon. At Seddon's insistence, the Hooks left his home within twenty-four hours of the eviction notice being served on them.

Two days later, Eliza Barrow was suddenly taken ill and on 2 September, Mrs Seddon telephoned her family doctor, Henry Sworn, and asked him to visit. Eliza had previously been cared for by another doctor, John Paull, who had treated her for a number of minor illnesses including congestion of the liver, mild asthma and constipation. Mrs Seddon told Dr Sworn that she had twice telephoned Dr Paull to request a visit but that he had been too busy to come and had advised her to contact another doctor. Now she was worried about Miss Barrow, who had been suffering from abdominal pain, accompanied by severe sickness and diarrhoea, since the previous day.

Sworn examined Miss Barrow and prescribed a mixture of bismuth and morphia. He visited Miss Barrow several times over the next few days but she showed no sign of improvement and, according to Mrs Seddon, was refusing to take her medicine. Sworn prescribed a different mixture, an effervescent cocktail of citrate of potash and bicarbonate of soda, which was prepared in separate containers and then mixed together at the last moment before being given to the patient. He threatened Miss Barrow that, if she didn't take her medicine, he would be forced to send her into hospital.

Miss Barrow's condition slowly improved and on 11 September, the doctor found her much better, although still very weak. He suggested that she should be given Valentine's meat juice, brandy and milk to build up her strength, progressing to milk puddings in a few days time, providing the improvement continued. However by 13 September, the sickness and diarrhoea had returned, her temperature was slightly raised and her pulse was weak. Sworn prescribed bismuth and aromatic chalk but at seven o'clock on the following morning, Mr Seddon visited his office to say that Eliza Barrow had died during the night.

Dr Sworn was not unduly surprised at this news and, having treated Miss Barrow for twelve days, was willing to issue Seddon with a death certificate, on which he gave the cause of Miss Barrow's death as epidemic diarrhoea and exhaustion.

As a result of Frank Vonderache's suspicions, it was decided to hold a formal inquest into the death of Eliza Barrow and on 11 November, coroner Mr Cohen signed an order for her body to be exhumed. This was done on 14 November and the body was then examined by Bernard Spilsbury, the pathologist at St Mary's Hospital.

Spilsbury's first observation was that the body was remarkably well preserved, which is often a side effect of arsenic poisoning. However, initially, he was unable to find anything about Miss Barrow's body that was not consistent with her having died from the causes certified by Dr Sworn.

Also present at the post-mortem examination was William Wilcox, the Senior Analyst to the Home Office. Wilcox removed portions of Miss Barrow's liver, stomach, intestines, spleen and brain for analysis and also took some muscle, bone, hair and fingernail clippings. He was able to isolate the equivalent of 2.01 grains of arsenic from Miss Barrow's body and estimated that she had taken a considerably larger dose, some of which had been expelled from her body by vomiting and purging. Between them, Wilcox and Spilsbury concluded that Eliza Barrow had died from the ingestion of arsenic, probably taken two or three days before her death, since it had had sufficient time to be traceable in her hair and fingernails. The true cause of Miss Barrow's death was therefore acute arsenic poisoning, most probably a single dose.

At the request of the police, Wilcox also analysed a sample of the medicine that Dr Sworn was known to have prescribed for Miss Barrow. He found it to contain minute traces of arsenic but estimated that the deceased would have needed to take at least 2cwt of the medicine to produce the amount of arsenic residue found in her body.

The Seddons were known to have purchased flypapers at the suggestion of Dr Sworn, since Miss Barrow's chronic diarrhoea, in combination with hot weather at the time of her illness, had not only been extremely foul smelling but had also attracted a huge number of flies to her bedroom. Wilcox analysed several different brands of arsenic-coated flypapers and was able to extract arsenic from all of them in varying quantities just by soaking them in water.

Having both the motive and opportunity to kill Miss Barrow, Frederick Seddon was the obvious suspect for her murder and he was arrested on 4 December 1911. 'Absurd!' was Seddon's reaction. 'What a terrible charge – wilful murder. It is the first of our family ever to be accused of such a crime' [*sic*]. Seddon then asked the arresting officers, 'Are you going to arrest my wife as well?'

If Miss Barrow had indeed been murdered, then realistically there were only four people who could have administered the fatal dose of arsenic. Servant Mary Chater had neither prepared nor served Miss Barrow's food. In fact she had never even been into Miss Barrow's room, which was somewhat surprising given that she had trained and worked as a nurse before entering the Seddons' service. The Seddons had five children and one of them, a daughter named Margaret, was known to have purchased flypapers from chemist Walter Thorley before Miss Barrow's death. However, although Margaret had prepared food for Miss Barrow prior to her illness, once Miss Barrow fell ill, her mother had taken over her care. The police soon established that only Mr and Mrs Seddon had been directly involved in caring for the deceased during her final illness. Thus, Mrs Seddon – also called Margaret – was arrested on 15 January 1912 and jointly charged with her husband with Miss Barrow's wilful murder. 'Yes, very well,' was her only comment.

Frederick Henry Seddon and his wife Margaret Ann were committed for trial at the Central Criminal Court, or Old Bailey, where both defendants pleaded 'Not Guilty' to the charges against them. The presiding judge was Mr Justice Bucknill and Richard D. Muir, S.A.T. Rowlatt and Travers Humphreys appeared for the prosecution while Edward Marshall-Hall, Wellesley Orr and Mr R. Dunstan conducted the Seddons' defence, with Mr Rentod acting specifically for Margaret Seddon, in a trial that was to last for ten days.

The prosecution called Robert Hook and Frank Vonderache and his wife, brother and sister-in-law, as well as several of Henry Seddon's colleagues from his job as a district superintendent for the London and Manchester Assurance Company, all of whom testified about Miss Barrow's financial affairs. Hook and the Vonderaches spoke of the money and assets she had before going to lodge with the Seddons, while Seddon's colleagues had all seen him counting out quantities of gold coins, which he had then placed in his safe. Hook stated that he had read a newspaper report of Miss Barrow's inquest in the newspapers, after which he had immediately contacted the police to voice his suspicions of foul play by her landlord.

The prosecution then summoned a succession of solicitors and bank managers, all of whom had had financial dealings with either Miss Barrow or Frederick Seddon. The police had been able to establish that several bank notes known to have been in Miss Barrow's possession had been paid into Seddon's bank account. It was also revealed that Seddon had sold Miss Barrow's India stock for the sum of £1,519 16s and had used the proceeds to buy several properties, from which he obtained a total annual rent of £200.

Solicitor Edwin Russell had acted for Frederick Seddon in the transfer of the Buck's Head and its adjoining barber's shop, while another solicitor, Henry Knight, had acted for Miss Barrow in the transaction, which took place on 11 January 1911. Knight told the court that, although Miss Barrow was partially deaf, he had read the relevant documents aloud to her and also handed them to her to read. He was happy that Miss Barrow knew what she was doing when she signed the leases over to Frederick Seddon in return for an annuity.

The prosecution also called medical witnesses Dr Paull, Dr Sworn, Bernard Spilsbury and William Wilcox and then ten-year-old Ernest Grant, who had shared a bedroom with Miss Barrow until the night before her death. Grant told the court that he too had seen Miss Barrow with money and gold coins, which she kept in a cashbox and would often count. Grant, who called Miss Barrow 'Chicky', stated that the Seddons had been kind to them and had nursed Miss Barrow throughout her illness. Ernest recalled that there had been a lot of flies in Miss Barrow's sickroom but could not remember ever seeing flypapers there.

Funeral director William Nodes told the court about the arrangements made by Seddon for Miss Barrow's funeral. Seddon had told Nodes that the funeral needed to be cheap since he had found the sum of £4 10s in his lodger's room, with which he needed to pay both her funeral expenses and her doctor's bills. Nodes offered to conduct the funeral for £4 but Seddon said that was too expensive and eventually the two men agreed on a total sum of £3 7s 6d. Nodes had seen nothing untoward in Seddon's apparent haste to get the body buried as the weather at the time was very hot and, when he went to collect Miss Barrow's body from the Seddon's home, he could not help but notice the foul smell of faeces and decomposition that permeated the entire house.

Next, chemist Walter Thorley related selling flypapers to the Seddons' daughter, Margaret. Thorley had subsequently picked Margaret from an identity parade and stated that she had purchased Mather's Arsenical Flypapers from him at some time after 26 August 1911 and that each paper contained between three and four grains of arsenic.

The police officers involved in the investigations into Miss Barrow's death told the court of arresting Frederick Seddon and afterwards making a search of his house. Among the items they found was a small paper packet containing a lock of human hair, which had been labelled in Seddon's writing 'Miss Barrow's hair for Ernest and Hilda Grant.' When tested, this too was found to contain arsenic.

With that, the prosecution rested and Mr Marshall-Hall spoke for the defence. He first pointed out that there was '...not a tittle of evidence' that either Frederick Seddon or his wife had ever possessed arsenic. Indeed, Marshall-Hall argued that there was absolutely no evidence that Miss Barrow had even died from arsenic poisoning. The fact that arsenic had been found throughout the hair sample found by the police indicated that Miss Barrow had been taking arsenic for some time and, as Marshall-Hall said, it was possible to buy pills and medicines containing arsenic from all registered chemists and druggists. The test carried out by Wilcox was qualitative rather than quantitative – in other words, it was useful for detecting the presence of arsenic but poor at proving exactly how much.

The defence counsels had strongly advised Frederick Seddon not to take the witness stand but he insisted that he wanted to give his own account.

Seddon described his job and told the court about his financial dealings over the few years prior to Miss Barrow's death. He described accepting Mr and Mrs Hook, Miss Barrow and Ernest Grant as lodgers at his house and how there had been frequent disagreements between them, until he felt that he had no alternative but to ask one of them to leave. He had originally intended to evict Miss Barrow but, faced with her tearful pleas to allow her to stay and her insistence that the Hooks had treated her cruelly, he relented and evicted the Hooks instead.

Until he actually evicted the Hooks, said Seddon, he had absolutely no idea that Miss Barrow had a cashbox in her room that contained large amounts of money. Seddon maintained that Miss Barrow had been fearful that the Hooks would try to steal it from her when they left the house and had brought it to him to ask if he would put it in his safe. However, she had then changed her mind and he had never had possession of the cashbox.

After the Hooks left, Miss Barrow was incapable of caring for herself so had agreed to pay the Seddon's daughter one shilling a day to take care of her. Miss Barrow had been very concerned about her financial affairs – her India stock was dropping in value and a recent budget by Mr Lloyd George had increased the taxes paid on licensed premises, which she felt was devaluing her lease on the Buck's Head. It had been Miss Barrow's idea to exchange her property and stock for an annuity and Seddon assured the court that, whenever possible, everything he had done on Miss Barrow's behalf had been with proper legal representation to ensure that her interests were protected at all times. However, Miss Barrow had shown a deep distrust of solicitors, particularly when it came to rewriting her will. She had been concerned about providing for Ernest and Hilda Grant and been aghast at the idea that her family or the Hooks might inherit her money. Thus she had asked Seddon to act for her and he had hurriedly drawn up a new will, which Miss Barrow had signed. Seddon insisted that he had fully intended to take the will to a solicitor to get it drafted in a proper legal form but had become too busy trying to care for the seriously ill Miss Barrow, who was still refusing to take her medicine and was being extremely demanding on both Seddon and his wife.

Seddon then admitted that he was slightly better off financially since Miss Barrow's death, since he no longer had to pay out her annuity. However, he told the court that he had promised Miss Barrow that Ernie Grant would always have a home with his family as long as he had no other relatives to care for him and that the cost of Ernie's keep and the loss of the seven shillings paid to his daughter each week for looking after Miss Barrow, as well as Miss Barrow's weekly rent of twelve shillings, were almost equal to the amount he had been paying out.

As far as Seddon was concerned, any money or possessions that Miss Barrow had left were to go to Ernest and Hilda Grant and he had merely been entrusted with managing the legacy until the children came of age. Nothing that he or his wife had done could account for the presence of arsenic in Miss Barrow's body, insisted Seddon, saying, 'How the arsenic came to be in Miss Barrow's stomach and intestines is a Chinese puzzle to me.'

Mrs Seddon also testified at length and her testimony corroborated that of her husband. She too vehemently denied having ever administered arsenic to Eliza Barrow. Looking much older than her thirty-four years, according to one contemporary newspaper, Mrs Seddon gave the impression that she didn't know why she was there and made no attempt either to seek her way out or to evade any dangerous questions.

It was the contention of the defence that, rather than a single dose of arsenic, Miss Barrow may have been dosing herself with patent medicine containing the poison for some time. Rather than there having been four people in the household who might conceivably have administered arsenic to Miss Barrow before her death, there were in fact five – the fifth being the deceased woman herself. It was suggested that Miss Barrow had either taken medicinal arsenic or might even have drunk the water in which the flypapers were soaking in her room during her final illness.

In his summary of the evidence for the jury, Mr Justice Bucknill told them, 'I should be astonished if you do not acquit her [Mrs Seddon].' The jury deliberated for almost an hour before returning with their verdicts – 'Not Guilty' for Mrs Seddon, at which her husband leaned over and kissed her. The jury then pronounced forty-year-old Frederick Henry Seddon 'Guilty'.

Before sentence was passed, Seddon was asked if he had anything to say. He immediately launched into a long, prepared speech in which he again refuted much of the prosecution's evidence before finally appealing to the judge as 'a brother Mason' to reverse the jury's finding. 'I declare before the Great Architect of the Universe I am not guilty,' said Seddon in conclusion to his speech, at which Mr Justice Bucknill broke down completely, before eventually pronouncing the death sentence against his fellow Freemason with some difficulty.

Pentonville Prison, 1914. (Author's collection)

John Ellis, assisted by Thomas Pierrepoint, executed Frederick Henry Seddon at Pentonville Prison on 18 April 1912. Shortly before his death, Seddon wrote a last letter to his sister, in which he continued to insist that he was innocent and, looking at the case with the benefit of hindsight, does raise some doubts about his guilt.

The lock of Miss Barrow's hair, which Seddon had asked the undertaker to cut as a keepsake for Ernest and Hilda Grant, tested positive for arsenic from root to tip, which appears to indicate that, rather than one single, fatal dose, the deceased had been taking arsenic for some time before her death. This does not exclude Seddon as the person who administered that arsenic but it does raise the question of why he did not simply have Miss Barrow's body cremated, which would have prevented her exhumation and thus ensured that his crime had gone undiscovered.

Note: In the contemporary newspapers there are numerous variations of the spelling of Vonderache, including Vonderake, Vonderahes and Vonderashe. There is also a discrepancy in names of the counsel for the prosecution, with some accounts suggesting that the prosecution was led by the then Solicitor General, Sir Rufus Isaacs. As always, I have taken the most commonly used names and spellings for this account.

23
'Excuse my fingers'

HAY-ON-WYE, HEREFORDSHIRE, 1921

Major Herbert Rowse Armstrong had practiced as a solicitor in the Herefordshire town of Hay-on-Wye for several years when, in 1921, he found himself in dispute with the town's other solicitors over the sale of an estate. Initially a junior partner with the firm Cheese and Armstrong, Armstrong had taken over the running of the practice after the senior partner and his wife died within a day of each other in 1914. Now, seven years later, he was being pressured by fellow solicitor, Oswald Norman Martin, to complete on the sale of a property, for which Armstrong held a deposit of £500 from Martin's client.

Given the dispute between the two men, it came as a complete surprise to Oswald Martin when, on 20 September 1921, he received an unexpected gift from Armstrong in the form of a box of chocolates, which were delivered to his house. As neither Martin nor his wife, Constance, were particularly fond of sweets, they each ate only one chocolate before putting the box away, to be brought out on 8 October after a dinner party.

Much to Constance Martin's embarrassment, one of her dinner guests reported being violently ill on the day after the get-together. Dorothy Martin – the wife of Oswald's brother, Gilbert – was the only guest to have partaken of the chocolates after the meal, although this fact wasn't noted at the time.

With the property deal still stalling, Oswald Martin's client finally felt that enough was enough and decided to withdraw from the transaction completely. When Martin communicated his client's instructions to Armstrong, it was suggested by Armstrong that the two solicitors should meet to thrash out the deal between them. Accordingly, on 26 October 1921, Martin presented himself at Armstrong's house, 'Mayfield', having been invited for afternoon tea.

The host poured tea and handed his guest a buttered scone, using his fingers rather than proffering the plate. 'Excuse my fingers,' he told Martin. Within a short time of returning home, Martin found himself inexplicably stricken by a mysterious illness. Throughout that night he vomited persistently, his heart raced and he had stomach pains and attacks of diarrhoea. When he awoke the next morning, he found himself extremely sensitive to light.

On hearing of Martin's illness, Herbert Armstrong seemed most concerned, offering to help with his fellow solicitor's work during Martin's enforced absence from his office.

Martin's wife, Constance, was the daughter of John Davies, the chemist in Hay-on-Wye. On hearing of his son-in-law's illness and of the similar symptoms suffered by Dorothy Martin after eating a chocolate gifted to the Martins by Armstrong, Davies realised that Armstrong had frequently purchased arsenic from his shop over the preceding few months, saying that he wanted to make up a weed-killing solution to deal with the dandelions in his lawn at home.

Davies put his suspicions to the doctor treating his son-in-law and Dr Hincks accordingly collected samples of Oswald Martin's vomit and urine, sending them with the remains of the box of chocolates to the Clinical Research Association in London. When tested, all were found to contain arsenic.

The police were notified and immediately began a discreet investigation into Armstrong's conduct. Major Armstrong, a prominent freemason and member of the Conservative Party, was a highly respected solicitor in Hay and his character was hitherto without blemish, hence the police enquiries were conducted in complete secrecy. Unaware that he was under investigation, Armstrong continued to issue invitations to Martin to dine with him, which Martin persistently declined, all the while trying not to alert Armstrong to the fact that he was under suspicion.

Broad Street, Hay-on-Wye, 1930s. (Author's collection)

Broad Street, Hay-on-Wye, 1970s. (Author's collection)

By 31 December 1921, the police had gathered sufficient evidence against Armstrong to pounce and he was arrested in his Broad Street office and charged with the attempted murder of Oswald Martin. However, the charge of attempted murder was little more than a holding charge as, during their investigations, the police had developed strong suspicions that Armstrong had been responsible for the death of his wife, Katherine, on 22 February 1921.

Herbert and Katherine Armstrong had been married since 1907 and had three children. Always a rather sickly woman, with a tendency towards hypochondria, Katherine Armstrong had begun to suffer from gastric illness in May 1920, shortly after making a new will. In her previous will, the majority of her estate had been divided between her children, with her husband benefiting only from an annual legacy of just £50. Now, according to the terms of her new will, Katherine's estate was left to her husband in its entirety.

By 22 August 1920, Katherine Armstrong's sickliness had progressed to a real illness and she was admitted to the Barnwood Hospital for Mental Disorders in Gloucester. On admission, having been certified as insane by a Justice of the Peace, doctors found her to have a heart murmur, as well as being confused and delusional. Between 5 October and 4 November, Mrs Armstrong was treated with a medicine containing four minims of arsenic in solution, which equated to a dose of three twentieths of a grain of arsenic per day. This treatment was discontinued after 4 November.

Armstrong appeared to show the greatest concern for his wife's wellbeing, visiting her as often as the doctors would allow him to and, by mid-January

1921, was keen that she should be allowed home. Her delusions now very much a thing of the past, Katherine was released from hospital on 22 January to find that her husband had engaged the services of a nurse to look after her. Yet Katherine was obviously still far from well and the nurse, Muriel Kinsey, was to hand in her notice just a few days later, claiming that she was unable to cope with her patient's threats of suicide. Katherine refused to take anything but her own homeopathic medicine, claiming that the doctors in the asylum had 'poisoned her with drugs'. She also frequently asked about the likely effects of throwing herself out of an upstairs window. On 27 January, Muriel Kinsey was replaced by nurse Eva Allen.

For the following few weeks, Katherine Armstrong suffered repeated attacks of vomiting, coupled with muscular spasms and, on 22 February, she finally died, just two weeks after her forty-eighth birthday. For the few days prior to her death, she was so weak that she could not get out of bed and had lost the use of her hands, legs and feet, having to be hand-fed by her nurse. The cause of her death was given as heart disease (one year), nephritis (six months) and acute gastritis (twenty-one days).

Armstrong was hardly the grieving husband. He immediately took a month's holiday abroad and, on returning to Hay, proposed marriage to a long-term acquaintance, Mrs Marion Gale. He had met Mrs Gale in 1915, while stationed at Bournemouth during his wartime service with the Royal Engineers.

On Armstrong's arrest for the attempted murder of Oswald Martin, he was searched and found to have a small packet containing one twentieth of an ounce of arsenic in his jacket pocket. Yet more of the poison was found in the drawers of his desk and his assertion that he had purchased it for killing dandelions was not believed. On 2 January 1922, Katherine Armstrong's body was exhumed from the churchyard at nearby Cusop and Sir Bernard Spilsbury conducted a post-mortem examination on her remains. On testing, her organs were found to contain three-and-three-quarter grains of arsenic. Her husband was formally charged with her murder on 19 January 1922.

Armstrong then faced the undoubtedly personally humiliating experience of appearing before the very magistrates to whom he had previously acted in a professional capacity as clerk. There, the presiding magistrate, Mr W. Mortimer Baylis, heard from numerous witnesses about the gradual deterioration of Katherine Armstrong's health leading to her eventual death. One witness in particular caused a buzz of interest in the packed courtroom – a mysterious veiled woman, known only to the court as 'Mrs X'.

Although her identity was ultimately revealed to be Mrs Marion Gale, as far as the magistrates' court was concerned, the woman remained incognito. A widow, she described her first meeting with the defendant in the autumn of 1915, when she told the court that she knew that he was married, although

Above: *High Town, Hereford in the 1920s. (Author's collection)*

Left: *Hereford Town Hall: location of the Assizes. (Author's collection)*

she had never met Mrs Armstrong. She had dined with Armstrong in London in 1920 and the couple had resumed their friendship after Mrs Armstrong's death in 1921. At that time, Mrs X had been invited to stay at Armstrong's home and Armstrong had proposed marriage. 'I was considering it,' Mrs X told the court. Although she was not cross-examined, she was asked by Mr

Micklethwait, Armstrong's defending solicitor, if she was aware that Armstrong had also proposed to another woman. 'I have no knowledge of that,' she replied.

While Armstrong was remanded in custody awaiting his trial, his three children and two of his servants were staying with a family friend in Hereford. It was reported on 11 February that the friend had received a box of chocolates doctored with tintacks and that police were investigating the matter.

Armstrong was eventually committed for trial at the Hereford Assizes before Mr Justice Darling, who stated that it might be necessary to hold a Special Assize solely for the purpose of hearing Armstrong's case. However, even before the case could come to trial, Armstrong's solicitors issued a writ for contempt of court against the *Daily Express* newspaper, which, in the course of their coverage of proceedings at the magistrates' court, had published a sketch purporting to be of Armstrong's eyes, describing him as '...the man with the harassed face and despondent attitudes.'

It was the contention of Armstrong's legal representatives that the article and picture published by the newspaper were prejudicial to their client receiving a fair trial. At the High Court of Justice, the Lord Chief Justice, Mr Justice Shearman and Mr Justice Roche agreed that the article in question had been in dubious taste but did not believe that it had prejudiced a fair hearing for the accused.

Thus Armstrong's trial opened at Hereford on 3 April 1922 and was to last for ten days. (The early days of the trial were marked by a fierce snowstorm both outside and inside the court, as snow blew unchecked through an open window.) Ernest Pollock prosecuted the case, with Sir Henry Curtis Bennett defending Armstrong, who was charged with the murder of his wife and the attempted murder of Mr Oswald Martin. In the judge's opinion, there was insufficient evidence to charge him with sending poisoned chocolates to Martin, so that charge was dropped and Armstrong pleaded 'Not Guilty' to the remaining two indictments.

One of the major issues at the trial was the question of whether or not Katherine Armstrong had actually wanted to die. Her first nurse, Muriel Kinsey, had left within days of taking up her appointment because she felt that Mrs Armstrong was suicidal. However her replacement, Nurse Allen, told the court that Mrs Armstrong had asked her, 'I am not going to die, am I, nurse? Because I have everything to live for, my children and my husband.'

Liverpool solicitor Arthur Edward Chevalier told the court that, in August 1920, he had cause to visit Mrs Armstrong at her home and, at that time, had formed the opinion that she was suicidal. He had recommended to Major Armstrong that his razor should be removed from the room as a precaution, which Armstrong immediately did, also removing a revolver at the same time.

It was also noted that Mrs Armstrong was a devotee of homeopathic medicine and that Nurse Allen was aware that she had two bottles in a cupboard at the end of the bed, one containing *nux vomica* and another mixture, the name of which Nurse Allen was unable to recall. However, given Mrs Armstrong's debilitated state, there was doubt as to whether or not she would have been able to reach the bottles. Pollock, for the prosecution, insisted that Mrs Armstrong had been given a fatal dose of arsenic in the twenty-four hours before her death and, as her physical condition at the time would have prevented her from taking the medicine herself, then she must have been poisoned. Her husband alone had the means, motive and opportunity. By process of elimination, Major Armstrong was the only person with access to his wife both in August 1920, when she was first taken ill, and immediately before her death.

The defence countered with the assertion that, while they did not dispute the cause of death as arsenical poisoning, they denied that Major Armstrong had been the person who administered the poison.

The mysterious 'Mrs X' testified again and although she was not veiled as she had been during her appearance before the magistrates, her identity was still concealed and the press were forbidden to take any photographs of her. Once again, she stated that she had always been aware that Armstrong was a married man with children and that, until the death of his wife, he had been just a family friend to her.

The court also heard from two gardeners employed by Major Armstrong, both of whom testified that his garden was 'a terrible place for weeds'. Neither gardener had ever seen Major Armstrong using weed killer on the garden himself, but one, Mr Jay, remembered Armstrong showing him a patch of garden where he had used weed killer that he had mixed himself. There had been some argument in court about the fact that Major Armstrong had bought arsenic to use for killing weeds in the winter. Mr Jay gave his professional opinion that it was better to kill weeds in January than in June, since the wet ground absorbed the weed killer and made it more effective. Both gardeners stated that they had used weed killer themselves in the Armstrongs' garden.

The court then heard from Dr Hincks, who had treated both Mrs Armstrong and Mr Martin throughout their respective illnesses. Hincks stated that, when Mrs Armstrong was initially taken ill, he had been of the opinion that she had been poisoned but that there had been nothing about her condition that was inconsistent with natural illness. He discussed autointoxication, informing the court that the body could poison itself for example, with decayed teeth or even just general illness.

Referring to Mr Martin, he told the court that he had treated the solicitor with a bismuth mixture that had contained no arsenic whatsoever. When chemist John Davies was called to the stand, he testified to having supplied Major Armstrong with white arsenic, stating that Armstrong had told him that he wanted the poison to make weed killer and that he had signed the Poisons

Register at every purchase. Davies admitted that, given the size of Armstrong's garden, at the time he hadn't considered the amount of arsenic purchased by the solicitor excessive.

Davies told the court that white arsenic was routinely coloured with charcoal before being sold. However, a packet of uncoloured arsenic bearing Davies's shop label was produced in court, much to Davies's surprise. His assistant, John Hird, was then questioned at length about selling poison to Armstrong in January 1921, with particular attention paid to the way the arsenic had been wrapped and whether or not it had been coloured with charcoal, as demanded by the law.

Sergeant Worthing testified to finding poison at Armstrong's house and also to finding a recipe for weed killer, which used half a pound of white arsenic and half a pound of caustic soda to a gallon of water. The ingredients were then boiled until the mixture was clear, after which one teacupful of the mixture was used in a gallon of water to treat weeds. Both Sergeant Worthing and Chief Inspector Crutchett of Scotland Yard stated that Armstrong had co-operated fully in their investigations and had at no time objected to a search of his home or office being made.

Oswald Martin had already testified about his illness and the persistence of Major Armstrong in inviting him for tea. Now the court heard from the medical witnesses. Home Office pathologist Sir Bernard Spilsbury concluded that Mrs Armstrong had clearly died from arsenical poisoning and that large doses of the poison had been administered to her throughout the last week of her life, culminating in a fatal dose within twenty-four hours of her death. Mr John Webster, pathological chemist to the Home Office and Sir William Wilcox, the Home Office medical adviser, both supported Spilsbury's evidence. According to the experts, this pattern was inconsistent with suicide, since a person intent on suicide would be more likely to take one large dose of poison, two at most. Webster, described as 'a nervous little man in a large frock coat', told the court that the amount of arsenic found in Mrs Armstrong's remains was the largest amount he personally had ever found in a body. However, he did concede that, although he would expect two grains of arsenic to be a fatal dose, he was aware of people taking up to fifteen grains and surviving. Once the medical witnesses had testified, the prosecution rested.

In a speech lasting for more than two hours, counsel for the defence Sir Henry Curtis Bennett then proceeded to attack every aspect of the case outlined by the prosecution. He pointed out that Mrs Armstrong had been in poor health prior to the alleged first attempt at poisoning her in August 1920, already displaying many of the symptoms that had since been attributed to her ingestion of arsenic.

Major Armstrong was a loving husband to her and the couple lived on affectionate terms. Anyone in the Armstrong household – including Katherine

Armstrong herself – could have administered the poison, said Bennett, and his client had no motive for so doing.

There was no question in anybody's mind that as soon as Mrs Armstrong was admitted to hospital her condition began to improve. Surely, said Sir Henry, if she had been suffering from arsenical poisoning, then the administration of a tonic containing yet more arsenic would have precluded any improvement in her health?

Bennett argued that the facts of the case pointed to suicide by Katherine Armstrong. He reminded the court of the affectionate relationship between Armstrong and his wife, suggesting that all the evidence that had been heard indicated that Katherine had received a large, fatal dose of arsenic on 16 February and that it had been self-administered.

He stated that there was nothing to suggest that Mrs Armstrong's second will was not her own work and ridiculed a suggestion by the prosecution that Armstrong had wanted to get rid of his wife in order to marry another woman. With regard to Oswald Martin, Bennett maintained that there was nothing to suggest that he had suffered from arsenical poisoning apart from analysis of his samples and he reminded the jury that there was some question about the cleanliness of the bottles used to collect these samples, which had come from Mr Davies's shop. Even if Martin had been poisoned, there was absolutely no proof that it had been Armstrong's doing.

Why was the arsenic found on Major Armstrong on his arrest not coloured with charcoal, asked Bennett? And did it naturally follow that because Armstrong had poison about his person for killing weeds that he was intending to use it to poison somebody he didn't like? It made perfect sense for Armstrong to divide the arsenic he had bought into smaller packets to guard against the risk of spilling it or of it blowing away. 'No one with any common sense will ever buy arsenic for weed killing again,' said Bennett.

It was left to the judge to sum up the case but when the foreman of the jury was later interviewed by the press, he revealed that eleven of the twelve jurors had already reached their verdict before the judge had even commenced his summary. The deciding issue for the jury was that Major Armstrong had divided the arsenic into little packets and then dosed his weeds with the individual packets. Although the jury praised both counsels for the prosecution and defence for the way in which they handled the case, they had no hesitation in finding Major Armstrong guilty of the murder of his wife, leaving the judge to pronounce the death sentence upon him. Armstrong remained calm and collected as he heard the verdict. Finally Mr Justice Darling told the court that the matter of the attempted murder charge against the defendant could be left until the next Assizes.

An appeal was immediately instigated, which was heard before the Lord Chief Justice and Justices Avory and Shearman on 11 May 1922. Sir Henry

Curtis Bennett continued to maintain that Mrs Armstrong had committed suicide, pointing out that there was absolutely no evidence to suggest that her husband had ever given her any food or drink containing poison.

Bennett then argued about significant dates in the case. Katherine Armstrong had been ill for several years with indigestion, neuritis and a loss of power in her hands and feet. On 4 August 1921, Mr Jay the gardener had bought ready-made weed killer. Jay had sworn in court that he had personally used half a tin and that the remaining half tin was still in the shed after Major Armstrong's arrest.

On 22 August, Mrs Armstrong was admitted to Barnwood House Hospital, at which point she was supposedly showing symptoms of arsenical poisoning. However, those symptoms could also apply to numerous other diseases. Arsenic administered in a tonic at the hospital should, at very least, have retarded her progress had she been poisoned with arsenic but on the contrary, while hospitalised she made a steady progress towards health.

Armstrong had purchased arsenic on 11 January 1922 and his wife had returned home on 22 January. When she again fell ill on 6 February, Armstrong himself sent for the doctor, telling him, 'My wife is not so well and I want you to keep an eye on her.' Nurse Kinsey had quickly left the Armstrongs' employ because she believed that Katherine Armstrong was suicidal.

Stating that Major Armstrong's behaviour throughout was more indicative of innocence than of guilt, Sir Henry went on to say that it was his belief that the prosecution had not satisfactorily proved the case against Armstrong.

The Court of Appeal failed to agree and Armstrong's appeal was dismissed. He was hanged by John Ellis at Gloucester Prison on 31 May 1922.

It was later suggested that Armstrong might even have been responsible for yet another suspicious death in Hay-on-Wye. In October 1921, estate agent William Davies died suddenly and unexpectedly – like Oswald Martin, he too was in dispute with Major Armstrong. Yet, in more recent years, questions have been asked about the possible involvement of Oswald Martin and his father-in-law, chemist John Davies, in Mrs Armstrong's death. It has been theorised that Davies – who was aware that Mrs Armstrong was suicidal and would have access to the arsenic that her husband had purchased from his shop to kill weeds – may have framed Armstrong for her murder in order to ensure that his son-in-law's was the most prominent and successful solicitor's practice in the area by eliminating Martin's only real business competitor.

Regardless of any conspiracy theories, Herbert Rowse Armstrong went to his death still strongly protesting his innocence, in spite of an offer of £5,000 by a contemporary newspaper for a last-minute confession of guilt.

24
'They will blame one of us'

BUDE, CORNWALL, 1930

In 1921 two sisters, Sarah Ann Hearn, known as Annie, and Lydia Everard, known as Minnie, moved from the Midlands to the small hamlet of Lewannick, near Launceston, to look after their ageing aunt. When she died in 1926, the aunt left everything to Annie, 'in appreciation of her devoted nursing'. However 'everything' was little more than her home, Trenhorne House, so although the women had a secure roof over their heads, they had no income.

For almost four years, the two sisters lived together in the house until Minnie fell ill. Once again, Annie's nursing skills were in demand, but by this time she had made firm friends with the married couple who lived less than 200 yards away at Trenhorne Farm. Throughout Minnie's illness, William Thomas was a regular visitor, dropping off newspapers and bringing custards and junkets baked by his wife, Alice, to tempt the invalid. At one time, when the two sisters were in even more dire financial straits than usual, William even lent them £38, which was a substantial amount of money in the 1920s.

After years of suffering from gastric complaints Minnie died in 1930, leaving Annie, then in her forties, living alone. William and Alice Thomas remained friendly and supportive, often including Annie in outings and picnics. In October 1930, William's mother had been staying at the farm and needed to be driven back to her home near Bude on the north coast. Annie was invited along for the ride. She was delighted by the prospect and happily joined the Thomas' in their car, leaving Lewannick at 3 p.m.

It was a very typical outing. After dropping off William's mother, the party parked their car in Bude. William went off to get his hair cut, while the two women walked around the shops. At 5 p.m. the three met in a local café where William ordered tea, cakes and bread and butter. Annie had made her own contribution to the meal, producing from her bag some tinned salmon sandwiches and chocolate cake, and these were shared between the three friends.

Bude in the 1930s. The buildings with the sun blinds in the centre of the picture are thought to be the café where the party ate. (Author's collection)

After tea they parted company again, with William making his way alone to the Grove Hotel. There he complained of nausea, but after a shot of whisky he felt much better. His wife was not so fortunate. When all three met up again, she complained of having a sickly-sweet taste in her mouth and asked if there was a fruit shop nearby. William found one and bought her some bananas.

On the drive home Alice began to feel terribly ill. William had to break the journey several times for her to be sick at the roadside, and when he kept a pre-arranged business appointment near Launceston, he returned to the car to find her in the public toilets vomiting again. As soon as they arrived home, Alice was helped to her bed and the doctor sent for. When he examined her, Dr Saunders found she was suffering pain in the stomach, coupled with a racing pulse and cramp in the legs. Hearing that she had eaten tinned salmon that afternoon, he immediately suspected food poisoning. Fortunately Alice was on hand to help and, once again, volunteered her nursing skills. She stayed at the farm for several days, cooking for William and caring for his bedridden wife.

Alice was expected to recover from her bout of food poisoning without any complications, but instead her condition gradually worsened. Some days she would seem better, only to relapse the following day. Soon she was complaining of a tingling sensation in her hands and feet and of having no control over her limbs. When the doctor noticed she had developed cold sores on her lips and chest, he suggested that she should go into hospital, but she resisted the idea. In desperation William sent for her mother, Tryphena Parsons, who promptly arrived to help Annie with the cooking and nursing.

Despite their best efforts, Alice continued to deteriorate. At the beginning of November she rallied sufficiently to eat some mutton, potatoes, vegetables and a sweet cooked by Annie, but after eating, complained of the lingering sweet taste in her mouth. In an effort to rid herself of this sickly taste, she asked for lemon juice, which was served to her by Annie, but soon afterwards she began vomiting again and suffering from nosebleeds. She became delirious, and her doctor was so concerned by her condition that he summoned a specialist from Plymouth City Hospital for a second opinion. Dr William Lister diagnosed arsenical poisoning and Alice was rushed into hospital, where she died three days later, aged forty-three.

William, who had been at his wife's bedside, returned home to Trenhorne Farm. There, according to Annie, he all but accused her of murdering his wife, saying, 'They will blame one of us and the blame will fall heavier on you than on me.' William was later to deny saying this, claiming to have little recollection of any conversation. He did recall asking Annie for a written IOU for the £38 she still owed him.

At a post-mortem, it was found that Alice's organs contained a residue of 0.85 grains of arsenic, consistent with her having consumed around ten grains. Since a dose of between two and four grains is normally fatal, her death certificate was issued citing the cause of death as 'Arsenical poisoning due to homicide' and also stating, '... but there is not sufficient evidence to show by whom or by what means the arsenic was administered.'

Annie had an uncomfortable time at Alice's funeral. She felt that the other mourners were looking at her with suspicion, particularly Alice's brother, Percy Parsons. The latter asked about the food that his sister had eaten on her trip to Bude and, when Annie mentioned that she had provided sandwiches, informed her that the matter 'would have to be looked into'. When the funeral party returned to the farm for refreshments, Annie soon made her excuses and left.

On 10 November, William received a letter from Annie, which read:

Dear Mr Thomas,
Goodbye. I am going out if I can. I cannot forget that awful man [Parsons] and the things he said. I am innocent, innocent [*sic*], but she is dead and it was my lunch she ate. I cannot stay. When I am dead, they will be sure I am guilty and you, at least, will be clear. May your dear wife's presence guard and comfort you still.
Yours, A.H.

In a postscript, Annie complained that her life was nothing without Minnie. She asked that her love be given to Bessie (another sister) and begged them not to worry about her, writing; 'I am all right. My conscience is clear. I am not afraid of afterwards.' Finally, she gave instructions that her goods should be sold and her debt to Thomas paid from the proceeds.

William took the letter straight to the police, who arrived at Trenhorne House to find it locked and empty. They soon discovered that Annie had taken a taxi to Looe, and a few days later her coat and hat were found there on a cliff top. It looked as though she might have committed suicide by flinging herself over the cliff into the sea, but there was no trace of her body on the shore below, apart from a solitary shoe that was washed up on the beach.

Meanwhile, in Torquay, a 'Mrs Ferguson' booked a room at a hotel, staying for one night and leaving early the following morning. She did not go far. Calling herself 'Mrs Faithful', she took lodgings in Torquay, later applying for a job as a live-in housekeeper to a local architect, Cecil Powell. Seduced by Mrs Faithful's excellent but fake references, Mr Powell hired her and, it seems, was highly satisfied with her work.

When Alice Thomas's inquest was opened on 24 November her husband was questioned about her death. William stated that, aside from the sheep dip and worming concoctions that any farmer might reasonably be expected to own, he possessed no poisons and certainly no arsenic. He also maintained that his wife had never objected to his friendship with Annie – and why should she, since he had never given her any reason to be jealous? Damningly, a member of staff at Shuker and Reed, a Launceston grocer and chemist shop, testified that he had sold an arsenic-based weed killer to Annie Hearn in August 1928. The signature against a 1lb tin of Cooper's Powder in the shop's poisons book matched that of Annie Hearn. Searches of Poisons Registers in chemist's shops at nearby Stratton, Holsworthy, Liskeard and Camelford produced no sales of poison that could be directly tied to either Hearn, William Thomas or any members of the Parsons family, although Shuker and Reed's register did reveal a sale to a Mrs Uglow some eight years previously. Mrs Uglow was a sister to Mrs Thomas, and it was Mrs Thomas herself who had introduced Mrs Uglow as a purchaser at the chemist's shop. A thorough search of Trenhorne House, conducted on 20 November, had revealed no arsenic in any form.

On 26 November the inquest returned a verdict of murder by arsenical poisoning by person or persons unknown. This was enough for police to initiate a search for the missing Annie, issuing a wanted poster that described her as 5ft 3in tall, brown haired and grey eyed, with a sallow complexion. It mentioned that she walked briskly, holding her head slightly to the left, that she was well spoken and had rather a reserved manner.

It was also sufficient cause for the police to exhume the bodies of Annie's sister Minnie and her Aunt Mary. Both bodies were found to contain arsenic, with Minnie's remains containing considerably more residue than those of Mary.

The possible poisonings in Cornwall were fast becoming national news and the *Daily Mail* offered a £500 reward for anyone finding the elusive Annie Hearn. Quite by chance, Mr Powell was a *Daily Mail* reader and he was also beginning to harbour suspicions about his housekeeper, 'Mrs Faithful'. He had noticed that a coat she had bought from a mail order firm had arrived addressed to a 'Mrs Dennis'. Moreover, his copies of the *Daily Mail* were being tampered with before he got to read them each morning, as someone was carefully removing all reports relating to the missing Annie Hearn.

Mr Powell alerted the police, and on 12 January 1931 Annie Hearn was detained on her way to an errand. At first she continued to protest that her name was Mrs Dennis but she eventually admitted her true identity when confronted by a police sergeant from Lewannick, Sergeant Trebilcock, who immediately recognised her. She appeared very cool and positively talkative. Superintendent William Morely Pill took a statement from her, and almost immediately her words resulted in some confusion. Sergeant Trebilcock claimed that Annie said, 'Mr Thomas used to come to our house every day with a paper. Of course, that was only a blind.' Pill and another officer present at the time did not hear her say this, and Annie later claimed that she had actually said, 'Mr Thomas used to bring a paper. He was very kind.' When describing the trip to Bude, she stated that on previous outings with William and Alice, they had always taken lunch with them. On the day she was invited to accompany them, she had cut some salmon sandwiches and chocolate cake, which she placed on the table at the café. Mrs Thomas had taken the first sandwich, Annie herself the second and Mr Thomas the third.

As for her argument with Alice's brother, Mr Parsons, at Alice's funeral, Annie said it had not really been a row. He had asked some searching questions about the sandwiches, leading her to believe that people suspected her of poisoning Alice. Thinking that either she or William were about to be charged with murder, Annie had fled, taking a taxi to Looe with the intention of killing herself on arrival. Her nerve failed her and she was unable to go through with her suicide.

Finally, Annie dismissed concerns about the roast mutton served to Alice shortly before her admission to hospital, stating that while she had cooked the meat, she had neither carved Alice's portion, nor helped with the gravy or other accompaniments to the meal.

Annie appeared on remand before Launceston magistrates no less than fourteen times. Initially charged only with the murder of Alice Thomas, on 24 February she was also charged with that of her sister, Lydia (Minnie) Everard. Minnie was described as an invalid, having previously suffered a nervous breakdown and with a long history of stomach troubles that had been variously diagnosed as chronic dyspepsia, bowel trouble, gastric ulcer, colitis and gastric catarrh. The most persistent of her symptoms was an inability to digest food. To aid digestion she was prescribed a mixture of bismuth, aromatics and pepsine, but by 19 April 1930, Minnie was complaining that the medicine was giving her pain. Her doctor, Dr Gibson, was surprised to hear this, but nevertheless gave her a check up, at which he noted that her heart sounded 'a little feeble'. He issued a new prescription for 'a soothing bowel mixture', but within a fortnight noted that his patient's condition had worsened and she was now vomiting.

Dr Gibson and his colleague Dr Galbraith continued to visit Minnie on a regular basis. By 4 July Dr Gibson observed that she had lost weight and was now complaining of rheumatic pains in her arms in addition to her usual digestion problems. At this time he checked Minnie for any signs of cancer, but his examinations did not reveal any malignancy. Two weeks later, Minnie was feeble and emaciated and seemed to the doctor to be only semi-conscious. She was so weak that she was unable to turn over in bed without assistance. The doctor believed that Minnie was slowly starving to death and made his concerns known to Annie. Her condition continued to worsen, until by 21 July she was barely able to speak and obviously in great pain. She died that night and Dr Gibson signed the death certificate, giving the cause of death as 'chronic gastric catarrh and colitis'. He described Annie Hearn as 'a good nurse and a devoted sister'.

Dr Roche Lynch, the Home Office analyst, testified for an entire day at Annie's hearing before the magistrates at Launceston. He explained that arsenic poisoning could be divided into three types – acute, sub-acute and chronic. Acute poisoning was normally, but not always, characterised by a swift death, usually within thirty-six hours of ingesting the arsenic, either through heart failure, poisoning of the heart muscle or by dehydration caused by persistent vomiting and diarrhoea. It could take two forms, either presenting with similar symptoms to gastroenteritis or in narcotic form, which gave only transient nausea and vomiting before unconsciousness. Sub-acute poisoning could result from either one dose of arsenic or several doses given over a period of time. It began with symptoms of gastroenteritis. The condition of the victim might appear to improve temporarily, before deteriorating into restlessness and neuritis culminating in unconsciousness and death. Chronic poisoning, on the other hand, gave rise to a variety of symptoms including digestive catarrh, disordered sensation and paralysis, with inflammation of the mouth, nasal passages and eyes. This would be accompanied by strange tingling sensations, almost as if the victim had ants crawling on their skin. Eventually the victim would experience a loss of power to the limbs with muscle pain and wasting. He was of the opinion that an initial dose of several grains of arsenic was administered to Mrs Thomas at around 5 p.m. on the day of the outing to Bude, and that her resulting symptoms were consistent with sub-acute arsenical poisoning.

As far as Minnie was concerned, Roche Lynch felt that she had been administered regular small doses of arsenic over a longer period of time, possibly around seven months. He confirmed this by testing a length of her hair and showing that it contained arsenic throughout its length. Knowing the rate at which human hair grows, he was able to establish a time period over which

Minnie had, in his opinion, been slowly poisoned. She was, according to the doctor, a textbook case of chronic poisoning.

Once all the evidence had been heard, the magistrates retired to debate their decision. After only fourteen minutes' discussion, they returned to commit Annie Hearn to Bodmin Assizes for both offences.

The trial opened at Bodmin on 15 June 1931, with the defendant pleading 'Not Guilty' to the murders of Alice Thomas and her sister, Lydia Everard. She was defended by Norman Birkett KC, assisted by Mr Dingle Foot, whose father, Isaac, was the Liberal MP for Bodmin. Cecil Powell paid for the expensive services of these gentlemen, generously donating the £500 reward he had received for being instrumental in Annie's capture.

The prosecution relied largely on the expert testimony of pathologist Dr Roche Lynch. He testified that Alice Thomas had died from arsenic poisoning and that, by examining her organs post-mortem, he had been able to calculate that she had ingested a dose of ten grains. Minnie also had large quantities of arsenic in her body.

The counsel for the defence instantly refuted these findings, pointing out that the soil at Lewannick contained high levels of arsenic. Although the exhumation of Minnie's body had been carried out in a snowstorm, just a tiny amount of local soil could have contaminated the specimens taken and accounted for the high results of the tests. The doctor who conducted the autopsy at the graveside was called, and was forced to admit that he had taken no precautions against contamination, and also that Minnie's organs had been left in open jars next to her grave for over an hour.

Having planted the idea of contamination firmly into the minds of the jury, the defence team then set out to discredit Dr Roche Lynch. Under questioning, he admitted that he had never seen or treated an actual case of arsenic poisoning, but only read about it. He conceded that the base level of arsenic in the soil at Lewannick was unusually high and that he had not taken this into account when calculating the levels of arsenic in Minnie's body. The prosecution maintained that Roche Lynch's calculations were fundamentally flawed, since he had analysed a portion of muscle from the dead woman. He had then assumed that muscle represented about 40 per cent of the human body, multiplying the amount of arsenic accordingly. Yet when Minnie died, her muscles had been severely wasted following her prolonged illness and would have accounted for only around 15 per cent of her total body weight.

The court heard testimony from the Launceston chemist who had stated at Alice's inquest that he had sold arsenic-based weed killer to the defendant. The defence team did not dispute this; merely pointing out that this particular brand of herbicide was bright blue in colour. It was demonstrated in court that, had it been used in the sandwiches, it would have turned the bread bright blue too.

Assize Court, Bodmin, 1930s. (Author's collection)

The defence called just one witness to the stand, Annie Hearn herself. Her calm demeanour as she maintained her innocence impressed itself on the jury. She vehemently denied poisoning either Alice or Minnie, admitting only to panicking and fleeing when she feared that she might be a suspect. It had been her intention to commit suicide, but she had eventually been too afraid to go through with it and had tried to start a new life in Torquay.

Mr H. du Parcq KC was left to sum up the case for the prosecution, even though he was clearly unwell and eventually fainted in the courtroom. He pointed out to the jury that both women had died from arsenic poisoning, both after having eaten food prepared by Annie. However, on the day of her panic-stricken flight to Looe, she had allegedly worn two coats, one on top of the other. To du Parcq, this clearly negated Annie's claims that she had intended to commit suicide, proving instead that she had been bent on duping people into believing that she was dead, leaving her free to make a new life for herself. And why, asked du Parcq, should an innocent woman flee in the first place, if not to avoid justice? Annie, he maintained, was a liar. She had lied about her intention to kill herself and, by inventing new names for herself in Torquay, had also lied about her identity. It was thus probable that she was also making false claims about her innocence.

For the defence, Birkett concentrated his closing arguments on undermining the testimony of the prosecution's expert witness. Having planted doubts in the minds of the jurors by referring to the high levels of arsenic in the Lewannick soil, he proceeded to labour the point, even though his contamination theory was not strictly true. While the arsenic levels in the soil were exceptionally high, they were not present in soluble form, so they would have been unlikely to affect the test results, even if contamination had occurred. He then tried to discredit Dr Roche Lynch, the Crown's analyst who, he pointed out, 'never attended a single person suffering from arsenical poisoning, yet he spoke of the symptoms with the same confidence that he spoke of other matters'.

Finally, Birkett asked the jury to consider the supposedly poisoned sandwiches. If a packet of sandwiches was placed on a table for three people to share, how was the poisoner supposed to ensure that the intended victim, Mrs Hearn, took the right sandwich, particularly as the bread would be bright blue?

After both sides had summed up their evidence, it was left for the judge, Mr Justice Roche, to address the jury. He quickly ruled that there was insufficient evidence in the case of the murder of Lydia Everard and instructed the jury to acquit Annie Hearn of that charge. They should focus instead on the murder of Alice Thomas, asking first if her death was due to arsenical poisoning and, if they decided that it was, did the defendant administer that poison?

Annie's guilt or innocence was dependent on whether the jury believed that she had administered arsenic to Mrs Thomas in the sandwiches eaten on the outing to Bude. If indeed the sandwiches had been laced with arsenic, then only

The grave of Alice and William Thomas, Lewannick churchyard. (© Nicola Sly)

two people could possibly have been responsible – Annie Hearn or William Thomas. The judge pointed out that it was up to the prosecution to satisfy the jury that the poisoner was not William Thomas, rather than the responsibility of the defence to satisfy them that it was. The jury deliberated for less than an hour before acquitting Annie Hearn of Alice Thomas' murder and were then instructed by the judge to acquit her of Minnie's murder too. Within minutes, Annie was a free woman again, vowing to settle her affairs in Cornwall, then never to set foot in the county again. However, her innocence was not as clear-cut in the minds of the jury as their verdict suggested. One juror was allegedly heard to say later in a public house that the jury had believed that Annie and William Thomas had acted together in murdering Alice. They had found Annie not guilty, even though they felt that she had committed the murders, because they had not wanted to see her 'swing' on her own.

As there was insufficient evidence to link William Thomas to the deaths, he was never charged with the murder of his wife. In fact, nobody but Annie was ever charged and the murder remains unsolved.

The case has become something of an enigma in the annals of true crime. Was there ever more than friendship between Annie and William and, if so, was Alice Thomas the only obstacle that stood in the couple's way? If their relationship was, as both claimed, merely friendship, then what motive did either William or Annie have for murdering either Alice or Minnie? And, was Minnie murdered at all, or was her early death simply the consequence of a long-standing battle with illness? Was William in any way to blame for his wife's death? Or did Annie Hearn literally get away with murder?

25

'It looks very black against me'

KIRKBY-ON-BAIN, LINCOLNSHIRE, 1934

By 1934, the relationship between forty-four-year-old Arthur Major and his forty-two-year-old wife, Ethel, had deteriorated to the extent that Ethel and the couple's son, Lawrence, no longer slept at home, instead going to the home of Ethel's father every evening. Although the only accommodation available to mother and son at Tom Brown's tiny cottage was either a sofa in the kitchen or an outdoor shed, if they tried to sleep at home Arthur would often turn them out of the house.

Arthur and Ethel of Kirkby-on-Bain, Lincolnshire had married in 1918 and, two years later, Arthur had found out from a neighbour that Auriel – the young girl he had always thought of as Ethel's sister – was in fact her illegitimate daughter. Wishing to avoid a scandal, Ethel's parents had passed off the child as their own and, to Arthur's fury, even when he discovered the truth Ethel flatly refused to name the child's father.

Almost from that moment on, the marriage appeared beyond saving. Arthur took to drinking and apparently began an affair with the couple's next-door neighbour, Rose Kettleborough, herself a married woman. Ethel discovered the affair when she found some letters in Arthur's pocket and immediately set out to make sure that everyone knew of his infidelities. She visited the Major's doctor, George Armour, with the letters, telling the doctor that Arthur was not fit to live and threatening to 'do him in'. She told the sanitary inspector responsible for the maintenance of the Major's council house, asking him if the tenancy might be transferred into her name. The letters were shown to Ethel's father and eventually Ethel confronted her husband about them, asking him what he was going to do about it.

'Nothing,' replied Major, effectively starting a public hate campaign instigated by his wife. Her next action was to write to the Chief Constable of Lincolnshire, informing him that her husband was using his company lorry for

Kirkby-on-Bain, Lincolnshire, 1920s. (Author's collection)

transporting passengers and that he was frequently drunk behind the wheel. She repeated these allegations to the village policeman, who kept a close eye on Major as a result, although he never found any evidence to support Mrs Major's accusations.

Next Mrs Major went to see the couple's solicitor, purporting to be visiting on behalf of her husband and getting the solicitor to send a letter to Mrs Kettleborough ending their association and demanding that she stop writing to him immediately. Solicitor's clerk Walter Holmes sent the letter according to Mrs Major's instructions, only to be confronted by a furious Arthur a couple of days later, insisting that his wife had acted without his knowledge or permission.

Arthur retaliated by taking out a notice in the local papers stating that he would no longer be responsible for his wife debts, an act that prompted Ethel into even more spiteful acts against him. Having been told by the local council that she could only assume the tenancy of the couple's house in her own name with her husband's consent, Ethel wrote to the sanitary inspector in Arthur's name giving up the tenancy. When the council acknowledged receipt of the letter, a surprised Arthur went straight to the clerk to deny all knowledge of it. Next Ethel went to her husband's employer and tried to have him dismissed from his job.

However, the final straw for Ethel was when she received an anonymous letter herself:

Mrs Majar,

You are slow. Don't you know how your husband spends his weekends? He has got a nice bit of fluff now. Besides, he would be done any day at the shop if it were not for Mrs sticking up for him. You could get rid of him easy if you had him watched. Everyone knows about him and Mrs. I hear there is now a little Majar to look after. [*sic*]

The discovery that her husband's behaviour was common knowledge around the village and that she seemed to have been the last person to know about it enraged Ethel Major even further.

Such was the Major's relationship that they both bought and prepared separate food for themselves, kept on different sides of the pantry at home. On 22 May 1934, Arthur came home from work as usual and made his own evening meal of his favourite corned beef. After eating he went into the back yard to repair his bicycle and it was while he was doing so that Lawrence saw him fall over.

Lawrence called to his mother and the couple rushed outside to find Arthur sagging against the shed, unable to stand unaided and in obvious pain. Between them, Lawrence and Ethel managed to get Arthur into the house, where he sat trembling violently in a chair for some time before finally staggering upstairs to bed with his wife and son's assistance.

Later that evening, Ethel's father called at the house and, on hearing that his son-in-law was ill, went up to the bedroom to see him. By then, Arthur was lying in bed, foaming at the mouth, his legs jerking convulsively. When Tom Brown asked if a doctor had been called, Ethel assured her father that Arthur had said that he didn't need one.

Mr Brown disagreed and sent for Dr Smith who arrived at ten o'clock that evening to find Arthur stiff and paralysed, unable to speak, with his body drenched in sweat.

Dr Smith carefully turned Arthur over in bed, at which the sick man promptly turned black in the face and began to convulse violently. By the time the convulsions had ceased some time later, Arthur Major was barely breathing and soon lapsed into unconsciousness.

Ethel Major seemed totally unconcerned by her husband's illness, blaming it on the corned beef he had eaten for his tea. Dr Smith however was afraid that Major was suffering from epilepsy and sent Lawrence off to fetch some medicine to sedate him.

That night, Ethel and her son slept at home, with Ethel rising at half-past seven the next morning and taking her husband a cup of warm water to drink. Throughout the day, Arthur lay semi-conscious in bed, moving only when his body was wracked by violent convulsions. However, by the time Dr Smith called later that day, he had recovered slightly and was even able to speak a few words. Meanwhile, Ethel was still showing little or no concern for her husband's condition and had even been out to do some shopping, leaving him unattended.

At some point during the afternoon, she prepared a cup of thin gruel for Arthur, leaving the cup on his bedside table. Later that evening, she also made him a cup of tea. Shortly afterwards, Arthur's convulsions returned and he became extremely sensitive to external stimuli, to the extent that the sound of a voice or even someone lightly touching his bed would trigger another attack of violent spasms.

By the following morning, Arthur's condition had improved slightly and when Lawrence took him a cup of tea he even managed to smile at his son. He grew even brighter during the day and, when Tom Brown called later that evening, he found his son-in-law to be a lot better. However the improvement was to be short-lived as, after drinking a cup of water, Arthur suffered a sudden relapse and he died in the throes of a fit at 10.40 p.m. on 24 May.

Mrs Major sent for her father and the undertaker but did not inform the doctor until the following morning, when she turned up at his surgery as if for a routine appointment. Smith asked if Mr Major had had another fit and, when Ethel confirmed that he had, asked why he had not been sent for. 'It happened so quickly that there was no time,' Ethel told him, pointing out that Arthur had regularly suffered from fits for the last two years. Dr Smith had no reason to disbelieve her and issued a death certificate.

Ethel immediately set about organising her husband's funeral with almost indecent haste. He had died on a Thursday evening and Ethel was determined that he should be buried at Roughton Church on the Saturday immediately following his death. When one of Arthur's brothers protested that this was too soon, she allowed the funeral to be delayed until the Sunday, although insisted that it must take place then since the vicar was due to go away on the next day.

Thus the funeral was set for 3 p.m. on Sunday 27 May. As the family waited at the Major's home for the start of the service, there was a ring on the doorbell. On answering the door, they found two policemen on the doorstep, who insisted that the funeral must be postponed. Ethel protested but her arguments were in vain. 'Am I suspected of something?' she asked the police, to be told that the delay was merely due to the fact that her husband had died so suddenly. 'It looks very black against me,' Ethel complained to the assembled mourners as she notified them of the unexpected change of arrangements.

Unbeknown to Ethel, the postponement of the funeral was the result of an anonymous letter received by the local coroner on the previous day. Signed 'Fairplay', the letter asked if the coroner had ever heard of a wife poisoning her husband and recommended that he should investigate Mr Major's death more closely. The letter writer stated that Major had complained that his food tasted 'nasty' and 'bitter' and suggested that when scraps of his food were thrown to a neighbour's dog, it had subsequently died.

The police immediately questioned the Major's neighbours and found that one of two dogs belonging to Mr Maltby, who lived next door, had indeed recently died. According to Mr Maltby, on 23 May his dogs had been shut in a garden shed while he was out and, when he returned at 9.30 p.m., he had checked and found one of them unaccountably stiff and paralysed. He had laid the dog on some sacking overnight and, when he saw it the next morning, it had died.

Another neighbour, Mrs Elsie Roberts, told the police that her garden overlooked that of the Majors. On the day before Arthur's death, Mrs Roberts had been feeding her chickens when she had seen Mrs Major come out of her house carrying a plate of scraps. Mr Maltby's dog had wandered into the Majors' garden and Ethel Major had scraped the plate onto the ground, watching in evident pleasure as the dog devoured the contents. The incident had stuck in Elsie Roberts' mind since Mrs Major had, in the past, shown an intense dislike for her neighbour's dogs and had thrown things at them whenever they had strayed onto her property.

The body of the dog, which had been buried in Mr Maltby's garden, was exhumed and sent for examination by veterinary surgeon Joseph Patterson at Horncastle. Meanwhile, Arthur Major's body was subjected to a post-mortem examination, with some of his organs being sent to Home Office analyst Dr Roche Lynch for testing.

Dr Roche Lynch found a total of 1.27 grains of alkaloid strychnine in Arthur Major's organs, the normal fatal dose for an adult male being between one and two grains. In addition, Roche Lynch analysed some of the organs removed from Maltby's dog, this time finding a total of 0.16 grains of strychnine. It was Roche Lynch's opinion that Major had taken two separate doses of strychnine amounting to between two and three grains in total, the first on 22 May and the second on 24 May. Opium was also found in Major's remains, although that was known to be present in the sedative medicine given to him by Dr Smith. Although Roche Lynch admitted that around 40 per cent of cases of death by strychnine that he had investigated were suicides, the fact that Major had ingested two doses of the poison indicated that the most likely scenario was wilful murder, since strychnine poisoning was so painful that, according to Roche Lynch, only a lunatic would take a second dose.

Detective Chief Inspector Hugh Young, who had been called from Scotland Yard to help the local police with their investigations, went to question Arthur Major's widow. 'I have never had any strychnine poison,' Ethel assured him.

'I have never mentioned strychnine,' said Young. 'How did you know that your husband died from strychnine poisoning?'

Assize Courts, Lincoln Castle. (Author's collection)

Lincoln Castle. (Author's collection)

'I must have made a mistake,' Ethel said, telling the officer that she was sure that her husband had been killed by the corned beef he had eaten shortly before his death. She had believed that it was 'bad' but had been so frightened of her husband's reaction that she hadn't dared to throw it away or even voice her suspicions to him.

Ethel Major was arrested and charged with the wilful murder of her husband, appearing before magistrates at Horncastle where she pleaded 'Not Guilty' to the charge against her. She was eventually committed for trial at the next Lincoln Assizes.

Her trial opened at the end of October 1934 before Mr Justice Charles. Mr Richard O'Sullivan KC prosecuted the case, assisted by Mr P.E. Sandlands, with Mr Norman Birkett KC defending, aided by Mr M.D. van Oss and Mr E.D. Lewis.

Mr O'Sullivan opened the proceedings with an assertion that Mrs Major had administered strychnine to her husband, causing his death. He first called Dr Smith to testify about the medicine that he had given to Major and then called Ethel's father, Tom Brown, into the witness box.

Brown worked as a gamekeeper and told the court that he kept a supply of strychnine in a locked wooden box at his home for the purpose of killing vermin. Ten years previously, he had lost the key to the box and had eventually had another one made. Brown identified a tiny key produced in court as the one that he had mislaid many years before – it had been found in his daughter Ethel's purse, although the defence counsel was quick to point out that the purse had previously been owned by Tom Brown's wife and had been given to Ethel after her mother's death. If she had anything to hide, said Birkett, Ethel could quite easily have disposed of the key rather than leaving it to be found in her purse after the death of her husband.

A bottle of strychnine found in Brown's box was produced and Brown identified it as his property, saying that, as far as he could tell, nothing had been taken from the bottle since he had last seen it before the alleged murder of his son-in-law.

Dr Roche Lynch informed the court of the results of his tests on the organs of both Arthur Major and Mr Maltby's dog, fielding questions from the defence counsel about the possibility that Major had in fact died from opium poisoning as a result of the medication prescribed to sedate him during his last illness. Roche Lynch assured the court that, in his opinion, Major had died from strychnine poisoning and although he conceded that there was a slight possibility that the opium in his medicine may have delayed the absorption of the poison into his body, he personally did not believe that the medicine prescribed by Dr Smith had in any way contributed to Major's death.

On the second day of the trial, the Major's neighbour, Rose Kettleborough, was called to answer questions about her alleged affair with Arthur Major. First denying that she had ever possessed any strychnine, Mrs Kettleborough next addressed the two letters found by Ethel in her husband's pocket, one of which read:

Mr Justice Charles. (Author's collection)

To my dearest sweetheart in the world. I thought I would like to write to you tonight, as I do not want to read. Thank you for your good-night kiss, darling. It is hard, so near and yet so far. So now, my dearest lover, I will close with all my fondest love to my dear one. Good-night, precious, I remain ever your loving sweetheart, Rose. [*sic*]

Rose categorically denied writing the love letters to Arthur Major and also denied any knowledge of the anonymous letter written to Ethel Major. Counsel for the defence Mr Birkett produced another letter, which Rose had written to her daughter, pointing out similarities in the handwriting between all of the letters, the most glaring of which was the incorrect spelling of the word 'Majar' in both the anonymous letter and the letter to Rose's daughter. Still Rose continued to deny authorship of the letters and, when they were shown to her husband, Joseph, he told the court that he did not think they were in his wife's handwriting.

'Do you mean that you are not sure?' pressed Birkett.

'Yes,' replied Joseph.

Ethel Major's daughter, Auriel, had already testified to the fact that Rose Kettleborough seemed to spend a lot of time hanging about outside the Majors' house, as if hoping to engineer an accidental meeting with Arthur, something that Rose also denied.

The court then heard from a number of acquaintances of the Majors' about their unhappy domestic life, which was common knowledge in the village of Kirkby-on-Bain. Most testified that they were unaware that Major was addicted to drink as his wife suggested. One of these was the wife of the local rector, for whom Arthur had tended the rectory gardens for almost a year, who stated that she had never once seen him the worse for drink. However, Mrs Pinning, who kept the village shop, told the court that she had seen Major topple off his bicycle into a ditch while under the influence of alcohol. None of the witnesses called had anything good to say about Mrs Major.

Detective Chief Inspector Hugh Young told the court that Ethel Major had consistently denied giving her husband poison and had suggested that Rose Kettleborough could have come into the house and poisoned the corned beef he had eaten for his tea. Young mentioned that Ethel had spoken to him about strychnine poisoning before it had been mentioned to her, although the defence was to maintain that Ethel had learned the cause of her husband's death from her solicitor before her interviews with the police.

The prosecution then addressed the matter of the corned beef to which Ethel Major had attributed her husband's final illness. Ethel had told the police that her son, Lawrence, had been sent by his father to purchase the tin of meat from the village shop, although Lawrence had initially denied this to the police, telling them that his mother had given him the money and sent him to buy the corned beef. Now called to the witness box, Lawrence changed his story, agreeing that his father had sent him. Mrs Pinning, the village shopkeeper, corroborated his new story, recalling that, on 18 May, Lawrence had arrived at the shop after closing time, apologising for his lateness and explaining that he had had to wait for his father to come home from work to give him the money. Another shopkeeper recalled Arthur Major buying corned beef himself on 21 May – it had been the last tin that she had in stock. On the following day, Major visited her shop again and asked for yet more corned beef. She had none to sell him, so he had purchased meat paste instead, along with some tea and condensed milk.

Lawrence was questioned about the relationship between his parents, and stated that for the three weeks prior to his death, his father had insisted on preparing his own food. His mother had always treated him kindly, said Lawrence, while his father was often unkind to him and was frequently drunk, during which time he was violent and abusive. The boy's grandfather, Tom Brown, agreed that Major was a drunkard who had frequently abused his wife. He told the court that in 1931 his daughter had begun legal proceedings for a separation from her husband but had been persuaded by Arthur to give their marriage a second chance after he promised to reform his ways.

It was expected that Birkett would call Ethel Major to speak in her own defence but this did not happen. This omission was eventually referred to no less than six times by the judge in his summary of the case for the jury and was obviously viewed as a lost opportunity for the defendant to make her own side of the case known.

Mr Justice Charles went on to commend Lawrence Major's evidence, stating that it must have been a terrible ordeal for the fourteen-year-old boy. It was obvious that the Majors lived in a state of marital disharmony, said the judge, and that Ethel hated her husband, being very jealous of his alleged extra-marital relationship with Mrs Kettleborough. Both parties in the marriage were capable of violence towards each other and it was a pity that inconsistencies in Ethel's statements had not been addressed by the defendant herself in the witness box.

Mr Justice Charles then pronounced himself 'puzzled' over the assertion by Dr Roche Lynch that Arthur Major had actually taken two doses of strychnine. Given that strychnine was known to taste exceedingly bitter, why would he take a second dose? And if, as the prosecution maintained, the poison was present in the glass of water given to her husband by Ethel Major then it would appear that the quantity of water in the cup was too small, since a fatal dose of the poison would need two and a half pints of liquid to fully dissolve it.

After the judge had finished his summary, the jury retired to consider their verdict, returning after nearly an hour's deliberation to pronounce Ethel Major 'Guilty' of the wilful murder of her husband but adding a strong recommendation for mercy. Ethel Major promptly fainted.

She was revived to hear the judge pronounce sentence of death upon her, protesting 'I am innocent' when asked if she had anything to say. Carried from the court in a state of collapse, she was taken by car to Hull Prison, one of the few in the country at the time with the facilities for accommodating women.

Mr Birkett promptly appealed the conviction. At the Court of Criminal Appeal in December 1934, before the Lord Chief Justice, Mr Justice Avory and Mr Justice Swift, Birkett argued that the judge's summary had been flawed since it failed to address the possibility that Arthur Major had committed suicide. Although there had been no evidence that Ethel Major had ever possessed any strychnine or that she had ever administered it to her husband, the burden of proof was not on the defence to establish that Major had committed suicide but was on the Crown to exclude the possibility that he had.

The Court of Appeal ruled that, while the matter of suicide had not been directly addressed, for the jury to convict Mrs Major they must have been satisfied beyond any reasonable doubt that this had been a case of murder rather than a hypothetical case of suicide.

Thus Ethel Major's appeal was dismissed. A public petition was sent to the Home Secretary, citing Ethel's domestic conditions as sufficient grounds for clemency and when Secretary of State John Gilmour sent a telegram to Alderman A. Stark, the Lord Mayor of Hull, declining to intervene in the process of justice, Stark responded by sending a telegram directly to the King and Queen:

> The Lord Mayor of Hull sends loyal and respectful greetings to their Majesties and respectfully pleads on behalf of the citizens of Hull for their Majesties' intervention on behalf of Mrs Major who is to be executed at Hull Prison tomorrow morning, despite the jury's strong recommendation to mercy. The impending execution is giving great distress to thousands of women, and it is earnestly pleaded that her Majesty may use her influence in mercy being shown at this eleventh hour to a woman and mother.

However, despite acknowledgement of the telegram from the King and Queen, saying that the message had been transmitted to the Home Secretary, the execution of Ethel Lillie Major went ahead at Hull Prison on the morning of 19 December 1934 with Thomas and Albert Pierrepoint sending her to an instantaneous death.

26

'I've been a good wife to him and nobody can say I haven't'

COOMBE, DORSET, 1935

Nineteen-year-old Charlotte McHugh, an illiterate Irish gypsy girl, once believed that she had found her prince charming in the form of an English soldier. Frederick John Bryant was a military policeman serving with the Dorset regiment and met Charlotte when he was sent to Londonderry, one of 60,000 English soldiers dispatched to assist in the repression of the Sinn Fein movement during the Irish Troubles of 1917–1922.

When Bryant left Ireland to return to civilian life and his job as a cowman in Dorset, Charlotte went with him. The couple married in March 1922 at Wells in Somerset and settled in a tied cottage at Nether Compton, near Sherborne.

However, life in rural Dorset wasn't the idyll of Charlotte's dreams. She had simply exchanged poverty and squalor in Ireland for the same in England. Frequently, she sought relief from her desperate circumstances by visiting the

Sherborne. (Author's collection)

223

local pub, where she became known amongst the locals as 'Compton Liz', 'Black Bess', or 'Killarney Kate'. As well as gaining several nicknames, Charlotte also gained a reputation for accepting drinks from strange men, many of whom were subsequently invited back to the cottage she shared with Frederick.

Not only were these liaisons extremely pleasurable for Charlotte, but they were also a means of supplementing the meagre 38s her husband received as his weekly wage. Bryant was well aware of his wife's extra-marital activities and even condoned them. 'I don't care what she does,' he told a neighbour who had informed him of Charlotte's visitors. 'Four pounds a week is better than thirty bob.'

Charlotte had pretensions to an extravagant lifestyle. On occasions, she was known to buy luxury foodstuffs and she also sometimes hired a car and driver for a day, the cost of which was almost the equivalent of a week's wage for her husband. To support her aspirations, Charlotte became adept at thinking of new ways to extract money from her gentleman callers. On one occasion, she managed to convince a Yeovil businessman that she was carrying his baby. The man – doubtless terrified of the likely scandal – quickly handed over £25 to pay for an abortion but, months later, Charlotte returned with a baby in her arms, demanding regular child support payments. In fact, the baby was fathered by neither the businessman nor Charlotte's husband, but was the progeny of one of her most regular lovers, Leonard Parsons.

Parsons – or Bill Moss as he was sometimes known – was a travelling salesman and horse dealer with a gypsy background and nomadic lifestyle similar to Charlotte's own. Moss lived with Priscilla Loveridge on Huish gypsy camp at Weston-super-Mare. Together they had four illegitimate children. However, once he met Charlotte and became her lover in 1933, Parsons all but moved in with the Bryant family. Surprisingly under the circumstances, he and Frederick Bryant became good friends, often drinking together at The Crown public house and even sharing a razor.

It was while Parsons was staying at the cottage that Fred Bryant suffered the first episode of what was to become a prolonged illness. On 13 May Bryant went to work as usual, while Parsons left to conduct some business, taking with him Charlotte and Ernest, the Bryant's oldest child. Fred ate the lunch of meat, potatoes and peas left for him by Charlotte and, shortly afterwards, became seriously ill with what appeared to be food poisoning.

Weakened by severe vomiting and diarrhoea, all Fred could do was to call out for his next-door neighbour, Mrs Ethel Staunton. When Mrs Staunton heard his cries, she immediately went to see if she could help, finding Fred sitting on the stairs, groaning and shivering violently. Fred asked her to fetch a tin bath from the garden, which she did, making him a solution of salt water to induce vomiting. She then went off to fetch her husband, Bernard.

By the time she came back, Frederick Bryant had managed to drag himself upstairs to bed. He had also vomited into the bath, bringing up a large quantity of what Mr Staunton described as 'green frothy stuff'. Staunton sent someone to telephone for the doctor and, while waiting for him to arrive, made up several hot water bottles for his neighbour who was complaining of feeling bitterly cold.

Dr McCarthy eventually arrived to find Frederick Bryant complaining of stomach pains and cramp in his legs and suffering from bouts of severe sickness and diarrhoea. Concluding that his patient had an attack of food poisoning, he gave him an injection and left him to rest. When he called back at the cottage the next day, he found Bryant's condition to have greatly improved. Charlotte Bryant was attending to him and McCarthy questioned her about what her husband had eaten over the previous couple of days. Charlotte assured him that Fred had eaten exactly the same food as the rest of the family and that nobody else had suffered any ill effects, which appeared to rule out food poisoning as the cause of Fred's illness.

Fred eventually made a full recovery but, on 6 August, he again fell ill with similar symptoms. This time he was diagnosed with gastroenteritis and, once more, after a few days he was back to his normal rude health.

In October 1935, the Bryant family moved to a new cottage at Coombe. It was around this time that Leonard Parsons' attraction for Charlotte began to show signs of waning. Afraid that he was about to leave her, Charlotte tried numerous ways to keep him by her side. First, she hid his clothes. A few days later she visited a garage where he had left his car for repairs. Posing as Mrs Parsons, she told the garage owner to be careful about working on the car since her husband had no means of paying the bill.

Her efforts were in vain as, in November, Parsons left the Bryant household never to return. Charlotte, however, had no intention of letting him get away and made a strenuous effort to track him down. She hired a car and driver to take her to the Huish Camp to see Priscilla Loveridge. Priscilla wasn't there on that day, but Charlotte managed to speak to her mother, Mrs Penfold, telling her that she wanted to open her daughter's eyes to the baby her partner had fathered. Mrs Penfold asked Charlotte if she had a husband, to which Charlotte replied that she had, but that he was seriously ill in a nursing home and she didn't think he would be coming home.

On the following day, Charlotte again secured the services of a driver and headed back to Weston-super-Mare, this time taking Parsons' baby with her and also her next-door neighbour, Mrs Lucy Ostler, with whom she had become firm friends. This time, she was more fortunate. Priscilla Loveridge was at home and she and her mother were shown the baby, which bore a strong resemblance to its father, Leonard Parsons.

On 10 December, Frederick Bryant was again stricken with a mystery illness. Working in a stone quarry on the farm, he suddenly doubled over with stomach pain. Having been sick on the grass, he was sent home to recover and, according to one of his workmates, appeared to be dragging his feet as he walked.

He was attended by Dr Tracey who, on examination, found him to be suffering from the symptoms of shock, with a temperature that was well below normal. A seemingly unconcerned Charlotte told the doctor that her husband had suffered similar attacks in the past.

On 20 December, an insurance salesman, Edward Tuck, called at the Bryants' cottage hoping to sell Fred a life insurance policy. One look at the weakened, haggard man was sufficient for Tuck to decide not to proceed with the sale. Later that very day, Fred collapsed again and the Bryants' daughter, Lily, was sent to a neighbour for help. The neighbour, Mr Priddle, accompanied her back to the cottage where he found Fred vomiting profusely, groaning and writhing in agony. Bryant asked for some water, but was unable to keep it down. When Charlotte put her husband's illness down to overeating, Priddle took matters into his own hands and telephoned for a doctor himself.

Dr McCarthy saw Bryant on 21 December and made up a prescription for medicine, which Charlotte was to collect from Sherborne that afternoon. Charlotte was away from home for three hours, during which time neighbours cared for Fred. He complained of awful pain, which he described as burning him inside like a red-hot poker, and was convinced that he was going to die. When Charlotte returned, she unsympathetically remarked to a neighbour that it was a pity she hadn't got him insured, saying that at least he could have a military funeral.

Fred received his first dose of medicine at six o'clock that evening, but said that it tasted foul. The medicine was promptly discarded and Fred spent an uncomfortable night in bed with his wife. Mrs Ostler also stayed overnight, sleeping on a pull-out bed in the same room.

By morning, Fred's condition had worsened considerably. The vomiting and diarrhoea had so weakened him that he was unable to raise himself from the bed. Dr McCarthy was called and arrived at noon when, finding Bryant now gravely ill, he arranged for his admission to the Yeatman Hospital in Sherborne. It was there that thirty-nine-year-old Frederick Bryant died in agony just a few hours later. The doctor was at his bedside and it occurred to him that Bryant's symptoms were exactly those of arsenic poisoning. He refused to issue a death certificate.

A post-mortem examination was conducted the following day. Charlotte Bryant and Mrs Ostler visited the hospital to collect a death certificate, but once again it was refused. There would have to be an inquest, Charlotte was told.

Charlotte was not sure what this procedure involved but Mrs Ostler explained that 'they must have found something in his body which didn't ought to be there.' On their way home, the two women bumped into Edward Tuck, the insurance agent, who gallantly offered to drive them back to Coombe. During the journey, Tuck was struck by Charlotte's conversation. 'They can't say *I* poisoned him,' she stated repeatedly, emphasizing the 'I'. 'I've been a good wife to him and nobody can say I haven't.'

The inquest opened on 24 December but was adjourned over Christmas. When it reopened on 27 December, a second post-mortem examination was ordered and Frederick Bryant's internal organs were sealed in jars and sent to Home Office analyst Dr Roche Lynch for testing.

Meanwhile, Dorset police began an intensive search at the Bryants' cottage. The investigating officers, led by Chief Inspector Alex Bell and Detective Sergeant Tapsell, sent Charlotte and her five children to the public assistance institution at Sturminster Newton, where she was shortly joined by her neighbour Lucy Ostler and her seven children.

With the widow Bryant and her children out of the way, numerous bottles, tins and items of clothing were removed from the cottage for testing. The floors were swept and the dust was also collected. The Bryants' cat, dog, chickens and pigeons were put to sleep so that their bodies could be analysed. While police were conducting their search, a puppy from the farm on which the cottage stood died suddenly and unexpectedly. It too was subjected to a post-mortem examination but no connection could be found between its death and that of Fred Bryant.

Charlotte and her children were interviewed, as were Lucy Ostler and other neighbours. However, police were initially unable to trace Leonard Parsons in spite of sending cars to search large areas of Dorset, Somerset and Devon.

The report from Dr Roche Lynch had, as expected, confirmed that Frederick Bryant had died from arsenic poisoning, so the investigating officers broadened their search to check the registers of every chemist's shop in the area. They also visited glove factories at Yeovil, where red arsenic was commonly used in the tanning of animal skins. Two particular chemist's shops attracted their attention. One in Sherborne had recorded a purchase of poison at the end of April 1935, just a few days before Bryant's initial bout of sickness. The second, in Yeovil, had sold a tin of weed killer on 21 December, the day on which Charlotte was absent from home for three hours on the pretext of collecting Fred's medicine.

By now, police had both Charlotte Bryant and Lucy Ostler in custody as prime suspects for the murder of Frederick Bryant. An identity parade was arranged in which the Yeovil chemist tried to pick out the woman who had bought poison from his shop shortly before Fred's death, signing the register with a cross. He was unable to identify either Charlotte or Lucy as his customer.

Certificate for the purchase of a Poison.
(RULE 31.)

For the purposes of subsection (2) (*a*) (i) of section 18 of the Pharmacy and Poisons Act, 1933,

I, the undersigned, a householder occupying (*a*) "NEWTON" FACTORY RD. HINCKLEY. LEICS. hereby certify from

my knowledge of (*b*) ARTHUR JOHN HIGGINSON of (*a*) 136, FACTORY RD. HINCKLEY that he is a

person to whom (*c*) POTASSIUM CYANIDE may properly be supplied.

I further certify that (*d*) A.J Higginson is the signature of the said

(*b*) ARTHUR JOHN HIGGINSON

H. Banks

Signature of householder giving certificate.

Date 24 - 6 - 41

(*a*) Insert full postal address.

(*b*) Insert full name of intending purchaser.

(*c*) Insert name of poison.

(*d*) Intending purchaser to sign his name here.

Endorsement required by Rule 31 of the Poisons Rules to be made by a Police Officer in charge of a police station, when, but only when, the householder giving the certificate is not known to the seller of the poison to be a responsible person of good character.

I hereby certify that in so far as is known to the police of the district in which

* HAROLD BANKS. resides he is a responsible person of good character.

Signature of Police Officer S. James

Rank Police Sergeant

In charge of Police Station at Hinckley

Date 24 - 4 - 41

Office Stamp of
Police Station.

* Insert full name of householder giving the certificate.

A certificate for the purchase of poison. (Author's collection)

Charlotte Bryant. (Daily Echo, Bournemouth)

Both women had consistently denied any knowledge of the cause of Fred's death. However, it must have dawned on Lucy Ostler that she was under threat of prosecution for his murder as she asked to make another statement.

This time, Lucy gave a version of events that directly conflicted with Charlotte's statement. She told the police that, on the night that she had stayed at the cottage to assist with Bryant's nursing care, she had woken at 3 a.m. to hear Charlotte coaxing her reluctant husband to take a drink of meat extract. Shortly afterwards she had heard him vomiting and, within twelve hours, he was dead. Charlotte had told officers that she had been so exhausted that she had slept through the night without waking. In fact, Lucy Ostler had mentioned the next morning that she had got up several times during the night to give Fred Bryant a drink of water – Charlotte maintained that she hadn't heard a thing.

In her second statement, Lucy also told police that soon after Bryant's death, Charlotte had pointed to a tin in the cupboard, saying, 'I must get rid of that.' Lucy's description of the tin matched that of the Eureka brand weed killer that the Yeovil chemist had sold to the unidentified woman. A few days later, Lucy had found the burned remains of a tin of a similar size in the ashes under the Bryants' boiler. She had thrown the ashes into the yard.

After revising her statement, Lucy Ostler was released from custody and on 10 February 1936, Charlotte Bryant was formally charged with administering poison to her husband Frederick John Bryant and wilfully murdering him. She denied the charge.

At Sherborne Police Court, she was eventually committed for trial at the next Dorset Assizes. Prior to her hearing before the magistrates, she was permitted to see her children for the first time in weeks, playing with them for an hour or so in an anteroom.

Charlotte Bryant's trial opened before Mr Justice MacKinnon at Dorchester on 27 May 1936. Immediately Solicitor-General Sir Terence O'Connor KC, for the prosecution, addressed the court, telling the jury that this would not be a case in which he could say that on a certain day, at a certain place, the accused woman went and bought some arsenic and took it home before putting it in her husband's tea, milk or whatever. Much of the evidence against her was circumstantial, but nevertheless strong.

Nobody was in any doubt that Frederick Bryant died as a result of the administration of arsenic and his wife had a motive for wanting him dead, that motive being Leonard Parsons. O'Connor pointed out that the one weakness in the evidence against Charlotte was that nobody had been able to show that she had ever purchased poison.

Among the first witnesses to testify were various neighbours of the Bryants who spoke of attending Fred during his bouts of sickness, including Lucy Ostler who stated that she had heard Charlotte say several times that she hated Fred.

On the second day of the trial, Leonard Parsons was called to the witness stand and caused some consternation in court when he was unable to understand the questions put to him about the nature of his relationship with the accused. Asked on what terms he was with Mrs Bryant, Parsons simply looked blank. O'Connor rephrased the question. 'Have you been intimate with Mrs Bryant?'

High West Street, Dorchester, 1946. (Author's collection)

Interior of the Court House, Dorchester. (© Nicola Sly)

'I cannot understand,' responded Parsons.

O'Connor tried again. 'Did you live with her as man and wife?'

'No,' said Parsons promptly.

In the end, O'Connor was forced to ask his question in much baser terms, which Parsons finally understood. 'Oh, yes,' he replied enthusiastically, going on to say that he had enjoyed sexual relations with Charlotte from 1933 to 1935, something that Charlotte had consistently denied in her statements to the police.

Parsons told the court that Charlotte had wanted to marry him and that, more than once, she had asked if he would marry her were she to be widowed. According to Parsons, his answer had always been no.

Parsons denied that he had once taken a bottle into the Bryant household, the contents of which fizzled when poured onto a stone. He also spoke of trying – and failing – to buy arsenic to use in the treatment of a sick mare. He was refused the poison at the chemist's shop in Sherborne because he was not known to the proprietor. He had even applied to the police to be allowed to purchase a small quantity of arsenic, but had been turned down.

Insurance agent Edward Tuck spoke of meeting Charlotte Bryant in 1934 and being told by her that she would like to insure her 'old man'. Having called at the cottage and seen how ill Frederick looked, Tuck didn't pursue the sale any further. However, he did tell the court of giving Charlotte Bryant and Lucy Ostler a ride home from the hospital and of Charlotte's strange remarks on that occasion about poisoning.

Dr Roche Lynch gave evidence about the scientific tests he had conducted, both on Frederick Bryant's internal organs and on items removed from the cottage. He stated that, when presented with Bryant's organs for testing, they showed a remarkable degree of preservation, something that was characteristic of ingestion of arsenic. The poison was present in every organ tested and, in total, he estimated that the body contained 4.09 grains of arsenic, the normal lethal dose being between two and four grains. Furthermore, the concentration of arsenic in the dead man's fingernails suggested that the poison had been administered over a period of time, rather than as a single dose.

Roche Lynch was then cross-questioned by Joshua Casswell, counsel for the defence. While conceding that, of the 146 items taken from the Bryants' cottage, 114 were found to contain no arsenic at all, Roche Lynch went on to say that the concentration of arsenic in the ashes from the Bryants' boiler was so abnormally high that something containing the poison had to have been burned there. He denied Casswell's suggestion that Bryant might have been accidentally poisoned, having eaten without washing his hands after he had been dipping sheep.

On the following day, Charlotte Bryant herself took the stand. 'I cannot tell you poison,' [*sic*] she stated firmly, while clutching the Bible tightly in her hands. 'I never had any weed killer in the house.'

On the fourth day of the trial, the jury retired, returning after an hour with a verdict of 'Guilty'. Mr Justice MacKinnon asked if Charlotte had anything to say before he passed judgement upon her.

'I am not guilty, sir, not guilty,' she told him.

As sentence of death was passed upon her, Charlotte let out a long, pitiful moan. 'Not Guilty,' she said again, before collapsing in tears in the dock. She was half carried away from the court, her loud sobbing being heard long after she left the courtroom.

When counsel for the defence, Mr Casswell, returned to his London office on the following Monday, after having enjoyed a short holiday with his family, he found a letter awaiting him, with a further copy of the same letter sent to his home address. It read:

> If I am right in supposing that you were the defending counsel in the case which ended at Dorchester Assizes on Saturday last would you please communicate with me as soon as possible because I have something to put before you arising out of that part of the evidence in the judge's summing up relating to the normal percentage of arsenic in coal ashes...

The letter continued in a similar vein and was signed by Professor William A. Bone of the Imperial College of Science and Technology.

Casswell immediately made contact with Professor Bone and received a second letter from him, in which Bone claimed that Dr Roche Lynch's evidence on the normal proportions of arsenic found in domestic fires was seriously flawed.

It was an established fact, wrote Bone, that the normal arsenic content of house coal was not less than 140 parts to the million and, more usually, around 1,000 parts to the million. Lynch had stated in court that the ashes from the Bryants' boiler had contained 149 parts of arsenic to the million and, rather than being unusually high and suggesting that something containing arsenic had been burned there, the arsenic content was substantially less than might normally have been expected, suggesting evidence to the contrary.

Having obtained a written statement from the professor, Casswell immediately appealed the conviction, adding that he would be taking the unusual step of asking Professor Bone to appear before the Court of Appeal so that they could hear for themselves what he had to say. The hearing was fixed for 10 July and Casswell was heartened when contacted by the Solicitor-General, who told him; 'Lynch has made a dreadful blunder.'

However any optimism that Casswell might have felt was dashed by the Lord Chief Justice, Lord Hewart, who dismissed the appeal and flatly refused to even listen to Professor Bone who was waiting outside the court of appeal to testify.

Questions were quickly asked in parliament about whether the Home Secretary, Sir John Simon, would consider introducing legislation to ensure that any verdict reached on mistaken evidence should be subject to enquiry on appeal. Casswell, sitting in the Stranger's Gallery of the House of Commons, was astounded by Simon's reply.

Referring specifically to the case of *Rex v Bryant*, Simon assured the House that both the appeal judges and the trial judge were of the opinion that Professor Bone's information did not affect the validity of the jury's verdict and that, even if Lynch's evidence were wrong, the remaining evidence against Charlotte Bryant was so strong that it could be conclusively determined that no miscarriage of justice had occurred.

No one had told Charlotte Bryant of the desperate efforts to secure a reprieve on her behalf, since her defence counsel did not want to get her hopes up. Hence, she remained confined in the condemned cell, where, for the first time in her life, she learned the rudiments of reading and writing. Shortly before her execution, she made a will in which she left the sum of 5s 8½d to be divided equally between her five children. It was the first ever document that she signed with her own name rather than with her mark.

She had made one final effort to secure a reprieve of her death sentence, sending a telegram to the new king, Edward VIII, which read: 'Mighty King.

Exeter Prison, 1905. (Author's collection)

Have pity on your lowly, afflicted subject. Don't let them kill me on Wednesday.' Unfortunately for Charlotte, the Home Secretary felt unable to advise the king to spare her life and she was executed at Exeter Prison on 15 July 1936.

At the time of her execution, a Mrs Van der Elst from Kensington, a notorious campaigner for the abolition of capital punishment, drove up to the prison in her car and allegedly broke through a cord, which was barring one of the entrances. She was promptly arrested and charged with causing a breach of the peace and obstructing a police officer in the course of his duty. Magistrates dismissed the first charge against her and fined her the sum of £5 for the second. Mrs Van der Elst paid her fine and, at the same time, handed over an equal amount as a donation to the police sports fund. She announced her intentions of starting a fund, with £50,000 of her own money, to provide for the children of people who had been murdered or executed and added that she planned to take care of Charlotte Bryant's children and pay for their education and upbringing. In the event, after Charlotte's death, the Dorset Public Assistance Committee formally adopted her five children.

'You need not worry about me as everything is all right'

W hen Dorothea Nancy Waddingham's husband, Thomas Willoughby Leech, died from throat cancer, leaving her with three children to bring up, Dorothea became romantically involved with the couple's lodger, Ronald Joseph Sullivan. In due course another child was born and, needing a means of supporting their family, Dorothea and Ronald decided to capitalise on Dorothea's nursing experience and open a nursing home on Devon Drive, Nottingham.

In reality, Dorothea's experience as a nurse was limited to a short period of working as a maid at the Burton-on-Trent Infirmary and a job in a chemist's shop.

Market place, Nottingham, 1930s. (Author's collection)

Nevertheless, she and Sullivan opened up a home catering for the elderly, as well as 'medical, surgical and chronic cases' and began accepting patients.

In December 1934, Miss Winifred Blagg began to be concerned for the welfare of her old friends, Mrs Louisa Baguley and her daughter Ada. Ada was nearing fifty years old and was crippled, in need of constant nursing care. She was a large woman, weighing around sixteen stones and suffered from progressive creeping paralysis, which left her unable to walk. Unfortunately, the task of looking after her daughter was becoming too much for Louisa, who was then in her late eighties. Miss Blagg began to look for suitable accommodation for the mother and daughter, finally settling on Dorothea Waddingham's establishment. It was agreed that the Baguleys should move in for a total fee of £3 a week and in January 1935, they took up residence in their new home. When Miss Blagg visited them, she was more than happy with the care they were receiving, as at first was Ada's cousin, Lawrence Baguley.

However, before too long, Dorothea and Ronald began to complain that the money they were receiving for the Baguleys' care was not nearly enough. It was suggested that Louisa and Ada should make new wills, leaving all their money and the proceeds of their life insurance policies to Dorothea in return for a guarantee that they would be cared for throughout the rest of their lives. The Baguleys' relatives objected to this arrangement and from then on, it was made blatantly obvious to them that they were not welcome to visit the nursing home. On 5 April 1935, Lawrence Baguley went to see his relatives and was turned away by Ronald Sullivan and, on the following day, Dorothea Waddingham consulted a solicitor to begin sorting out the legalities of the new wills.

On the death of her father, Ada Baguley had been the sole beneficiary of his will, with the conditions that all the income from his £1,600 legacy should go to his wife, Louisa, and that, if Ada predeceased her mother, the estate was to pass to Louisa. New wills were made in favour of Waddingham and Sullivan on their undertaking to continue caring for Louisa and Ada until their deaths.

Ada Baguley at least seemed quite happy with the plans as Lawrence Baguley received a letter signed by his cousin, in which she told him, 'You need not worry about me as everything is all right.' The letter ended 'Everything is carried out straightforward here and if you are not careful you will regret it.'

The new wills came into effect on 7 May 1935 and, just five days later, Louisa Baguley died. As she was eighty-seven years old and had been in failing health for some time, the cause of her death was recorded as 'cardiac degeneration' and accepted as being mainly down to old age.

On 11 September 1935, Ada Baguley followed her mother to the grave. Dr Manfield had attended her throughout her stay at the nursing home, and it was he who Dorothea Waddingham called to come urgently when she grew concerned about Ada's condition on the morning of her eventual death. When Manfield arrived, Ada Baguley had just died.

Manfield had last seen Ada on 2 September and, when told by Dorothea that Ada had been in a coma for four hours prior to her demise, he made an external examination of the body and concluded that she had died from a stroke. He recorded the cause of death as due to 'cerebral haemorrhage due to cardio-vascular degeneration'.

On the following day, Dr Cyril Banks, the Medical Officer of Health for Nottingham, received a request for the cremation of Ada Baguley's body. A letter dated 29 August 1935 accompanied the death certificate, purporting to be a written request from Ada that she should be cremated. The letter was witnessed by 'R.J. Sullivan' and Banks noted that the entire letter appeared to have been written in the hand of the person who had signed his name as a witness. Dr Banks was sufficiently disturbed by this to order a post-mortem examination.

Dr Leonard Taylor conducted the post-mortem and initially formed the opinion that Ada's death had been caused not by a stroke but by pneumonia. However, he removed some of Ada's organs for further testing and an examination by analyst William Taylor revealed the presence of a total of 3.102 grains of morphine. The analyst concluded that Ada Baguley had died as a result of acute poisoning by either heroin or morphine, a fatal dose of which had been administered between six and twelve hours before her death.

An inquest into Miss Baguley's death was opened by Nottingham City Coroner Mr W.S. Rothera, which eventually concluded on 30 January 1936. The coroner's jury returned a verdict of wilful murder against Dorothea Waddingham and Ronald Sullivan, saying:

> The unanimous verdict of the jury is that Ada Baguley met her death by a fatal dose of morphine or heroin or both. Our considered opinion is that there was a joint conspiracy. Our verdict is one of wilful murder against Ronald Sullivan and Nurse Waddingham.

Dorothea, who had been asked to leave the courtroom because of her constant interruptions to the proceedings, was promptly arrested along with Ronald Sullivan and charged with Ada Baguley's murder. When the body of Mrs Louisa Baguley was subsequently exhumed, Home Office Analyst Dr Roche Lynch found pseudo-morphine to be present in her remains. He concluded that the presence of pseudo-morphine – the chemical to which heroin and morphine eventually convert – and the absence of any natural causes of death suggested that she too had died from acute heroin or morphine poisoning. Both Waddingham and Sullivan were subsequently additionally charged with Mrs Baguley's murder and committed for trial at the next Nottingham Assizes.

The trial opened before Mr Justice Goddard on 24 February 1936 and was to last until 27 February. Norman Birkett KC served as prosecuting counsel, while J.F. Eales defended Dorothea Waddingham and Mr A. Lyons defended Sullivan. It was made clear at the outset that the only charge being tried at present was that of the murder of Ada Baguley, to which both Waddingham and Sullivan pleaded 'Not Guilty' but, before the trial had reached its conclusion, the judge determined that there was insufficient evidence to convict Ronald Sullivan and ordered that he should be discharged.

Detective Inspector Pentland, who had headed the enquiries into the deaths of Mrs Baguley and her daughter, stated in court that both defendants had co-operated fully with his questioning and had made no attempt to hinder his investigations. Pentland also agreed that the general impression he had received throughout the investigation was that both of the alleged victims had been happy and comfortable at the nursing home.

The police enquiries had established that Nottingham chemist, Mr Leonard Leader, had dispensed thirteen prescriptions for heroin tablets for two previous residents of the home, Mrs Kemp and Mrs Harewood, both of whom had predeceased the Baguleys. In addition, Leader had supplied barbitone tablets for Mrs Baguley and a regular batch of chlorodyne medicine prescribed for Ada by Dr Manfield, which contained two and two-elevenths grains of morphine per bottle.

Manfield stated in court that he had never prescribed either morphine or heroin for either of the Baguleys, with the exception of the chlorodyne mixture. Furthermore, he told the court that, after the death of Mrs Kemp in February 1935, Dorothea had returned six unused heroin tablets to him. Dorothea initially said that she had never given morphine to Ada Baguley but, in a later statement to the police, added that, on 27 August 1935, Manfield had left a prescription for six tablets of morphine for Ada Baguley to be used at Dorothea's discretion and a further prescription for four tablets on 2 September, even though she told him she had not used the first tablets. Manfield denied leaving any such prescriptions.

Several friends and relatives of Ada Baguley testified, including a Mrs Briggs, who had visited Ada on the day before her death and spent three-quarters of an hour chatting with her in the garden, finding her to be 'quite bright'.

Solicitor Mr Lane talked of advising the Baguleys on making new wills after having first discussed the matter with them in the presence of Dorothea and Ronald Sullivan. However, neither Dorothea nor Ronald had been present when he had actually drawn up the new wills for the Baguleys and Mr Lane was satisfied that he was acting in accordance with their wishes.

The prosecution called Dr Frank Jacob, who had been treating Ada Baguley for twenty years for a progressive disease, disseminated sclerosis. Although he had prescribed no treatment while Ada was resident at the nursing home, he had for many years prescribed a chlorodyne mixture known as 'BP 1914'. Jacob believed that, by the time she entered the home, Ada had been rapidly nearing the end of her life and had a life expectancy of between one and three years at most. Dr Manfield had been shown Dr Jacob's prescription and had continued to prescribe it, although he had switched to a weaker strength mixture in August 1935.

Manfield admitted that this had been a mistake on his part – he had intended to prescribe a stronger mixture. He had also prescribed a kaolin mixture for Ada, which contained morphine, but insisted that he had never prescribed either morphine or heroin. He did concede that he had given Dorothea Waddingham morphine tablets 'from his pocket' and that, in addition to the morphine he had prescribed for Mrs Kemp and Mrs Harewood, this would have amounted to around one hundred half-grain tablets of morphia sulphate. Calling Ada Baguley a 'chronic and hopeless case', Manfield agreed that her post-mortem examination had shown a degeneration of her heart valves, which would have caused her considerable pain He added that he had no complaint about Dorothea Waddingham's nursing skills and that he had always found her most anxious to do the best she possibly could for all of the patients in her care.

William Taylor, the assistant to the senior Notts City analyst, related finding morphine in Ada Baguley's remains, admitting that it was the first time that he had ever found morphine in a sample. The defence pointed out that no representative for Dorothea Waddingham had been present during the tests and that, since testing had mostly destroyed the samples, there was no opportunity for his results to be checked.

For the defence, Mr Eales first dealt with the question of the will, reminding the jury that there had never been any secrecy about it and that the solicitor had been confident that, in drawing it up, he was acting in accordance with the Baguleys' wishes. Eales reminded the jury that the report of the presence of morphine in Ada Baguley's remains had been solely down to William Taylor and that it was the first time he had ever found morphine in any remains.

Dorothea Waddingham had assisted with the investigation throughout and had been prepared to testify in court, even though it laid her open to cross-examination by 'one of the most brilliant members of the English Bar'. Eales suggested that Dr Manfield's memory might have failed him with regard to the nature of the tablets actually prescribed.

Eales then played his trump card. The one thing that conclusively destroyed the prosecution evidence and established the innocence of his client was the fact that, on the morning of Ada's death, Dorothea Waddingham had been so concerned by her condition that she had called a doctor. 'I venture to submit that it is impossible to believe that any person who had administered a fatal dose of poison would be so utterly and incredibly stupid as to endeavour to get a doctor there during the lifetime of the patient.'

With that, the defence closed, leaving the judge to sum up the case for the jury. Mr Justice Goddard first instructed the jury to ignore any lack of professional qualifications of Dorothea Waddingham, even though she referred to herself as 'Nurse'. What they should focus on was whether or not the Crown had proved that the prisoner administered a poisonous drug to Ada Baguley, and, if so, had it been administered feloniously rather than negligently and had the administration resulted in Ada Baguley's death?

Dorothea Waddingham had admitted in court to giving Ada Baguley morphine but had stressed that she had only done so '…in the exercise of the discretion given to me by the doctor'. Dr Manfield had left tablets to be administered at her discretion and she had administered them – she believed she had done nothing wrong. Although stressing that the court was trying Dorothea not Dr Manfield, the judge told the jury that, if what she said were true, then she deserved to be acquitted. The jury must also satisfy themselves that a fatal dose had actually been administered, given that they only had William Taylor's report to rely on.

There were points in Dorothea's favour as well as against her, continued the judge. Mrs Blagg, who had originally chosen the home for the Baguleys, was the Secretary of the County Nursing Association. In addition, Dorothea had made repeated appeals to the Baguleys' friends and relatives, saying that she could not possibly keep the Baguleys for £3 a week, before arriving at the solution of changing the Baguleys' wills in her favour. The business with the wills had been conducted openly and the solicitor acting for the Baguleys was happy that he was working on their instructions alone. In addition, said Mr Justice Goddard, not one person had come forward to suggest that the Baguleys were not happy with Dorothea, or that they were not being properly cared for. The prisoner had mentioned cremation to Dr Manfield before Ada's death, which might suggest that the defendant had not tried to arrange it in haste to destroy evidence.

Yet although these points were all in the prisoner's favour, Dr Jacob had testified that Ada Baguley's medical condition was not likely to have caused her severe pain and there would have been no cause to administer morphine. Also, Dr Manfield had categorically denied prescribing it.

Dorothea had testified that, on the day before her death, Ada Baguley had eaten a meal of pork, baked potatoes, kidney beans and fruit pie and that she had asked for and been given second helpings. If, as Dorothea had stated, Ada Baguley had been in sufficient pain for the previous three nights to require the administration of morphine as an analgesic, why would she be given such a large meal?

Finally, the judge dealt with the change in Dorothea's testimony from an initial statement of 'I have never given Miss Baguley any morphia' to her current stance, which was that she had given it under doctor's orders. She had stated that Dr Manfield had asked her not to mention morphine but Manfield had no interest in Miss Baguley's death unless it was one of protecting his professional reputation.

The jury retired at the conclusion of Mr Justice Goddard's summary, which had lasted in excess of two hours. On their return, they found Dorothea Waddingham 'Guilty' of the murder of Ada Baguley, although they made a strong recommendation for mercy.

'I am innocent,' Dorothea protested in a whisper, before the judge passed the death sentence on her, promising to forward the jury's recommendation to the appropriate quarter.

The judge then ordered that Ronald Sullivan should be placed in the dock and, since the prosecution had indicated that they would not be proceeding with the charge of the wilful murder of Louisa Baguley, Mr Justice Goddard had the jury re-sworn in order to formally acquit Sullivan of the charge.

On 5 March the defence filed an appeal, which was heard by Lord Chief Justice Lord Hewart and Justices Humphreys and du Parcq on 30 March 1936. It was the contention of the defence that the trial had boiled down to the simple question of whether the jury believed the defendant or Dr Manfield and that Mr Justice Goddard had not satisfactorily addressed the option of manslaughter, which would have applied had Mrs Waddingham given the

Winson Green Prison, Birmingham, 1934. (Author's collection)

tablets negligently and unskilfully, rather than with intent to kill. The doctor had given her the morphine and, unable to get medical assistance for her patient, she had administered the tablets simply to relieve pain. The appeal judges could see no justification for a verdict of manslaughter and the appeal was consequently dismissed.

The Home Secretary refused to recommend a reprieve in spite of the express wishes of the jury and even though Dorothea was still breastfeeding her fifth baby. Thirty-six-year-old Dorothea Nancy Waddingham (also known as Leech and Sullivan) was executed by Thomas and Albert Pierrepoint at Winson Green Prison in Birmingham on 16 April 1936. The execution was marked by a noisy demonstration from a crowd of between 2,000 and 3,000 people outside the prison, led by the noted opponent of the death penalty Mrs Van der Elst, who played the hymns 'Abide with Me' and 'Nearer my God to Thee' through a loudspeaker as the hanging of Dorothea Waddingham took place.

28

'She was ill, ill, ill on many occasions'

For some weeks, Mrs Bown had been troubled by a foul smell emanating from the garden of her flat at Goring Way, Greenford in Middlesex. With the heat of the early summer, the odour gradually became more and more pungent until Mrs Bown finally mentioned it to Lionel Watson, who lived in the flat below hers.

By that time, Watson had technically moved out of his flat, which he had previously occupied with a woman named Phyllis Crocker and her eighteen-month-old daughter, Eileen. Phyllis left the flat with her daughter on 21 May 1941 to live in Scotland and soon afterwards, Watson had also vacated his home, returning to live with his mother, although he still called at the flat regularly to make sure that everything was in order. Now Watson promised to check the property's drains and, on 27 June, Mrs Bown noticed him pouring disinfectant over the offending area.

However, the application of the disinfectant did nothing whatsoever to alleviate the stench and three days later Mrs Bown decided to investigate for herself. In the company of another neighbour, she lifted some flagstones in the garden and began to dig beneath them. She immediately noticed some white powder and what appeared to be human flesh and notified the police. When the garden was dug up, the decomposing bodies of Phyllis Crocker and her daughter were found buried beneath the flagstones at a depth of around 2ft. A post-mortem examination on the bodies revealed the presence of sodium cyanide and the cause of the deaths of both mother and child was deemed to be cyanide poisoning.

Watson and Phyllis Crocker had lived together since September of 1940, even though he was already married to another woman with whom he had four children. Although Phyllis had been very keen to legitimise their relationship, Watson's wife refused to grant him a divorce. On 18 January 1941 he had finally yielded to pressure from Phyllis and married her bigamously, his new wife being under the impression that her husband was divorced and was free to marry her.

Thus, when he arrived home from a trip to the cinema on 20 May 1941 and found baby Eileen lifeless in her cot and Phyllis lying dead on her back on the bathroom floor, Watson found himself in a quandary.

He told the police, 'I was in a bit of a fix because I had bigamously married her. I could not call in a doctor owing to that. I thought of my children, my job and my people.' He sat and stroked Phyllis's hand while deciding what to do.

In his statement to Detective Inspector John Smith and Divisional Detective Inspector Richard Deighton on 1 July 1941, Watson explained that he had first met Phyllis at the Hoover factory where they both worked. At that time, Phyllis had lived with her mother, Mrs Smith and daughter Eileen at 9 Goring Way. Mrs Smith had been terrified of air raids and had decided to move to Scotland, where she believed she would be safer. As soon as Mrs Smith left, Watson moved in to her home, living as man and wife with Phyllis.

Mrs Smith returned from Scotland six weeks later in a very nervous condition and, two weeks later, tried to drown herself at Twickenham. She was rescued but died soon afterwards in Tooting Hospital, leaving the way clear for Watson to move into the property at Goring Way on a permanent basis.

Watson told the police that soon after her mother's death, Phyllis had informed him that she was pregnant. She had taken something to induce a miscarriage but it had just made her ill and she was taken to Isleworth Hospital. Having lost the baby while there, she discharged herself from hospital and, according to Watson, '…was never the same after that'.

After their marriage, Phyllis told her husband that she was pregnant again. 'She was ill, ill, ill on many occasions,' Watson told the police, adding that Phyllis had visited her doctor numerous times. Dr Stuart had assured her that she was not pregnant but Phyllis had seemed unable to accept this and had begun to take 'stuff' to get rid of the baby she believed that she was carrying.

The day of her death had been Watson's day off work. He had asked Phyllis to come for a walk with him but she had claimed to have a bad headache. She had taken two aspirins and said that she intended to go to bed, so Watson had gone to the Granada Cinema at Greenford alone, arriving at 6.10 p.m. When he returned home at 10 p.m. he had found Phyllis lying dead in the bathroom, with Eileen dead in her cot. He covered the baby with bedclothes and picked up Phyllis and carried her to the couple's bed, where he sat with her body all night, mulling over what he should do next.

Watson went to work as usual the next morning and, when he got back to the house that evening, he dug a hole in the back garden and buried the bodies. 'There is nothing more to say,' he told the police.

Two days later, he was to make a further statement dealing with the aftermath of the deaths. Watson told the police that he had sold some of Phyllis's jewellery to Brown's pawnbrokers at West Ealing, receiving the sum of £4 17s 6d for her wedding ring, engagement ring, a brooch and a gold padlock bracelet. He had removed two rings from Phyllis's fingers before burying her and insisted that he had thrown these away.

Three or four weeks later, he had given several of Phyllis's possessions to a seventeen-year-old girl, Joan, who worked at Hoover's. These included a dress, some shoes, a powder compact, a steel ring with a stone and a bracelet. 'Don't think I have been familiar with Joan because I haven't,' Watson told the police, adding, 'I just took her out after my wife died to kill time and for company.'

Watson had also given away a baby's bracelet and a monogrammed serviette ring, gifts that he said he had personally bought for baby Eileen. He had tried to have Phyllis Crocker's Post Office Savings Account transferred to him, intending to use the balance of £43 to make the hire purchase payments on the furniture at the couple's home. The Post Office had sent Watson a form for Phyllis to sign, on which Watson had forged her signature. However, the Post Office weren't happy with the signature and wrote back asking Phyllis to sign her name in front of a clerk. Watson sent back a letter saying that Phyllis was in Scotland and that he would get her to do this when she returned.

Watson was charged with the murders of twenty-eight-year-old Phyllis Elizabeth Crocker and her daughter Eileen Alice Crocker and was brought to trial at the Central Criminal Court, or Old Bailey, in London, where he pleaded 'Not Guilty'. The trial opened on 15 September 1941, with Mister Justice Cassels presiding, Mr G.B. McClure prosecuting and Mr J.P. Valetta defending.

'The case for the prosecution is that Watson is a poisoner,' opened McClure. He went on to describe the relationship between Phyllis and Lionel and their bigamous marriage, telling the court that nobody had seen Phyllis alive since 20 May 1941.

McClure described the finding of the bodies in the garden at Goring Way and pointed out that Mrs Bown had actually seen Watson digging in the very spot where the bodies were later discovered on 26 May. Watson, who worked as a Bakelite moulder, had access to sodium cyanide in the case hardening department at his place of employment and had been seen handling it by several of his colleagues. Three of Watson's workmates – Frederick Heath, Ernest Bradshaw and Alfred Hall – later testified that Watson had discussed poisons with them. 'The very method of causing death suggests not a quick impulse but long planning – waiting for the opportunity,' said McClure.

Watson took the stand in his own defence, sticking to his story that he had been out and returned to find Phyllis and Eileen dead, after which he had been too afraid to contact the police in view of his bigamous marriage and had buried the bodies in the garden. Watson's counsel, Mr Valetta, insisted that his client had no motive for killing Phyllis and Eileen but the prosecution maintained that he had tired of Phyllis and wanted her and her baby out of the way so that he could pursue a relationship with Joan, the woman to whom he had given some of Phyllis's belongings.

Having heard medical evidence that Phyllis and Eileen had died from cyanide poisoning, the jury, whose members included three women, needed only twenty minutes of deliberation to return with a verdict of 'Guilty'.

'You planned to poison Phyllis Crocker and you did so,' said the judge in his address to the prisoner. 'The law provides one punishment for murder, the punishment of death.'

Mr Valetta appealed Watson's conviction on the grounds that the judge had not dealt satisfactorily with evidence suggesting that Phyllis Crocker had poisoned Eileen herself before committing suicide. The proceedings were held at the Court of Criminal Appeal before the Lord Chief Justice, Mr Justice Humphreys and Mr Justice Lewis on 28 October 1941. The Lord Chief Justice ruled that there were no grounds for the allegation that the question of suicide had not been adequately dealt with and that there was 'a great body of evidence' connecting Watson with the deaths, which was sufficient to 'prove to the hilt' the charge made against him, if the jury believed it.

Hence thirty-year-old Lionel Rupert Nathan Watson was executed at Pentonville Prison on 12 November 1941 by Thomas Pierrepoint, who was assisted by Henry Critchely.

Note: The actual date of Phyllis Crocker's murder is uncertain and is variously given as 19 and 20 May 1941. Initially, Watson couldn't recall the exact date but he was later to say he 'reckoned' that it was on 20 May 1941.

29

'I am looking after them that look after me'

BLACKPOOL, LANCASHIRE, 1953

At seventy-nine years old, Mrs Sarah Ann Ricketts of Devonshire Road, Blackpool, believed that she was still perfectly capable of taking care of herself. However, Mrs Ricketts, who had lost two husbands, both of whom had gassed themselves, was prepared to admit that she was having difficulty with the upkeep of her bungalow. Accordingly, on 10 March 1953, she placed an advertisement in her local newspaper offering free accommodation to a couple in exchange for help around the house.

On the same day, Mr and Mrs Alfred Merrifield responded to the advertisement. Alfred Edward Merrifield was seventy years old and was the

Blackpool, 1954. (Author's collection)

Princess Parade, Blackpool. (Author's collection)

View over Blackpool. (Author's collection)

third husband of Louisa, who was twenty-four years his junior. Louisa had a somewhat dubious past. She too had been twice widowed, her second husband dying just ten weeks after their marriage. Her four children from her first marriage had all been taken into care and she had served a prison sentence, having been found guilty of ration book fraud. Yet it is doubtful that Louisa revealed these details at her interview with Mrs Ricketts, since the old lady seemed completely satisfied with the couple and, on 12 March, Alfred and Louisa moved into her bungalow.

It took just twelve days for Louisa to approach a firm of local solicitors and request them to visit Mrs Ricketts, so that she might make a new will. On 31 March, William Arnold Darbyshire called at the house with his clerk, where he found the new will already prepared and awaiting signatures.

Under the terms of Mrs Ricketts's new will, Louisa Merrifield was to be both the sole executrix and the sole beneficiary. In the course of the conversation between the solicitor, Mrs Ricketts and the Merrifields, Alfred raised some objections to being excluded and it was decided to amend the will so that he became a joint beneficiary with his wife.

According to Mr Darbyshire, neither Alfred nor Louisa Merrifield had the opportunity to read the revised will, which he took away with him for safekeeping. Darbyshire felt that Mrs Ricketts was acting on her own free will and that she was not being coerced or pressured in any way. 'I have made things right for you,' she told the Merrifields in his presence.

On 10 April, Louisa Merrifield went to visit a doctor, asking him to come and examine Mrs Ricketts and give his opinion on whether or not she was of sound mind when she had made the new will. Dr Burton Yule went to the bungalow later that day and spoke quite bluntly to Mrs Ricketts, telling her that Mrs Merrifield had told him that she had made a new will, in which her bungalow had been left to the Merrifields. Was that what she really wanted, asked the doctor?

'I am looking after them that look after me,' replied Mrs Ricketts, who was estranged from her two daughters. She assured Dr Yule that she was quite aware of what had happened and that this was what she had intended to do. She insisted that she felt perfectly well and Dr Yule believed that she was *compos mentis*, so didn't examine her further.

On 13 April, Mrs Merrifield visited a different doctor, Dr Woods, telling him that Mrs Ricketts seemed to be seriously ill, asking the doctor, 'What would happen if she died in the night?' Dr Woods went to see Mrs Ricketts that evening and, as far as he could see, there was no danger of that occurring since, apart from a touch of mild bronchitis, Mrs Ricketts was fit and well for her age. However, he left a bottle of medicine for the old lady.

On the following day, Mrs Merrifield left a message at his practice to say that Mrs Ricketts was worse. Dr Woods' partner, Dr Page, visited the bungalow at around midday when he found Mrs Ricketts to be in a critical condition and left a second bottle of medicine. Just under two hours later, Dr Yule visited the house and found the old lady dead.

Having seen Mrs Ricketts just four days earlier and formed the opinion then that she was perfectly healthy, Dr Yule found himself unable to explain her sudden and unexpected death. He discussed his concerns with the Merrifields and Louisa volunteered an opinion that Mrs Ricketts had suffered a stroke. The Merrifields appeared totally unconcerned when the doctor told them that he would have to report the matter and could not issue a death certificate.

Dr George Bernard Manning, a consultant pathologist attached to the North-West Science Laboratory, carried out a post-mortem examination on

An advertisement for
Rodine – rat poison.
(Author's collection)

the body of Mrs Ricketts. Manning found bran and yellow phosphorous in
Mrs Ricketts's stomach and, as a result, formed the opinion that she had been
poisoned with 'Rodine', a commercial rat poison. When the contents of her
stomach were analysed, Alan Thompson, a staff chemist at the Laboratory, found
0.042 grains of free phosphorous, with a further 0.099 grains in the intestines.
There was no evidence of any solid food in Mrs Ricketts' stomach, other than
some bran, such as that found in Rodine, a poison that could legally be bought
in most chemist's shops without the necessity to sign the Poisons Register.

Thus it was the pathologist's opinion that Mrs Ricketts had died as a result
of phosphorous poisoning, either from a single dose or from the accumulation
of several small doses ingested on 13 April. Manning believed that the average
fatal dose of phosphorous would be between one and two grains, but was also
aware that death had been known to occur after taking as little as one-eighth
of a grain. Manning felt that Mrs Ricketts had taken more than one grain of
phosphorous, although he was unable to measure or even estimate the exact
amount with any great accuracy. The police were informed of his findings and
began an immediate investigation into the old lady's death.

On 17 April, Detective Superintendent Colin Macdougall of Scotland Yard
called on Mrs Merrifield at the bungalow in Devonshire Road and told her that
there were strong suspicions that her employer had died as a result of something
that she had eaten or drunk. 'That's funny,' Louisa mused. 'There has been nothing
in the house since I have been here that would hurt her.' Louisa Merrifield told
the police that, when she and Alfred first moved in with Mrs Ricketts, there had
been no food in the house and the old lady appeared to be surviving almost
solely on a weekly delivery of alcohol, which mainly comprised bottles of stout
and rum. Louisa said that she had taken over the food shopping and that, as a
result, Mrs Ricketts's health had begun to improve. However, shortly before her
death, Mrs Ricketts had objected to not being allowed her alcohol and had
taken back control of the shopping, once again neglecting to buy any food.

Describing the days immediately before Mrs Ricketts's death, Louisa
Merrifield told the police that her employer had stopped eating and, by 9 April,

was beginning to show the effects of a lack of proper nourishment. She had asked Louisa to call a Dr Bruce, who practiced on Raikes Parade in Blackpool. However, Louisa had been unable to find that particular doctor and her employer had stubbornly refused the attentions of any other.

One the day of her death, Louisa said that she had heard the old lady get up at about 1 a.m. to go to the toilet and by 3.15 a.m., Mrs Ricketts was sitting on the hall floor, moaning and rubbing her stomach. Louisa told the police that she had put Mrs Ricketts back to bed then sat up all night with her, feeding her spoonfuls of brandy to quench the old lady's obvious thirst. At 8.30 a.m. on 14 April, she had walked across the road to Dr Woods' surgery and Dr Page had arrived at about midday, advising her to telephone Dr Yule.

The police had found no marks of violence on Mrs Ricketts's body nor had they found any trace of Rodine in the house or grounds, despite thoroughly digging the garden to see if anything had been buried there. However, in the course of their enquiries, they spoke to several people who told them that Louisa Merrifield had discussed her expected inheritance before Mrs Ricketts had actually died. Hence Louisa Merrifield was arrested and charged with the murder of Mrs Ricketts and, when the police also found witnesses who believed that Alfred Merrifield had purchased Rodine rat poison in the days prior to Mrs Ricketts's death, he too was arrested and charged some two weeks after his wife.

The Merrifields appeared before magistrates at Blackpool at the end of May 1953 and were committed to stand trial at the Manchester Assizes before Mr Justice Glyn-Jones. Sir Lionel Heald prosecuted the case, while Mr J. Di V. Nahum acted for both defendants, who pleaded 'Not Guilty' to the charge of murder by poisoning against them.

The prosecution pointed out that as soon as Mrs Ricketts changed her will in their favour, the Merrifields had an obvious interest in the old lady's death. They outlined the circumstances of Mrs Ricketts' death to the court, detailing the various visits that she had received from doctors in the last days of her life. Sir Lionel then called two witnesses, both of whom were prepared to testify that Louisa Merrifield had talked about Mrs Ricketts' demise and also her own inheritance of the bungalow before the old lady had actually passed away.

Mrs Veronica King of Lancashire Street in Blackpool told the court that she had met Louisa at the house of a friend on 12 April. Louisa had said that she had to go home to 'lay the old lady out.' When Mrs King asked if Mrs Ricketts had been ill, Louisa told her that she was not yet dead but would be before too long. On 25 March, Louisa had also told an acquaintance, David Brindley, that an old woman had died and left her a bungalow worth £3,000. She planned to sell the bungalow, she told him, and use the proceeds to buy a hotel for use as a nursing home. Brindley was absolutely sure of the date as he remembered that he had drawn his pension on that day, which was also two days before his landlady's birthday.

On the day before Mrs Ricketts's death, she had told her milkman that she was not getting sufficient food and that the Merrifields seemed to be taking all her money. George Forjan, the van driver who regularly delivered the old lady's order of rum and bottled Guinness, confirmed this account, stating that he had delivered the drinks on 13 April and unusually Mrs Ricketts, who always paid in cash, could not find the money to pay him. 'I don't know what they are doing with my money,' she told Mr Forjan. She had told Forjan that she had not eaten properly for three days and that she wanted to change her will, asking Alfred Merrifield in Forjan's presence to fetch her solicitor. Merrifield had simply said that the solicitor's office was too far for him to go to and told the driver that Mrs Ricketts was 'telling stories' about not being fed.

Immediately after her employer's death, Louisa had secreted papers relating to Mrs Ricketts's financial affairs in a handbag, which she had given to a friend, Mrs Alice Hands. According to a witness who was present at the time, Louisa had said that the bag contained mostly insurance policies and she was anxious that they should not fall into her husband's hands. The handbag had eventually found its way to Mr John Budd, the Merrifields' solicitor, who had handed it to the police. As well as documents, the handbag also contained a spoon on which were the remnants of something slightly sticky. Tests on the spoon revealed absolutely no trace of Rodine, yellow phosphorous or bran.

A local chemist, Harold Hague, gave evidence that a man resembling Alfred Merrifield had bought Rodine in his shop in mid-March. His shop assistant, Mavis Atkinson, corroborated his story and although both witnesses identified Merrifield in court, both had previously failed to pick him out at an identity parade. After Mrs Ricketts's death, the court was told that Louisa Merrifield had tried to make very hurried arrangements to have the body cremated as soon as possible.

Naturally, much of the trial, which lasted for eleven days in total, was taken up by evidence from the medical witnesses. These included Dr Manning, who had carried out the post-mortem examination and Alan Thompson, who had performed the chemical analysis on Mrs Ricketts's remains. Mr Nahum, the counsel for the defence, elicited from Manning that this was the first case of phosphorous poisoning that he had ever seen.

Manning pointed out that Rodine had an unpleasant taste – he had even tasted some himself to make sure – and that he didn't think that anyone could take it by mistake. However, the taste could be disguised by mixing the rat poison with foods like blackcurrant jam or alcohol.

Both Louisa and Alfred Merrifield testified in their own defence, with Louisa again relating the story of sitting up all night with her employer before her death. Now she added the detail that Mrs Ricketts had complained of having a nasty taste in her mouth and had rinsed her mouth out with glycerine. Both Merrifields continued to insist that they had never given the old lady anything that might have harmed her and that they certainly didn't know anything about phosphorous poisoning.

However, the defence counsel went on to shock the court by calling another witness, Professor J.M. Webster, the director of the Home Office Forensic Laboratory in Birmingham. It was Webster's opinion that, rather than being poisoned, Mrs Ricketts had died a natural death from necrosis of the liver, coincidentally just after the phosphorous had been administered. There was no evidence that the phosphorous found in her stomach and intestine had been absorbed into her body, none of the poison had been found in any of her other organs and she had shown none of the symptoms of shock that he would normally have associated with the ingestion of poison. Additionally, he had rarely seen a case of poisoning in which the minimum fatal dose had been administered – normally a much larger dose was given.

Thus it was the contention of the defence that the prosecution had not satisfactorily proven that Mrs Ricketts had even been murdered, let alone that the two defendants were guilty. Even if Mrs Ricketts had died from ingesting Rodine, it could just have easily been by suicide or accident.

With regard to Mrs Ricketts's will, Mr Nahum told the jury that Mr Merrifield had believed that Mrs Ricketts was amending it in his favour, thus he had no motive for murdering his employer. Nahum also dismissed as ridiculous the idea that Louisa had murdered Mrs Ricketts because she had caught her employer and her husband engaged in sexual practices together. He reminded the jury that the police had found absolutely no trace of Rodine on the premises at Devonshire Road.

When the judge had summed up the case, the jury retired for almost six hours, returning to find Louisa Merrifield 'Guilty' of the murder of Mrs Ricketts. They were unable to agree on a verdict for Alfred, who was eventually released. Although Mrs Ricketts's two daughters immediately contested her will, it was announced in June 1956 that he was to benefit from a one-sixth share of his employer's estate.

Meanwhile, Louisa's defence team immediately filed an appeal against her death sentence, which was heard before Mr Justice Cassels, Mr Justice Barry and Mr Justice Slade. One of the grounds for the appeal was that the defence believed that the judge had already decided on Louisa Merrifield's guilt before his summary of the case and that this decision had prejudiced the jury. However, the appeal was dismissed and Albert Pierrepoint hanged forty-six-year-old Louisa May Merrifield at Strangeways Prison on 18 September 1953. Yet, if Professor Webster was correct in judging the cause of death to be necrosis of the liver, then all Louisa should have been tried for is attempted murder.

30

'Nothing to say'

GOSPORT, HAMPSHIRE, 1955

An urgent call to attend a sick child is one that most doctors take extremely seriously and Dr Bernard Johnson of Portsmouth was no exception. Even though Dr Johnson's partner, Dr Ian Buchanan, had already seen the child in question that morning and found nothing much wrong with him, when Dr Johnson received a call from John Armstrong to say that his five-and-a-half-month-old baby, Terence, needed a doctor, Johnson interrupted his lunch to respond to the call.

Dr Johnson arrived at the Armstrongs' home in Perth Road, Gosport at 1.30 p.m. on 22 July 1955, just ten minutes after he had received the telephone call to attend. Sadly, when he arrived, baby Terence had just died. His mother, Janet, aged nineteen, told the doctor that, before his death, the baby had been a poor colour, very sleepy and difficult to rouse. Dr Johnson informed her that, as the child had died so suddenly, he would be unable to issue a death certificate. To his surprise, Janet immediately asked him, 'Will there have to be an inquest?'

Dr Johnson reported the infant's death to the coroner, who requested that Dr Harold Miller, a pathologist from the Portsmouth Hospital, carry out a post-mortem examination on the baby, which was done later that day. Dr Miller could find no reason to explain the baby's sudden death, although, in the course of his examination, he recovered what looked like berry skins from the child's throat and stomach.

Meanwhile, the police had visited Mr and Mrs Armstrong at home and had been astounded to find them sitting in the living room watching television. Neither parent appeared unduly upset at the death of their child and remained detached and unemotional as Sergeant Bulley questioned them about the events leading up to the child's demise.

According to twenty-four-year-old John Armstrong, baby Terence had been unwell the previous evening. He had appeared to choke after his feed,

Gosport in the 1950s. (Author's collection)

after which he had been exceptionally drowsy and was wheezing. Armstrong, who worked as a sick-berth attendant at the Royal Naval Hospital at Haslar, had been sufficiently concerned about his child that, at 11 p.m., he had given him artificial respiration until he was happy that the child was breathing more normally. He had also pushed his fingers into Terence's throat in an effort to clear any obstruction and make him vomit, but this had been non-productive. Dr Buchanan had been called, but the Armstrongs had failed to communicate any sense of urgency in the telephone conversation and seemed to the doctor to be calling more for reassurance than anything else.

Hence Dr Buchanan had not attended the baby until 8.40 a.m. on 22 July, when he had been unable to find much wrong with him. He was later to say that Terence was an apparently normal, well-nourished and healthy baby who was crying lustily and did not appear to be ill. After the doctor's visit, Terence had slept for most of the morning until his father returned home from work for his lunch at about 12.15 p.m. At that time, John Armstrong had noticed that Terence's breathing was very shallow. He touched his son's hand and the child turned blue in the face. Armstrong again gave artificial respiration until his son's colour returned to normal, but since the baby was still unnaturally sleepy, he decided to seek medical help. He then cycled the four miles back to work, before ringing Dr Buchanan again. Buchanan was, by that time, off duty and enjoying a game of golf, so his partner took the call.

Sergeant Bulley found it incomprehensible that John Armstrong, who would have acquired some medical knowledge from working at a hospital, would

Haslar Hospital, 1907. (Author's collection)

not have called for medical help for his son sooner. Nevertheless, he collected some items from Janet Armstrong, including a vomit-stained pillow and the baby's last feeding bottle, which was still unwashed, and took them to Dr Miller. There he learned that the doctor suspected that Terence might have ingested poisonous berries, so he went straight back to the Armstrongs' home and searched the garden. He found a *daphne mezereum* bush, covered in clusters of bright red berries. It was obviously unlikely that baby Terence had fed himself the berries, but he had an older sister, three-year-old Pamela who, according to her parents, had also vomited shortly after her tea on 21 July. Could Pamela have eaten the poisonous berries and also given them to her baby brother? Mrs Armstrong thought that she could – she had apparently spoken to Pamela, who had admitted to feeding her brother some 'sweeties'.

Sergeant Bulley reported his findings back to Dr Miller, who sent the contents of Terence's stomach to the county analyst, with a note saying that he suspected that the child had been poisoned by *daphne* berries. By now, the skins had completely dissolved, although the milky fluid extracted from the child's stomach was pink in colour.

The results of the analysis of the gastric fluid showed no trace of *daphne* or indeed any other berries. However the analyst did find uncooked maize starch and also traces of a synthetic dye, eosin. No trace of any harmful bacteria was found.

With no ready explanation for Terence's death, his burial was authorised by the coroner and he was interred at Ann's Hill Cemetery in Gosport. Yet the Hampshire police were still far from satisfied that they had uncovered all there was to know about the child's death. Thus, Detective Inspector Gordon Gates decided to talk to Dr Miller, who pointed out to him that both maize and eosin were constituents of capsules of the drug Seconal, a barbiturate used for treating severe insomnia.

Gates immediately sought authority to have Terence's stomach contents reanalysed for the presence of the drug and the gastric fluid was sent to the laboratory at Scotland Yard. There, analyst Dr Lewis Nickolls extracted the equivalent of a third of a grain of Seconal, with a further fiftieth of a grain being isolated from the vomit stain on the baby's pillow. It was his opinion that the fatal dose of Seconal for a child of Terence's age and size would be about three grains.

Inspector Gates returned to question Mr and Mrs Armstrong, who strenuously denied ever having had any Seconal in the house. The house was searched, as was John Armstrong's locker at work, but no drugs were found. However, while conducting his enquiries at the Naval Hospital, Gates learned that, in February 1955, around fifty pink one-and-a-half-grain Seconal capsules had been stolen from the poisons cupboard there.

An exhumation order was issued for the body of Terence Armstrong and Home Office pathologist Professor Keith Simpson was called upon to conduct another post-mortem examination. This time, a further twentieth of a grain of Seconal was recovered from the child's remains and that, in conjunction with the amount of Seconal already recovered, led Professor Simpson to the conclusion that baby Terence had ingested between three and five capsules, which would have killed him within the hour.

Simpson put forward a theory that the baby had been given a small dose of the capsules on the evening before his death. As well as causing sleepiness, Seconal also has a side effect of causing rapid, shallow breathing, symptoms reported by the Armstrongs to the doctors who examined the baby on the day of his death. By 8.40 a.m., when Terence was examined by Dr Buchanan, the effects of the evening dose would have largely worn off and a second dose would have been necessary to kill the infant. If Simpson's theory was correct, then Janet Armstrong was alone with the baby when he received the initial dose.

It emerged that another of the Armstrongs' children – nine-week-old Philip – had also died suddenly on 10 March 1954. The cause of his death had been certified as broncho-pneumonia, although the eighty-two-year-old doctor who had issued the death certificate admitted to having some doubts about his diagnosis, being more concerned about a severe rash on the baby's buttocks. It was decided to exhume baby Philip's body from his grave at Highland Road Cemetery, Southsea, but unfortunately the remains were found to be too decomposed for any analysis to be successful. John Armstrong accompanied the police to the cemetery for the exhumation and apparently asked Inspector Gates, 'How long does a body take to decompose?'

The police asked John Armstrong to attend the police station for an interview about the death of baby Terence, but Armstrong refused to do so unless he was first charged and arrested. An inquest into the baby's death was opened before Coroner Mr F.A. Maxwell-Wells, at which neither John Armstrong nor his wife were prepared to answer any of the questions posed by the coroner, responding to every one with the words 'Nothing to say'. The jury eventually returned a verdict of death from the effects of Seconal poisoning, although they felt unable to determine how and by whom the drug was administered.

The Director of Public Prosecutions did not feel that there was sufficient evidence against Janet or John to convince a jury that either was guilty of murdering their son, so reluctantly the police had to let the matter drop. John and Janet Armstrong remained free, with John Armstrong even giving his account of his son's death to a Sunday newspaper.

However, the case was not to end there. The Armstrongs' marriage broke up and, in July 1955, Janet applied to magistrates at Gosport for a separation order and maintenance. She told the court that her husband had ill-treated her and that he persistently told her that if she had looked after baby Terence properly, he would not have died. Her application for maintenance was turned down and, as she left the magistrates' court, Inspector Gates was waiting for her. 'Is there anything you would like to tell the police, Mrs Armstrong?' he asked and Janet said, yes, there was. She then made and signed a statement saying that, at the time of Terence's death, there had been Seconal capsules in the house and that John had asked her to get rid of them in case he had been blamed either for Terence's death or for stealing them from his place of work. Janet Armstrong said that she had thrown some of the capsules onto the compost heap at the bottom of the garden and some down the drain.

Since it was believed that Janet had been alone with baby Terence when the capsules were first given to him, but that John would also have had the opportunity to administer the fatal dose while his wife was busy preparing his lunch, both were subsequently charged with the murder of Terence John Armstrong. After appearing before magistrates at Gosport, both were committed for trial at the next Winchester Assizes.

The trial opened on 3 December 1956, before Mr Justice Pilcher, with both Janet and John Armstrong pleading 'Not Guilty' to the murder of their son.

Armstrong denied ever having stolen any tablets from his workplace, but did admit to finding five or six Seconal capsules, three or four Amytal and three Nembutal tablets in a bedside locker and taking them home, planning to keep them in reserve in case he had difficulty sleeping after working a nightshift.

It emerged at the trial that the medical evidence given by Professor Simpson and Mr Nickolls at the earlier proceedings had, through no fault of their own, been flawed. Both of the medical witnesses had assumed that the Seconal given to baby Terence had been normal, gelatine-encased capsules. However, shortly before the trial, they had found out that the capsules missing from the Naval Hospital had been a new type made from methylcellulose, which didn't dissolve as quickly as gelatine. Professor Simpson had carried out some experiments with the new capsules and determined that the time they took to dissolve would just about allow for John Armstrong to have administered the fatal dose, although Simpson conceded that it would have been 'a near thing'.

Janet Armstrong was questioned by the prosecution and admitted to having suspicions that her husband had given Terence the capsules. Since she denied having given him any drugs herself, then there was only one other possible suspect – John. According to Janet, her husband had not been pleased to hear that she had been expecting baby Terence as he maintained that the couple could not afford another child. John not only had access to the Seconal capsules but also had the chance to give them to the baby while she was busy preparing lunch. And it had been John who had asked her to dispose of the tablets after the baby's death. Meanwhile, John continued to deny having poisoned his baby, placing the blame for his death squarely on Janet's shoulders.

In his summing up of the case for the jury, Mr Justice Pilcher reminded them that they did not have to find both Armstrongs guilty or not guilty but could record either verdict on just one of them. The jury deliberated for forty-three minutes, returning with a verdict of 'Not Guilty' for Janet Armstrong and 'Guilty' for John. Janet was promptly discharged, while John was given the death sentence, in spite of his assurance of 'I am innocent, my Lord' when the judge asked if he had anything to say before sentence was pronounced.

Armstrong's solicitors immediately appealed the conviction but the appeal was dismissed, although his sentence was later commuted to one of life imprisonment.

Sensationally, Janet Armstrong was later to admit that she had given the baby a capsule of Seconal to help him sleep but, since she had already been tried and acquitted, she was unable to be tried again. In 1958, in response to a campaign by Mr D. Johnson MP to have Armstrong's conviction quashed in the light of his wife's statement, Home Secretary Mr Butler wrote to Johnson with his conclusions. He claimed to have studied the new evidence and found that it in no way exonerated John Armstrong, since it did not amount to a confession from Janet that she alone had murdered her son. Butler stated that he had found no grounds to suggest that John Armstrong had been wrongly convicted and therefore his life sentence would stand.

31
'Has the old bugger got any money?'

John Knowles of Felling, County Durham, had been married to his wife Mary for forty-six years when he died from tuberculosis in 1955 aged sixty-six. The couple first met when Mary was in service to the Knowles family and their marriage produced six children.

After her husband's death, Mary took a job as a housekeeper for Mr John Russell, a painter from Jarrow. Unfortunately, the job lasted only until January 1956, when Mr Russell fell ill with bronchial trouble, eventually dying a week later from pneumonia. Russell had formerly lodged with John and Mary Knowles and, it was rumoured, had been her lover while staying in her marital home. Before his death, he had made a will naming Mary Knowles as his sole beneficiary and he conveniently died just after receiving his post-war credits. (Because of the cost of the Second World War, the rate of Income Tax for individuals was raised and people were permitted to claim back the tax paid at a higher rate after the war ended.) Thus, Mary inherited the princely sum of £70 on Mr Russell's death.

In September of 1956, Mary was introduced to Mr Oliver Leonard, a retired estate agent from Hebburn. At that time, Leonard was lodging with a Mrs Alice Connolly, who was shocked when Mary asked her about Leonard, saying, 'Has the old bugger got any money?'

'A little, as far as I know,' replied his landlady and, within days, seventy-five-year-old Mr Leonard had moved out of his lodgings and in with Mary Knowles. Soon afterwards, Mary went to see Mrs Connolly with a desperate request. 'Get that old man out of my house. He won't sign any money over to me until I marry him.' Mrs Connolly agreed to take her former lodger back but, by the following day, Mary had changed her mind and decided that she would marry Mr Leonard after all. They married at Jarrow Register Office on 20 September 1956 and almost immediately the new Mrs Leonard contacted an insurance agent to ask about insuring her husband's life. She was told that he was too old.

On 1 October, Mr Leonard visited his doctor, Dr John Laydon, complaining of being a little breathless. The doctor examined him and found him to be in good health for his age although suffering from slight bronchitis and the possible early signs of degeneration of the heart muscle. Dr Laydon prescribed some cough mixture.

Two days later, Mrs Leonard called for help from her neighbours in the early hours of the morning because her husband had fallen out of bed. After helping her to get him back into bed, one of the neighbours suggested that Mr Leonard might benefit from a glass of brandy. Mary said that she had none in the house and made a cup of tea instead. When the neighbour gave Leonard the tea, he took one mouthful and spat it out, knocking the cup out of the neighbour's hand. The neighbour believed that the old man was delirious at the time and advised Mrs Leonard to contact a doctor, which she said that she would do as soon as the surgery opened.

Oliver James Leonard died on 3 October 1956. A doctor was only called to the house after his death and, not having treated Leonard before, he contacted Dr Laydon, who eventually issued a death certificate based on his examination of the dead man just two days earlier, on which the cause of death was recorded as 'myocardial degeneration and chronic nephritis' (kidney disease). Leonard's widow wasted no time in winding up his financial affairs, eventually obtaining around £50 from his will, once all his bills had been settled.

She wasted no time in remarrying either, as on 28 October 1957 she made another trip to Jarrow Register Office, this time on the arm of seventy-six-

The Infirmary at Hebburn Park, c. 1911. (Author's collection)

year-old Ernest George Lawrence Wilson, a retired engineer from Felling. The couple threw a small reception to celebrate their union, at which Mr Wilson played the piano while his wife joked about saving some of the wedding cake for the funeral.

On 11 November, Mrs Wilson called the doctor to see her new husband, who was ill in bed. Dr Wallace found symptoms of heart disease in the previously healthy old gentleman and prescribed some tablets and cough medicine for him, arranging to call back and see him again in a few days. On the very next morning, he received an urgent telephone call to say that Mr Wilson's condition had worsened. He went straight round to the Wilsons' home but by the time he got there, Ernest Wilson was dead. Dr Wallace certified the cause of death as 'cardio-muscular failure' and, as before, the widow Wilson wasted no time in burying her husband in Jarrow Cemetery and settling his affairs, claiming the proceeds of two insurance policies totalling around £25. She also tried to withdraw money from her husband's bank account but was not allowed to do so.

Unfortunately for Mary Wilson, the authorities became suspicious about the sudden death of not one, but two of her husbands less than a fortnight after she married them and it was decided to hold post-mortem examinations on Ernest Wilson and Oliver Leonard, whose bodies were exhumed on 30 November 1957. On examination of the stomach contents of both men, Dr William Stewart found wheat bran and elemental phosphorous and, knowing that, along with syrup, these were the ingredients of rat, cockroach and beetle poison, concluded that each man had taken some before his death. Whatever had been noted on their death certificates, the actual cause of death was phosphorous poisoning.

The bodies of John Knowles and John Russell were also exhumed and the same ingredients were found in their stomachs too. Dr Ian Barclay of the Forensic Science Laboratory at Gosforth eventually managed to isolate one-thirtieth of a grain of elemental phosphorous from Wilson's stomach and a further one-hundredth of a grain from his intestines. Analysis of Leonard's remains produced one-eightieth of a grain from his stomach and one-twentieth of a grain from the intestines. According to Barclay, a fatal dose would be between one and two grains and both Wilson and Leonard had ingested sufficient elemental phosphorous to kill them.

Mary Wilson was arrested and charged with the murders of Ernest Wilson and Oliver Leonard. She denied the charges and, even when the results of the post-mortems were explained to her, could only say, 'It must have been something they ate when they went out.' In spite of her denials, magistrates at Jarrow committed her for trial at the next Assizes in Leeds.

Her trial opened before Mr Justice Hinchcliffe in March 1958, with Mary Wilson pleading 'Not Guilty' to both of the charges against her. Mr R. Withers

Payne and Mr Geoffrey Veale QC prosecuted and Miss Rose Heilbron, who, in 1949, was one of the first two women ever to be appointed KC, defended Mrs Wilson. Miss Heilbron asked for the murders of Oliver Leonard and Ernest Wilson to be tried separately but Mr Justice Hinchcliffe refused, saying that he didn't think that separate trials were desirable in the interests of justice.

The prosecution maintained that Mrs Wilson was nothing more than a 'wicked woman', who married two men in quick succession and then deliberately poisoned them for her own financial gain. The testimony of the medical witnesses showed that the stomachs of these two men contained a mixture of wheat bran and elemental phosphorous, from which the only conclusion that could be drawn was that both had ingested rat, beetle or cockroach poison, which was freely available from any chemist's shop.

No tins or packets of poison had been found at 'Windy Nook', the bungalow Mrs Wilson shared with her last husband, which, according to the prosecution, eliminated both accidental ingestion of the poison and suicide since, had the men's deaths been by accident or suicide, the poison containers would remain in the house. Only a murderer – or murderess – could have disposed of the external evidence of poisoning and it was surely beyond all possibility of coincidence that two of the defendant's husbands would both accidentally or purposely take the same kind of poison so soon after they were married.

The prosecution went on to discuss the haste with which Mary Wilson had set about claiming insurance payouts after the deaths of her husbands, calling Mrs Grace Liddle who testified that Mrs Wilson had tried to sell her Ernest's gold watch only hours after his death.

Miss Heilbron, for the defence, first challenged the conclusions of the medical witnesses, particularly with regard to the post-mortem examination carried out on Mr Leonard, who had been buried for thirteen months when he was exhumed. Making the point that none of the medical witnesses had much experience in examining victims of phosphorous poisoning, she asked whether they found it at all unusual that phosphorous should be recovered from a body after so long. Dr Barclay told the court that, according to literature on the subject, in a similar case, phosphorous had been discovered after six months. Miss Heilbron pointed out that there was a lot of difference between six and thirteen months, to which Barclay responded that there must always be a first time and that this was the first time at which phosphorous had been discovered in a body after so long a period of burial.

The counsel for the defence then tried to suggest that, in view of their advanced age at the time of their marriages, both Mr Leonard and Mr Wilson had taken pills as a sexual stimulant. Was Dr Barclay aware that phosphorous pills could be bought at chemist's shops? She mentioned a particular brand, Dalmania pills, which were used by men to revive flagging sexual appetites and facilitate erections, asking if Barclay was aware that they contained yellow phosphorous.

Barclay was forced to admit that he had not heard of them and seemed surprised to hear that Miss Heilbron had engaged the services of a private investigator, William Dixon, to visit pharmacies and purchase the pills, which she produced in court.

Dr A.S. Curry, the senior scientific officer from the Home Office Forensic Science Laboratory at Harrogate admitted that he had heard of phosphorous being used in pills by the French at the turn of the century but that, even if pills were called phosphorous pills, they were more likely to contain phosphates rather than the elemental phosphorous believed to have poisoned the victims in this case. Miss Heilbron gave him one of her Dalmania tablets, which he crushed on a piece of paper with the edge of a coin. After sniffing the crushed tablet, he conceded that it did appear to contain phosphorous but went on to say that it was only in a minute quantity and that, in order to die from phosphorous poisoning as a result of taking them, the deceased would need to swallow a very large number of pills.

Miss Heilbron also challenged the death certificate written by Dr Laydon for Mr Leonard, saying that parts of the counterfoil seemed to have been written in different ink at different times. After examining the document in question with a magnifying glass, Dr Laydon disagreed.

Having announced that Mrs Wilson would not be testifying in her own defence, Miss Heilbron then faced a problem. She had intended to call Home Office pathologist Dr Francis Camps as a witness but Camps was unexpectedly otherwise engaged at a trial in Sussex. Mr Justice Hinchcliffe grudgingly adjourned the trial for a day to allow Camps to finish giving evidence at the other trial.

When Camps appeared the following day, he challenged the evidence of the medical witnesses saying that '…the findings were contradictory pathologically' and that, without examining the remains microscopically, he personally would not have been prepared to exclude natural death and would have deemed the cause of death for both of the alleged victims as 'unascertainable'. Miss Heilbron had already drawn an admission from pathologist Dr Stewart that he had not found it necessary to use a microscope at the post-mortems, since he believed that he could see the evidence clearly enough with his naked eye.

After closing speeches by the prosecution and defence, Mr Justice Hinchcliffe summed up the case for the jury. He pointed out that Mrs Wilson had initially promised the police that she would help them all she could with their enquiries. By choosing not to give evidence, which left the jury without explanations for many important matters in the case, had she helped all she could? The prosecution, said Hinchcliffe, maintained that both husbands died from the very same unusual cause and that only the prisoner stood to gain from their deaths. No doctor was called to attend Mr Leonard in his final illnesses and furthermore, if one or both men had taken poison either deliberately or accidentally, would the tin not have been found?

It was the contention of the defence that both men, who were after all in their mid-seventies, had taken phosphorous as a sexual stimulant after their marriage, even though no evidence that they had taken or even possessed such pills had ever been found. However, the jury must consider this suggestion, as they must also consider the testimony of Dr Camps, and they should not find the defendant guilty unless they were absolutely sure that such a verdict would be the right one.

The jury of nine men and three women retired for one hour and twenty minutes before returning to pronounce Mary Elizabeth Wilson 'Guilty' of both murders.

Thus Mrs Wilson became the first woman to be sentenced to death after the Homicide Act of 1957, which restricted capital punishment for murder to only five specific types of murder – in this case the criteria being two murders committed on different occasions. She stood impassively in the dock as the judge passed sentence on her, setting a provisional date of 16 April for her execution.

Her defence counsel immediately filed an appeal on the grounds that the two murders should have been tried separately. This was heard at the Court of Criminal Appeal on 19 May 1958 and was dismissed after the presiding judges backed Mr Justice Hinchcliffe's decision to try both murders at once and stated that he had summed up the case concisely and fairly and decided it admirably. Mrs Wilson's execution date was set for 4 June 1958.

However, just five days before her scheduled execution, Home Secretary Mr R.A. Butler recommended a reprieve on the grounds of her age and the sentence was commuted to one of life imprisonment.

The 'Widow of Windy Nook' as Mary Elizabeth Wilson was dubbed in the press, died in Holloway Prison on 5 December 1962, aged seventy-one.

Holloway Prison at the turn of the century. (Author's collection)

32

'What I feel is the emptiness of my soul'

After a difficult pregnancy and labour, Mrs Margaret Young finally gave birth to a son – Graham Frederick – on 7 September 1947. Soon after the baby's birth, Mrs Young was diagnosed with tuberculosis and, by the time Graham was three months old, she was dead.

Graham's father, Fred, was distraught at the tragic loss of his young wife. Fortunately, he was surrounded by his family, who immediately swung into action to help him. His sister, Winifred Jouvenat, and her husband, Jack, took in baby Graham, while Fred and Margaret's daughter, eight-year-old Winnie, went to her grandmother's home. Fred stayed alone in the family home, making an effort to visit both of his children every evening after work and at weekends. However, Fred was understandably lonely and, in April 1950, he married for the second time.

By now, Fred had sold the home where he had shared so many happy times with Margaret and had moved in with Winnie and her grandmother. Wanting a proper home for his new wife, he purchased the Jouvenats' house in St Albans from them and set about rebuilding his family.

Graham was still under three years old at the time of his father's remarriage and apparently adapted quite well to the presence of a father and older sister he had never lived with, as well as a new stepmother, Molly. A quiet, obviously intelligent little boy, he taught himself to read at an early age and spent a lot of time at the local library with his sister. He was expected to do well at school but hated it, finding his lessons tedious. In his school reports he was often described by his teachers as lazy – if a subject interested him, he was happy to apply his mind to it but he rebelled against subjects like maths, which he found boring.

As he progressed through school, Graham told his classmates time and time again that he hated his stepmother, saying that she was too strict, that she refused to buy him clothes or give him pocket money and that on occasions she locked him out of the house. (Disturbingly, Molly was later to find a wax model of herself in the pocket of Graham's school blazer, stuck through with numerous pins.) Graham daydreamed endlessly about his real mother, constantly wondering how his life would have turned out had she not died.

By the age of nine, Graham was showing a passionate interest in chemistry and was reading widely on a variety of adult subjects from black magic to Nazism. His stepmother found bottles of ether and acid in his pockets and, when she questioned Graham about them, he admitted to rifling through the dustbins of a local chemist's shop. Molly went straight to see the chemist to remonstrate with him about his casual disposal of dangerous chemicals and also visited the library to discuss her stepson's bizarre taste in books. Little did the family know that Graham's most abiding interest was in toxicology and that he had already conducted experiments on mice and cats. Somewhat surprisingly, given what the family obviously viewed as an unhealthy interest, Graham's reward for passing the eleven plus examination was a chemistry set!

Graham's move to secondary school brought him the long-awaited chance to practice chemistry in a properly equipped laboratory. While other boys in his class planned their careers, Graham had only one ambition in life, which was to become a famous poisoner. He openly spoke of his future plans to his classmates, a practice that earned him the nickname of 'The Mad Professor'. As other teenagers idolised pop singers and film stars, Graham came to admire some of the more infamous British poisoners, telling his school friends that, one day, he would be just as well known.

At the age of thirteen, Graham managed to con a local chemist into selling him antimony. Although the minimum age for buying poison was seventeen, Graham somehow managed to convince Geoffrey Reis that he was old enough and, when questioned by the chemist, Graham was able to describe in detail the experiments he intended to carry out with the poison.

It was at about that time that Graham had a childish argument with his best friend, Christopher Williams. From that moment on, Christopher began to suffer a series of mysterious illnesses, which were eventually diagnosed as migraines. When Christopher's illness failed to respond to any conventional treatment, his parents were advised to take him to a psychiatrist. Nobody realised that Chris only ever became ill after spending time with Graham Young and sharing food or drink that Young had prepared.

The Young household was thrown into turmoil yet again when Graham's stepmother found a clearly labelled bottle of antimony in his bedroom. Molly went to see chemist Geoffrey Reis, whose name was on the label, and alerted him to Graham's real age and Graham's father banned him from conducting any experiments in the house. Graham promptly went to another chemist, Edgar Davies and, as he had done to Geoffrey Reis, he conned Davies into selling him poisons.

Two views of St Albans in the 1950s. (Author's collection)

Meanwhile, Graham's own family were suffering frequent similar bouts of unexplained illness to those of his school friend and they began to question whether Graham could possibly be carelessly using the household crockery to conduct his chemistry experiments. Nobody even entertained the idea that Graham could be deliberately poisoning them, particularly his father, who could not believe that his son would defy him by carrying out any experiments at all after he had been expressly forbidden to do so. The most frequent sufferer was Molly Young, although on one occasion Graham's sister, Winnie, was taken ill after drinking a cup of tea, prepared for her by her stepmother. Winnie managed to reach her office but was so ill that her workmates rushed her to the Middlesex Hospital where, after a day of tests, she was told that she seemed to have been poisoned with belladonna.

Angry and frightened, Winnie openly accused Graham of carelessness when she got home and a family row ensued, ending with Graham storming off to his bedroom in tears. He was so distressed that Winnie eventually apologised to him, little knowing that at the time he had sufficient poison concealed in his bedroom to kill 300 people.

By 1962, Molly Young was literally fading away. She suffered from constant crippling stomach pains and had lost a huge amount of weight but in spite of undergoing numerous tests in hospital, nobody could even begin to hazard a guess at the cause of her illness. On 21 April 1962, which was Easter Sunday, Fred went to the pub at lunchtime and returned home to find his wife writhing in agony on the back lawn. To Fred's horror, Graham was watching his stepmother intently through the kitchen window and had made no attempt to help her or to call for medical assistance.

Molly was taken to Willesden Hospital, where doctors wanted to admit her for observation. Molly was far from keen on the idea but Graham was sent home on the bus to fetch her nightclothes. By late afternoon, Molly was telling the doctors that she wanted to go home and cook Fred's dinner – just minutes later, she was dead.

A post-mortem examination was carried out by Dr Donald Teare but, during the summer of 1961, Molly had been involved in a serious road accident when a bus that she was travelling in crashed. Teare therefore certified the cause of Molly's death as a prolapsed bone at the top of her spinal column. Graham immediately began to pester his father to have Molly cremated rather than buried and was so persistent that Fred finally agreed just to get some peace and quiet.

Just days later, Fred was stricken with a severe bout of sickness and diarrhoea, coupled with severe stomach pains. He was eventually persuaded to see his doctor who could find no obvious cause for his symptoms and suggested admitting him to hospital for observation. Fred wasn't happy to leave his recently bereaved children and put up a spirited argument against hospitalisation, which

A poison bottle from the turn of the century. (© Martin Latham)

ended abruptly when he collapsed in the doctor's surgery. An ambulance was called and Fred found himself in the same hospital where his wife had so recently died.

Graham and Winnie came to visit him but Fred found himself feeling strangely uneasy as Graham sat silently by his bedside, saying little to his father but apparently anxious to discuss his father's condition with the doctors and nurses. Eventually, when a family friend brought Graham in to visit his father one evening, Fred was sufficiently disturbed by his son's demeanour to hiss at his friend, 'Get that boy away from me.'

Fred was eventually released from hospital but was quickly readmitted when his symptoms returned two days after he arrived home. When his family went to visit him, the doctors told them that Fred was suffering from either arsenic or antimony poisoning. As Fred's sister and daughter looked on in shock, fourteen-year-old Graham began to lecture the doctor on how to distinguish between the effects of the two poisons. Antimony poisoning was confirmed the following day and Fred was told that he would recover but that his liver would be permanently damaged.

Graham's aunt Winifred actually asked Graham if he had poisoned his father, a question that seemed to hurt him. He flatly denied having anything to do with his father's illness but, at school, he was telling a different story. One of his classmates, Clive Creager, was so convinced that Graham had poisoned both Molly and Fred that he went to his parents. Unfortunately, the Creagers found the idea so incredible that they didn't contact the police.

Eventually, Graham's science teacher, Mr Hughes, grew suspicious and searched the boy's school desk, finding several bottles of poison and also a notebook that contained dozens of macabre drawings of gravestones and dying men, along with poems and essays about poisons and poisoners. Hughes took his findings to the school's headmaster and the two men decided to consult the Young's family doctor, Dr Wills. Even then, the police weren't contacted but instead it was arranged for a psychiatrist to talk to Young in the guise of a careers advisor. So enthusiastic was Graham Young about poisons and toxicology in this interview that the psychiatrist went straight to the police.

On 21 May 1962, Detective Inspector Edward Crabbe called at Young's home while he was at school and made a thorough search of his bedroom. As well as an impressive collection of true crime books on poisoners, Crabbe found bottles of antimony, thallium, atropine, digitalis and several other dangerous chemicals. When Young returned from school, two small phials of what was later proved to be thallium were found in his shirt pocket and he was taken to Harlesden police station for further questioning.

Initially, Young denied all knowledge of administering any poison to anyone, appearing hurt that he might be considered capable of such acts. However, the next day, he reconsidered and confessed to poisoning his sister with belladonna and went on to make a statement in which he also admitted to putting various poisons in the milk, water and food at home. He claimed to be addicted to poisoning people, knowing all the while that what he was doing was wrong but being unable to stop himself. He appeared before magistrates later that day, charged with poisoning Fred and Winifred Young and Chris Williams. Since Molly Young's post-mortem examination had concluded that she died from natural causes and her body had subsequently been cremated, the police could not charge Graham with her murder due to lack of evidence, even though the boy was later to admit that he had been systematically poisoning her for a year before her death. He had added regular small doses of antimony to her food until she had built up a tolerance for the poison. Graham neglected to add to his statement that he had then given her the single fatal dose of thallium that finally killed her.

Graham Young was committed for trial and, on 6 July 1962, aged just fourteen years and nine months, he appeared at the Old Bailey before Mr Justice Melford Stevenson. Much of the evidence came from medical witnesses who had been asked to examine the boy and assess his mental condition and the future risk of him poisoning again. Graham had a self-confessed 'obsession' with poisons and, since he had shown no remorse whatsoever for the suffering that he had caused his victims, the judge determined that the most appropriate outcome for him would be treatment in a maximum-security hospital. Thus Graham Young was committed to Broadmoor under the 1959 Mental Health Act, with the court adding a rider that stated that he must remain there for at least fifteen years. He became the youngest person to be admitted to the secure hospital since 1885.

Even the strict confines of a secure hospital setting could not deter Graham Young from trying to achieve his lifelong ambition of infamy. Soon after his admission, another patient, John Berridge, died from cyanide poisoning. Graham claimed to have poisoned him by extracting cyanide from laurel bushes in the hospital grounds, but his confession was not taken seriously and Berridge's death was ultimately recorded as suicide. Trusted to make tea and coffee for the nurses as part of his rehabilitation, Young experimented by adding an extremely caustic brand of toilet cleaner to the beverages. Luckily the coffee tasted so foul that the nurses were alerted to the fact that it had been tampered with.

After three years in Broadmoor, Graham Young made a legal application to be transferred to an ordinary mental hospital. His father and Aunt Winifred travelled to Broadmoor for the hearing, where they told the panel that, in their opinion, Graham should never be released from hospital and that, if he were, no members of the family were prepared to offer him a home. Graham's

Graham Young. (Rex Features)

application was turned down and the boy showed his annoyance by adding an entire packet of sugar soap to the hospital tea urn. Fortunately, an alert patient noticed that the sugar soap was missing from its usual place and the tea trolley was intercepted before anyone could drink any of its contents. Had anyone done so, his or her stomach would have been burned out by the strength of the chemical.

After that, Graham seemed to realise that any hope of his early release was dependent on his good behaviour and he became a model patient. By 1970, Mr E.L. Unwin, the psychiatrist treating him, felt able to recommend his release to the Home Office in a written report that read. 'He is no longer obsessed with poisons, violence and mischief. And he is no longer a danger to others.' By November, Graham had been granted a week's home leave, as a preparatory move towards his eventual release.

It was decided that he would stay with his sister, Winnie, her husband, Dennis, and their new baby. The visit was a success, with Graham behaving like a 'normal' young man and Winnie agreed that he could return to spend

Christmas at her home. Once again, Graham seemed to adapt readily to life in a family setting and he was eventually released on licence on 4 February 1971, in spite of the serious concerns of some of the nurses at Broadmoor, to whom Graham had openly boasted that he intended to kill one person for every year that his freedom had been curtailed. His release was conditional on him living at a fixed address, being supervised by the probation service and regularly attending a psychiatric clinic as an outpatient.

Graham Young moved into a hostel on his release, although his sister stayed in close contact with him. Winnie soon became concerned that Graham still seemed to be obsessed by his past crimes and, while staying in the hostel, another resident became seriously ill after sharing bottles of wine with Graham. Trevor Sparkes experienced bouts of chronic sickness and diarrhoea and what he described as 'a loss of control' of his legs. Doctors were mystified by his illness, which continued on and off throughout his association with Graham Young.

During his residence in the hostel, Graham Young was given vocational training as a store man and in April 1971, he applied for a job at John Hadland Laboratories in Bovingdon, a company who specialised in the manufacture of optical and photographic instruments. Interviewed for the position, Graham took with him a medical certificate signed by Mr Unwin, explaining that he had been hospitalised throughout his adolescence for 'a deep going personality disorder' but was now capable of undertaking any work without any restrictions as to travel, residence or environment. Graham himself explained his hospitalisation by saying that he had suffered a nervous breakdown following the death of his mother in a car accident.

On 10 May 1971, Graham started his new job as a store man at Hadland's and less than a month later, his boss Bob Egle was taken ill, suffering a bout of chronic diarrhoea. Having rested at home for a few days, Egle was well enough to return to work but on the day after his return, another employee, Ron Hewitt, also developed diarrhoea along with stomach pains and a terrible burning sensation at the back of his throat. Initially diagnosed with food poisoning, Hewitt took a week off work but for the next three weeks his symptoms came and went and he suffered no less than twelve bouts of sickness and diarrhoea.

Meanwhile, Bob Egle was still far from well and decided to take a week's holiday at Great Yarmouth. The sea air apparently worked wonders for his health and he returned to work feeling much better. On the day after his return he felt ill again, complaining of numbness and a lack of feeling in the end of his fingers. Noticing that her husband was staggering when he walked, his wife called the doctor who prescribed some tablets for him. When Egle was unable to keep the prescribed medication down, his wife called the doctor again. This time peripheral neuritis was diagnosed and Bob Egle was admitted to hospital in Hemel Hempstead.

On his arrival at hospital, Egle was suffering from excruciating pain in his back, which was so severe that, on the following day, he was transferred to the bigger St Albans Hospital, where he was placed in the intensive care unit. The numbness in his fingers gradually spread throughout his entire body so that he became completely paralysed and on two occasions, his heart stopped and he had to be resuscitated. On 7 July 1971, eight days after his admission to hospital, Bob Egle died. The cause of his death was recorded as broncho-pneumonia and Guillain-Barre polyneuritis, a rare disease of the nervous system. As one of his closest colleagues in the stores at Hadland's, Graham Young was asked to accompany managing director Godfrey Foster to Egle's funeral to represent the staff. Back at Hadland's, Ron Hewitt was still feeling far from well and eventually handed in his notice, leaving the firm on 9 July.

At the beginning of September, there were yet more illnesses at Hadland's. First Fred Biggs complained of stomach pains and vomiting then, on 20 September, manager Peter Buck suffered the same symptoms, although having left work early because he felt so ill, he was sufficiently recovered to return the next day. On 8 October, David Tilson was the next member of staff to fall ill, his chief complaint being a numbness of his legs, which gradually eased, giving way to agonising pain. Three days later another employee, Jethro Batt, was experiencing exactly the same symptoms.

On 18 October, both Tilson and Batt visited their doctors, Tilson complaining of pains in his chest and stomach and difficulty breathing and Batt of excruciating pain in his legs. Tilson was admitted to St Albans Hospital on the following day, where he continued to suffer from vomiting and pain and noticed that his hair had begun to fall out. Batt's condition also worsened. He was still experiencing intense pain and he too began to lose his hair. As the days passed, he gradually became paralysed and, by the time he was hospitalised on 5 November, he was completely bald, in constant pain and suicidal. Meanwhile, Tilson was released from hospital on 28 October, the doctors treating him suspecting that his unexplained illness was psychosomatic, and Fred Biggs was admitted to hospital on 4 November, suffering from chest pains and numbness in his limbs.

By now, the staff and management at Hadland's were concerned and frightened by the plague of mystery illnesses that seemed to be affecting the plant. Rumours began to circulate that there was a problem with the water and some people expressed concerns about possible radioactivity on a disused airfield owned by the government, which was located next to Hadland's buildings. The management insisted that the illnesses were simply reoccurrences of a local virus nicknamed 'The Bovingdon Bug', but the workforce remained unconvinced by that explanation.

Hence it was decided to call in a specialist to investigate and Dr Robert Hynd, the Medical Officer of Health for Hemel Hempstead, was asked to visit the firm. He brought in a team of doctors and factory inspectors who went over Hadland's with a fine toothcomb, although they failed to find any possible explanation for the strange epidemic of illness, which claimed its latest victim on 19 November with the death of Fred Biggs.

The atmosphere at Hadland's was by now one of complete panic among the staff. Several handed in their notice and John Hadland called in local GP, Dr Iain Anderson, who acted as medical officer to the firm.

Addressing the entire staff in the work's canteen, Anderson outlined the three possibilities currently under consideration by the authorities – radiation poisoning, heavy metal poisoning and a virus. The first two options had been discounted. Investigation had shown that there was no possibility of radioactive contamination from the airfield and, although the symptoms shown by the members of staff who had fallen ill were consistent with poisoning by thallium, no thallium was ever used at Hadland's. This left 'The Bovingdon Bug' as the sole viable explanation and this was under vigorous investigation by medical experts. Anderson told the staff that he was confident that a solution would soon be found.

Having reassured the workforce, Anderson asked if anyone had any questions. Immediately a young man stood up and began to fire a barrage of questions at the doctor, asking why heavy metal poisoning had been discounted. Anderson tried in vain to field the diatribe from the young man, who seemed to have an encyclopaedic knowledge of poisons and medical matters. When he was eventually able to close the meeting, Anderson sought out the man – Graham Young – in the relative privacy of the storeroom. Such was the depth of Young's knowledge on heavy metal poisoning that Anderson grew suspicious.

Anderson consulted with John Hadland who, having witnessed Young's lengthy outburst at the meeting, had entertained the same doubts as the doctor. After first consulting with his solicitors, Hadland made a telephone call to the police.

Chief Inspector John Kirkpatrick responded to the call by visiting Hadland's and inspecting their employment records. Noting that the start of the illnesses seemed to coincide with the arrival of Graham Young, Kirkpatrick sent a number of employee records to Scotland Yard for background checks, including those of Young.

On the following day, Kirkpatrick tried to contact the head of the Hertfordshire CID, Detective Chief Superintendent Ronald Harvey. By a stroke of good fortune, Harvey was at a formal lunch, in the company of a group of forensic scientists and when Harvey returned to his table after talking to Kirkpatrick, he discussed the outbreak of strange illnesses with his fellow diners. All of the men at the table were in complete agreement – the symptoms Harvey was describing were consistent with thallium poisoning.

Harvey had never heard of thallium or its effects and decided to read up on the heavy metal. Unfortunately, literature on the subject was scarce and there was only one book, of which there were only two known copies in England. One of these was at the police laboratories in Cheshire and a squad car was immediately sent to fetch it. When Harvey read it, he too believed that the problem at Hadland's could indicate that there was a poisoner at large and when the results of the investigations from Scotland Yard revealed that Graham Young had spent nine years in Broadmoor for poisoning three people, Harvey ordered his immediate arrest.

With Graham in custody at Sheerness police station, the police went to search his bed-sit room. To their amazement, they found it decorated from floor to ceiling with pictures of Hitler and other Nazi leaders, along with crude drawings of gravestones and dying men. Not only that but every available surface was cluttered with phials, bottles and tubes of chemicals. The most significant find was a handwritten diary hidden under the bed, which detailed the work of a poisoner, describing the compounds used and their terrible effects on the victims.

Graham Young was arrested on suspicion of murder and taken to Hemel Hempstead police station, where his main concern seemed to be whether he was suspected of murder or murders. He began a battle of words with Inspector Kirkpatrick, demanding to know the precise details of the charge against him and the name of the person he was charged with murdering. When told it was Fred Biggs, he confidently assured Kirkpatrick that Biggs had died from a virus. However, his arrogance led him to tell Kirkpatrick that he had once committed the perfect murder – that of his stepmother, Molly.

Young continued to try and baffle the police with his technical knowledge of toxicology. Confronted with the diary, he insisted that it was a work of fiction that he was planning to use as the basis for a novel he was writing. Eventually, when the police persisted, he admitted that the initials in the diary were those of his workmates at Hadland's. Young effectively confessed to committing two murders and several attempted murders but challenged the police to prove it.

Meanwhile, a post-mortem was conducted on the body of Fred Biggs, during which the doctors even consulted with an expert on thallium poisoning from Belgium. Initially, no trace of thallium could be found in Biggs's body and his death was recorded as 'Cause not established'. However, once tests had been conducted on his internal organs, analyst Nigel Fuller was able to isolate thallium in most of them. An application was made to exhume the ashes of Bob Egle, who had been cremated after his death. These too showed large amounts of thallium and, as a control, Fuller also tested the remains of another cremated man, which showed no trace of the poison. He concluded that both Biggs and Egle had died of thallium poisoning, estimating that Biggs had probably ingested hundreds of grams of the poison, of which one gram would constitute a fatal dose.

Graham Young was committed by magistrates to stand trial but continued to insist that he was innocent, in spite of the fact that the evidence against him was so strong. The trial was postponed as Young's solicitor struggled to find a barrister who was prepared to defend his client but eventually the services of Sir Arthur Irvine QC and Mr Freddie Beazely were secured and the trial opened before Mr Justice Eveleigh on 19 July 1972. Graham Young pleaded 'Not Guilty' to the ten charges against him – two counts of murder for the deaths of Frederick Biggs and Robert Egle, two charges of attempted murder for David Tilson and Jethro Batt and charges of the malicious administration of poison with intent to cause grievous bodily harm to Trevor Sparkes, Ronald Hewitt, Peter Buck, Diane Smart (another worker at Hadland's), Jethro Batt and David Tilson. It was believed that the poison involved in the lesser charges was antimony, while that which had killed Biggs and Egle was thallium.

Mr John Leonard QC prosecuted the case and informed the jury that no rational motive could be found for the poisonings at Hadland's other than the use of the victims as scientific 'guinea pigs' by Young, who simply wanted to observe what happened to them after poison was administered. Leonard did however argue that the attempt to poison Diane Smart might have been made because she irritated him, having accused him of being a carrier of 'The Bovingdon Bug'. He also pointed out that, with Bob Egle dead, Young would stand a chance of promotion at work. The prosecution produced evidence that, on the day after Young was given his job at Hadland's, he had travelled to London and visited a chemist, where he had purchased twenty-five grams of antimony, signing the Poisons Register with the fictitious name 'M.E. Evans'. He was later to use the same chemist's shop to purchase thallium, outlining a series of experiments he wished to carry out to the chemist as reason for his purchase and again using the same pseudonym.

The prosecution's key evidence was the diary, which seemed to document all the illnesses at Hadland's, referring to the victims by their initials. Many extracts from the damning notebook were read out in court including one dated 3 November, which was believed to refer to David Tilson. 'D's loss of hair is almost total. The hospital feels it might be due to poison. I must watch the situation very carefully. If it looks like I will be detected then I shall have to destroy myself.' Another entry, apparently referring to Fred Biggs, read, 'I have administered a fatal dose of the special compound and anticipate reports of his illness on Monday. He should die within the week.'

The defence was able only to call one witness to speak on Young's behalf and that was the defendant himself. Graham Young remained cool in the witness stand, exhibiting his characteristic arrogance as he fluently parried the questions put to him. He continued to insist that the diary was a work of fiction and that all the information contained within it was his attempt to create a character with homicidal tendencies for a novel. Young went on to disagree with all the medical evidence presented by the prosecution, insisting that the deaths and illnesses at Hadland's had been down to 'The Bovingdon Bug' rather than poisoning.

He explained the confession he had made shortly after his arrest as his part of a bargain struck with the police officers in order to gain access to the food, clothes and legal representation that had been denied him. He had been in 'absolute desperation' at being kept wrapped up in a blanket 'like a Sioux Indian' for more than fifteen hours.

The evidence against Graham Young made for an open and shut case and neither the prosecution nor the defence spoke for long in summing up the evidence for the jury, both concluding their closing speeches in less than an hour. It was then left to the judge to summarise the case. Mr Justice Eveleigh reviewed the medical evidence and warned the jury to consider Young's confession very carefully, since it was not unknown for people to confess to things that they hadn't done. Discussing Young's diary, the judge pointed out that there were some discrepancies contained within it, citing the example of the 'fatal dose' administered to Bob Egle, which Young had recorded as a total of fifteen or sixteen grains. In an interview with the police, Young had told them that he had administered a total of eighteen grains in three doses. The judge also reminded the jury that on one occasion, Young had openly given Fred Biggs some thallium to use as an insecticide in his garden and had at that time issued a warning to Biggs about its toxicity, advising him to handle it with extreme caution. Finally, the judge advised the jury not to overlook the existence of 'The Bovingdon Bug', which had indisputably affected not only workers at Hadland's but also several inhabitants of the village of Bovingdon and some of its neighbouring villages, who had no connection whatsoever to the plant.

The jury deliberated for a little under an hour, returning to pronounce Graham Frederick Young 'Guilty' of the murders of Egle and Biggs and of the attempted murders of Batt and Tilson. He was acquitted on all of the more minor charges due to lack of evidence. With their verdict, the jury delivered a strong recommendation that there should be an immediate review of the present system whereby poisons could be so easily purchased. Only then was Young's previous criminal history revealed to the court, with defence counsel Sir Arthur Irvine heavily criticising Young's release from Broadmoor. Indeed, on the day of the end of the trial, the Home Secretary, Reginald Maudling, was to announce that a complete review of procedures had been carried out and several measures had been introduced in order to tighten up the safeguards against another dangerous prisoner being released in the future. Investigations were continuing to determine whether or not more changes were necessary.

Parkhurst Prison, Isle of Wight. (Author's collection)

Young was sentenced to life imprisonment for each of the murders and attempted murders and was taken to Wormwood Scrubs Prison. He was later transferred to the maximum security Parkhurst Prison on the Isle of Wight. Asked if he felt remorse for his actions, Young said, 'What I feel is the emptiness of my soul.'

On 1 August 1990, he was found dead in his cell aged just forty-two years. The official cause of his death was given as heart failure, although there were rumours that Young had either committed suicide or that he might even have been poisoned by other inmates at the prison.

Bibliography and References

Newspapers and Magazines

Bournemouth Daily Echo
Chamber's Journal, July 1856
Cornish and Devon Post
News of the World
Nursing Record and Hospital World, 12 October 1895
The Guardian
The Manchester Guardian
The Scotsman
The Times

Books and Articles

Bell, Gail. *The Poison Principle*, Macmillan, London, Oxford and Basingstoke, 2002
Browne, Douglas G. and Tullett, E.V. *Bernard Spilsbury: His Life and Cases*, George
    G. Harrap and Co. Ltd, 1951
Casswell QC, J.D. *A Lance for Liberty*, George G. Harrap and Co. Ltd., 1961
Eddleston, John J. *The Encyclopaedia of Executions*, John Blake, London, 2004
Emsley, John. *The Elements of Murder: A History of Poison*, OUP, Oxford, July 2006
Fielding, Steve. *The Hangman's Record Volume One 1868–1899*, Chancery House
    Press, Beckenham, Kent, 1994
Holden, Anthony. *The St Albans Poisoner*, Panther, St Albans, 1976
Marshall, Walter. 'The Bude Enigma Revisited', *True Detective*, November 1997
Watson, Katherine. *Poisoned Lives: English Poisoners and their Victims*, Hambleden
    Continuum, 2003

Various websites have also been consulted during the compilation of this book.
However, since they have a tendency to disappear without notice, to avoid
disappointment, they have not been individually listed.

Index